# ASPECTS OF DEVIANCE

# ASPECTS OF DEVIANCE

## E.W. Vaz

Department of Sociology
University of Waterloo

Prentice-Hall of Canada, Ltd.,
Scarborough, Ontario

Canadian Shared Cataloguing in Publication Data

Vaz, Edmund W., 1924-
  Aspects of deviance

Bibliography: p.
Includes index.
ISBN 0-13-049312-0.   0-13-049304-X pa.

1. Deviant behavior.   I. Title.

HM291.V39                   301.6'2

Prentice-Hall, Inc., Englewood Cliffs, New Jersey
Prentice-Hall International, Inc., London
Prentice-Hall of Australia, Pty., Sydney
Prentice-Hall of India, Pvt., Ltd., New Delhi
Prentice-Hall of Japan, Inc., Tokyo
Prentice-Hall of Southeast Asia, (PTE.) Ltd., Singapore

ISBN−013-049304-X (paper)
       013-049312-0 (cloth)

1   2   3   4   5   JD   80   79   78   77   76

Printed in Canada

# Contents

**1   Deviance as Social Action**   1
Structure of Deviant Action   2

**2   Norms**   6
The Function of Norms   13
The Institutionalization of Norms   21

**3   Deviance**   26
Deviance and Roles   29
Deviant Roles   32

**4   Social Definitions of Deviance**   43
Canadian Narcotic Legislation: An Example   47

**5   Socialization and Deviance**   53
Deviance and Motives   60
Reference Groups and Motivation   62
Vocabularies of Motives   64

**6   Acquiring a Deviant Self**   73
Stigma: The Labeling Process   78
The Organizational Web   82
Getting Hooked   86

**7   The Incidence of Deviance: How Much is There?**   92

**8   Socioeconomic Location and Deviance**   105
Age   115
Sex   117

**9   Subcultural Worlds**   122
The Emergence of Subcultural Worlds   133

**10   The Social Organization of Deviant Behavior**   140

The Social Organization of Gang Delinquency   145
Thrasher's Gangs   146
Fighting Gangs   148
Delinquent Subcultures   150
Subcultural Variety   153

**Conclusions**   164

# Preface

It is not intended that this book be used as a textbook although it may be; it does not contain any critical reviews of the literature on deviance, nor does it advance any special argument or theoretical perspective on deviant behavior. Instead it presents a brief discussion of some selected areas in the study of deviance. Although the book is not exclusively Canadian in content, except for the section on the organization of gang delinquency much of the discussion and most of the examples apply to the Canadian scene.

Unfortunately, we know very little about deviance and the varied worlds of deviants in Canada. Yet deviance is common to all walks of life and is generally easy to find and investigate. Even the presumably inaccessible forms of deviance like organized crime are not unavailable for study. But the paucity of sociological research on deviance in Canada suggests that Canadian sociologists do not know where the action is. Are there no professional criminals, hustlers, highly paid call-girls, con-men, or pick-pocket teams working in Canadian cities? What about the networks of drug addicts and dealers? What kinds of rackets operate in Canada and how do they function? Is there an underworld in Canada? What about the 'goon squads' operating perennially in our two major cities, whose members are expert in breaking bones and damaging other people's property? Are there no street-corner societies in Canadian cities? Where are the sociological accounts that lay bare the different forms of organization and cultures of these *sub rosa* worlds, and the careers of their inhabitants?

Statistical data are an important source of information about deviance, for example about crime and delinquency, and much of the Canadian research that has been conducted on deviance has relied on this kind of material. But more than one kind of information is required for the explanation and understanding of deviant behavior. Not all deviance looks the same even when it goes by the same name; we should be able to characterize it before we try to theorize about it. The 24-hour-a-day street work of gathering information about criminal activities and other forms of deviant conduct in Canada remains to be done. Perhaps more time should be spent on the streets, in all night restaurants, third-rate hotels or taverns and bars — places where contacts can be made, and where the action can be learned about. It is in precisely such places that sociologists can learn about the burglarizing, gambling, prostitution, drug trafficking, rackets and affiliated criminal activities that go on in a city. This kind of do-it-yourself research is sometimes exciting and usually extremely rewarding in the quest for explanation and understanding of crime in a society.

We need carefully detailed descriptive accounts of the deviant transactions of people, the deviant worlds in which they do business, and the kinds of deviance that occur within those worlds. We must explore their social settings and their interconnections with the legitimate straight worlds, examine the rules by which deviants organize their lives, inspect the social arrangements to which they grow accustomed and study the costs and payoffs of their deviant ways. We need to know of deviance as vocation and avocation, as work and play. This includes information on the day and night lives of people of all ages who roam the streets of large Canadian cities (are there worlds of juvenile gangs in these cities?), on the overlapping worlds of night people — their intimacy and collusion — and on the seamier worlds of petty criminals, run-down prostitutes, drug addicts and other partial outcasts. Aside from Letkemann's study of bank robbers, and West's work on 'serious thieves' in Toronto, what do we know of the work and cultures of criminals in Canada? We need to learn first hand of their occupational cultures and behavioral apparel, the selective relationships and contacts that their work entails, the multifarious experiences it engenders, and the manifold illusions, aspirations and heartaches that it generates. In another context, we require information concerning the daily forms of deviance and crime among middle class, striped-collar workers; worlds of the *infra dig.* service occupations; the sometimes off-color entertainment worlds; the violence-infused worlds of professional sports; the so-called respectable worlds of the professions — the doctors, lawyers, university professors and clerics, and the much pressured worlds of the police.

When deviance or crime in uncovered in these conventional worlds, it is attributed customarily to individual misbehavior. For the sociologist, such an explanation is naïve and unsatisfactory. Deviance is seldom a solitary matter; almost inevitably it assumes shapes and patterns that betray its normative nature. Surely there are tales to be told sociologically of these worlds, of their cultural patterns and behavioral contours, and of the institutionalized immorality, fraud and chicanery that transpire within them. Much remains to be done sociologically if we are to learn more about deviance on the Canadian scene. Perhaps this little book will help students to think systematically about the subject, and encourage them to examine sociologically the many unexplored worlds of deviance in Canada.

Few persons can have had the luxury of as much help as I have had in writing such a small book. I wish to acknowledge my gratitude to the following students for reading and commenting on various parts of the manuscript: Mary Ann Coe, Fred Desroches, Mohamad Nawaz, Uldis Kundrats, Joan Lyons and Nancy Suits. Professors Frank Fasick, Linda Fischer, Abdul Lodhi, Bill Scott and Audrey Wipper were also helpful with their comments. Professor Taylor Buckner of Concordia University deserves a special note of thanks for making available to me his data bank of student research papers on the day-and-night life-styles in Montreal. Miss Barbara Steel of Prentice-Hall was very helpful with editorial suggestions. I am especially grateful to Harold Fallding for his advice. Professor Albert K. Cohen, on whose work I have relied heavily, was my teacher at Indiana University. I am happy to acknowledge publicly my continuing indebtedness to him.

To my wife Cecile, who is French, I am grateful for having read carefully the entire manuscript, and for helping me to write clearly in English. The typing and retyping of the manuscript was done generously and cheerfully by Mrs. Beverly Taylor. I wish to express my gratitude to her.

Edmund W. Vaz

"It has always seemed strange to me," said Doc. "The things we admire in men, kindness and generosity, openness, honesty, understanding and feeling are the concomitants of failure in our system. And those traits we detest, sharpness, greed, acquisitiveness, meanness, egotism and self-interest are the traits of success. And while men admire the quality of the first they love the produce of the second."

*Cannery Row*
*John Steinbeck*

# Deviance as Social Action

**1**

Any discussion of deviance must involve the topic of social action—the activities in which people engage and the relationships that they form. Social action refers to socially acceptable activities such as making friends, helping others, falling in love, or going on a picnic, and to illegal activities like stealing money, pushing dope, picking pockets, and chiseling the government. It also includes legal, but nevertheless deviant conduct such as peddling sexual favors for higher grades in university, playing for an edge among friends and cribbing on examinations. This is the social stuff of everyday living—the ground level of social interaction.

There is nothing unusual about this because conformity and deviance are essentially a single category of action. Social acts that conform to the rules—obeying the speed limit and remembering your wife's birthday—and behavior that violates the rules—hustling women, hotel prowling or cheating at cards—are normative kinds of social action. Although they are oriented towards different sets of norms, all are permitted by the rules that govern the respective activities taking place.

The common characteristic here is interacting persons. The 'social' in 'social action' means that by virtue of the meaning that persons attach to what they are doing, their conduct 'takes account of the behavior of others and is thereby oriented in its course.'[1] Thus the nocturnal activities of a second-story man are greatly influenced by the regular patrol of the neighborhood police cruiser. Failure to accept a bribe is as much a social act as is the feigned ignorance of the offer. Also, social action may be oriented to the past, present, or anticipated conduct of others. In order to fulfill a 'contract', a 'trooper' must lay plans to murder his victim. These calculated arrangements are very likely influenced by the past relationships, present habits, and future appointments of his victim. Murder is social action.[2] On the other hand, action is not social when it is directed to the behavior of inanimate objects as it is in the case of the person who enjoys collecting guns solely for their aesthetic appreciation. And, if the meaning of the action is not oriented to the conduct of others, for example when persons engage in religious contemplation,[3] social action is not occurring.

## Structure of Deviant Action

To speak of the structure of social action, whether it is deviance or conformity, is to refer to the relative presence or absence of a continued pattern to the ongoing activity. It is a social process that is appreciably orderly, recurrent (when there is that need), and stable. Structure occurs because others want to know what to expect of us, and we are more at ease when we know what to anticipate of others. Thus, expectations are shared and organized and each person's actions are structured insofar as they engage the actions of another.[4]

Social structure does not refer to the psychology of persons, but to the positions or roles that they occupy, and how these roles are coordinated. It is likely that the coordination of positions that comprise the structure of La Cosa Nostra is largely independent of its current membership.[5] Persons come and go, but the system (the coordination of interdependent positions) remains intact. Roles remain relatively stable, irrespective of the role occupant. The actions of a person, as an actor occupying a role in a system

---

1   Max Weber, *The Theory of Social and Economic Organization,* London: William Hodge and Company, 1947, 80.

2   See Burton B. Turkus and Sid Feder, *Murder, Inc.,* New York: Farrar, Straus and Young, 1951; Donald R. Cressey, *Theft of the Nation,* New York: Harper & Row, Publishers, 1969, 31-35.

3   Weber, *op. cit.,* 102-104.

4   Harold Fallding, *The Sociological Task,* Englewood Cliffs, New Jersey: Prentice-Hall, Inc., 1968, 53.

5   Cressey, *op. cit.,* esp. 109-110.

of interaction, have a relationship to, and a bearing on the actions of the other actor as role occupant.[6] This reflects the coordination of social roles and is evident in the structure of a small, but complicated part of an illegal gambling operation described in the following excerpt.

> The gambler wishing to place an illegal bet on the outcome of a legitimate horse race usually gets in touch with a man occupying a 'solicitor' position, one of the many positions making up the structure of the illegal betting organization. There are three types of solicitor positions. All three types may be subsidiary to a single 'bookmaker' position. Occasionally a bookmaker also occupies the position of solicitor, and the street name for what I call 'solicitor' is, in fact, 'bookmaker.' The two positions are distinct, however, even if one man fills both of them. Ordinarily, a solicitor serves a bookmaker, in exchange for a percentage of the profits or in exchange for a straight salary. The person playing the role of 'stationary solicitor' accepts bets at a fixed location, such as a newsstand, store, office, house, or factory floor. Gamblers go to him. A few stationary solicitors operate 'horse rooms,' where wagers are accepted on each race just before it is run, as at the track. Horse rooms tend to be small operations because the solicitor, who also functions here as bookmaker, has no opportunity to reinsure his bets. We shall see that, accordingly, he must live in hope that his patrons will bet approximately like the bettors at the track will bet. He gets by because most bettors, at the track or elsewhere, simply bet on the 'favorites' selected by morning newspapers and racing forms. The returns on the gambler's investment are small when a 'favorite' wins.
>
> Men occupying the position of 'traveling solicitor', or 'walking solicitor,' go to the bettors. Each traveling solicitor has a rather fixed route, which takes him through office buildings and factories. He, like the stationary solicitor, is likely to think of himself as a bookmaker, and he is popularly, but erroneously, called a 'walking bookmaker,' or 'walking book.' He issues small slips of paper on which bets are recorded, keeping a duplicate copy which he later turns over to the bookmaker. The solicitor may set limits determined by the bookmaker: 'I'm a ten-dollar man' means that his bookmaker is

---

6   William M. Dobriner, *Social Structures and Systems,* Pacific Palisades: Goodyear Publishing Co., 1969, 107.

**a small operator who permits him to take bets no greater than ten dollars.**[7]

In the social system of making and collecting bets, the activities of the 'travelling solicitor' are linked to those of the 'bettor', and the actions of the 'runner' are related to those of the 'telephone solicitor'. Similarly, there are mutually oriented actions between addict and pusher and stool pigeon and detective. In his study of the police, Westley found that the stool pigeon and the informant were the 'life blood of the good detective'. The element of reciprocity is clear from the following detectives' remarks:

**Pigeons account for the solution of between 40% and 50% of the tough cases. The way you get pigeons is to bring them in for a minor crime and give them the idea you are bargaining with them. Then you can go to them for information when you need it. We keep our pigeons quiet.**

**To get informants you should cultivate friendships. You should associate with them—with the person, and find a chance to give them a break.... Get him out of a jam or cover up for him in some way, or help him financially. Sometimes a small amount of money or giving him a chance to make money in some way. Hold something over his head.**[8]

In the detective-informant relationship each party knows what to expect of the other, and both benefit. The detective gets his information; the informant gets a break, a suspended sentence or a few dollars. When they get together their behavior is predictable, stable, and structured.

Even within correctional institutions there is a structure to the considerable amount of deviance (for example, the merchandising of contraband) that transpires. The artificial scarcity of desired articles—clothing, sweets, toilet articles, drugs, homemade wine, obscene literature, tobacco—and the need for conspicuous consumption are two contributing variables to the patterns that emerge. Although they are not always highly structured, definable patterns are evident, and they provide a viable economic structure within the prisoner community. Besides the importance of social status and the willingness to take risks, the

---

7  Donald R. Cressey, *Theft of a Nation,* pp. 127-128. Copyright © 1969 by Donald R. Cressey. By permission of Harper & Row, Publishers, Inc.

8  William A. Westley, *Violence and the Police,* Cambridge, Massachusetts: The MIT Press, 1970, 40-41.

distribution of unequal opportunities to engage in specific forms of crime helps generate a network of roles, i.e., a structure which fosters the deviant transactions within the reformatory. In his study of a Canadian reformatory, Mann reports that,

> ... since the cleaners can legitimately move between various prison areas as they sweep the corridors—they have occasionally, opportunities to pick certain cell locks; they are also in a special position to lug contraband, take messages or 'kites' from one prisoner to another and act as go-betweens arranging deals on other activities. Fifth floor men have access to privileged information on parole and bed change lists, etc. Again, cafeteria and kitchen men can steal fruit, cookies; stores men can slip out better quality shirts, slippers, etc.; hospital personnel have opportunities to order in uncalled for quantities of oranges, etc., and to merchandise vasolene [sic] and hair tonic, etc.[9]

The patterns of social action also depend, to a considerable extent, on the common definitions that persons share of the ongoing situation. When participants agree that certain activities constitute an assembly line, a caper, or a pot party, they are more apt to continue their joint endeavors. Their common knowledge of the activities, trust in their fellow participants, the extent of their role commitment, and their relative belief in the shared rules of the activity help keep the operation going.

---

9   W.E. Mann (ed.), 'Deviant Behaviour in a Reformatory' in *Deviant Behaviour in Canada,* Toronto: Social Science Publishers, 1968, 88-89.

# Norms

# 2

The idea of things being good or bad, right or wrong, deviant or non-deviant is in the nature of social action. The structure of social action is seldom a happenstance affair, but emerges because, for the most part, men and women behave according to the norms they share. Norms are the differentially obligatory rules by which persons run their affairs, and although we usually infer them from the regularity of their actions, we can also enquire of people what they ought or ought not to do. Formal and informal norms are mental agreements among men and women, and are, therefore, difficult to grapple with. Although interdependent with social action, norms are a different dimension of social reality, but they are no less real for being so.

Norms of conduct are differentially important in governing men's activities. Some practices are so pervasive and deeply felt that they become an indelible part of our daily lives; they become habits of thought as well as of action.[1] These norms are 'automatically expressed in behaviour', and usually 'lead to the phenomena of conscience, of guilt feelings, of striving, of elation and depres-

---

1   Kingsley Davis, *Human Society,* New York: The Macmillan Company, 1949, 58-59.

sion.'[2] However, such informal norms (sometimes called folkways and mores),[3] and public opinion, moral conscience and other informal means of social control are insufficient to ensure order in a highly complex, industrialized society. In contrast to these informal norms, enacted law is a formal, deliberately planned, consciously designed set of rules that is 'not only necessitated by complex society but ... also makes such a society possible.'[4] Enacted law does not determine the basic sentiments of society, but is a product of them, and serves to give precision to the mores in the larger secular society. Moreover, laws are announced by a legislative body; they are embodied in a written code or constitution, and are enforced by a specially authorized agency that is permitted to use force.

Formal and informal norms comprise the framework of society, but the largest part of our daily interaction is regulated by informal norms. Norms may either prescribe or proscribe certain courses of action because they are deemed desirable or undesirable, and they imply a sense of obligation on the part of the person. They either restrict or extend an individual's range of conduct. Norms indicate what kinds of conduct are prescribed, preferred, permitted or merely tolerated.[5] For example, at an illegal gambling casino a regular customer who has gone broke may borrow from the resident loan shark. Should he win on the next pass of the dice or look at a winning poker hand he *must* repay the loan, at 10 percent interest, on the spot. If he loses he is permitted an extra twenty-four hours, no more. As security for the loan the gambler puts up his body.[6] In a different context, among gang boys, fellatio for money with a stranger is permitted but not encouraged,[7] while among gay lovers fellatio is certainly expected.

---

2  *Ibid.,* 55.

3  Rules that are relatively unimportant for the upkeep of the society are called folkways. They are fairly obligatory practices and are enforced by informal social controls. Rules that are more directly related to the basic requirements of society are called mores. Mores are considered to be morally right, and their violation morally wrong. Perhaps they are the optimum measuring rod of what is considered right and wrong in society. The classic work is William Graham Sumner, *Folkways,* New York: New American Library, 1960. First published in 1907. An excellent discussion is found in Davis, *op. cit.,* 52-82.

4  Davis, *op. cit.,* 67.

5  Robert K. Merton, *Social Theory and Social Structure,* New York: The Free Press, (revised edition) 1967, 133.

6  Donald R. Cressey, *Theft of a Nation,* New York: Harper & Row, 1969, 80.

7  Albert J. Reiss, Jr., 'The Social Integration of Queers and Peers,' *Social Problems,* 9, 1961, 102-119.

Norms may call for very strong to only superficial support; they may range from positive compulsive rules to strongly proscribing ones. For example, one of the first norms strongly impressed on the rookie cop is to 'Keep your mouth shut; never squeal on a fellow officer; don't be a stool pigeon.'[8] La Cosa Nostra's code makes disloyalty a major offence. In this respect both La Cosa Nostra and the police employ similar rules in governing their personnel.[9]

There is a wide range of formal norms—laws forbidding the possession of heroin or stolen goods; offences against public order, for example treason, piracy or sedition; offences against property rights, for example theft, robbery, breaking and entering or forgery; sexual offences, for example incest, rape, or acts of gross indecency and others. Informal norms are also varied: the implicit, but highly valued rules among some groups that prescribe how to turn on with grass; the rules among some west coast drug communities which proscribe being rowdy, lame, or uncool—that is, forbid one from engaging in nervy, unlimited, public displays of violence; the informal, but crucial rule of secrecy among the police, especially regarding mistakes in arrests, the violation of departmental rules, handling criminal suspects, illegal actions and personal misdemeanors.[10] Some professional baseball teams encourage players who visit night clubs to do their drinking seated at a table, with the belief that this creates a more favorable impression than being seen standing at a bar. On professional football teams veterans seldom talk to rookies.[11] A cardinal rule among poolroom hustlers is never to reveal 'your real speed'.[12] This resembles the apparent norm, among highly competitive graduate students in some university departments, which discourages sharing ideas and knowledge with fellow students. Swingers operate within a complex system of rules. 'The most important rules are the sanctions against the development of interpersonal involve-

---

8  William A. Westley, *Violence and the Police,* Cambridge, Massachusetts: The MIT Press, 1970, 111-112.

9  Evidence for the existence of a code governing the behavior of La Cosa Nostra members is difficult to come by. Moreover, since there is apt to be little honor among thieves, it is perhaps the fear of reprisals that regulates the conduct of men in the underworld. See Cressey, *op. cit.,* 162-185; Walter Lippman, 'The Underworld as Servant' in Gus Tyler (ed.), *Organized Crime in America,* Ann Arbor: The University of Michigan Press, 1962, 62; Tyler, *Organized Crime in America,* 228-231.

10  Westley, *op. cit.,* 112.

11  George Plimpton, *Mad Ducks and Bears,* New York: Bantam Books, 1974, 62.

12  Ned Polsky, *Hustlers, Beats and Others,* Chicago: Aldine Publishing Company, 1967, 80.

ment. There are also rules on who may participate in swinging . . . . physical attractiveness is important, and this means that one must be up to minimal standards . . . . if people are too heavy they are usually excluded. Also the rules tend to restrict people to similar ages.'[13]

Although rules for conduct are usually unwritten, it does not lessen their applicability or significance for the group. The fact that the code of La Cosa Nostra is unwritten does not deny its existence or its force in governing the members of that organization. Rules can vary from purely technical norms—how to boil an egg without breaking it, roll a joint, 'blow a box,' or apply third degree tactics without leaving any bruises—to moral norms— rules against laughing at a person's mishap, squealing on a friend to the police, forcing heroin on someone, or trying to make it with your best friend's wife.

Norms may also be differentiated on the basis of sanctions applied against the offender. Sanctioning itself is governed by rules, and varies widely from the amused smile, the crushing wisecrack, and the flared nostril to the silent treatment, hanging someone upside down from the twentieth floor of a hotel room, and the death penalty. Sanctions are especially powerful when they are administered by members of the group with whom the individual identifies.[14] Yet they may also be applied by the victim of the deviant act or by special agencies such as the law courts. In some instances sanctions may be administered by interested observers to the deviant act; a person may take action against the offender even when the deviant act does not interfere with the performance of his role. Should he feel that the act threatens the social validity of a strong moral norm, it is moral indignation that underlies the reprisal.

Minor transgressions in the course of social interaction elicit gentle rebukes. A slight nod or frown may bring the offender back into line; indeed, it is in this manner that the person often learns the true meaning of a rule. Similarly, for minor crimes which comprise the bulk of criminal offenses, relatively minor penalties such as fines, probation or reprimands are administered. Thus, in 1971 in Canada, 92.5 percent of persons convicted for relatively minor offenses were fined.[15] In some countries, for example Ger-

13　Robert R. Bell, *Social Deviance,* Homewood, Illinois: The Dorsey Press, 1971, 80.

14　Laurie Taylor, *Deviance and Society,* London: Thomas Nelson and Sons Ltd., 1971, 38.

15　Canada: Statistics Canada, *96th Annual Report of Statistics of Criminal and Other Offenses,* Ottawa: Information Canada, 1971.

many and Yugoslavia, motor offenses are settled on the spot. A serious criminal act like first degree murder elicits a severe penalty such as life imprisonment; treason and trafficking in narcotics also call for long prison terms.

The seriousness of an offense is always relative to the social system in which it occurs, and often to its defined danger to the persons involved. The junkie who squeals to the police runs the risk of serious physical injury should his conduct be discovered by fellow junkies. Some years ago cabdrivers in Montreal were strongly encouraged to steal from their bosses. Drivers were forbidden to give the boss their full take for a shift. The amount to be cashed in varied with the 'speed', the average gross intake for each shift. Usually this ranged from thirteen to sixteen dollars on weekdays and eighteen to twenty-two dollars on weekends. Business improved at night, and the range was a few dollars higher. Violation of these limits—cashing in thirty dollars on a Friday night—resulted in verbal abuse, threats of violence, and on one occasion physical injury. Stealing from the boss was the expected, normative behavior; failure to steal was deviant among the drivers, and elicited relatively strong sanctions.[16]

Norms vary from one society to another, in time, place and with social class. The magazine advertisement that says, 'You've come a long way baby!', and shows a sophisticated-looking female smoking a long 'Virginia Slim' cigarette leaves no doubt that at an earlier period women were forbidden to smoke. Today cigar-smoking women still elicit snide remarks in most groups, reflecting their breach of role expectations. Among nudist campers, body contact, staring, and sex talk are taboo,[17] but in the larger society similar acts such as girl-watching, are often encouraged. Until recently smoking pot was confined largely to jazz circles, and to some bohemian, minority, and criminal groups. Today it has expanded to include many students, teachers and younger business people, and in their groups, smoking pot is an acceptable leisure activity.

---

16  Edmund W. Vaz, *The Metropolitan Taxi-Driver: His Work and Self Conception,* Unpublished Master's thesis, Department of Sociology, McGill University, 1955.

17  Martin S. Weinberg, 'Sexual Modesty, Social Meanings, and the Nudist Camp', *Social Problems,* 12, 1957, 311-318. It is true also that the taboos against women exposing their nudity to men other than their husbands have greatly relaxed over the past fifty years. Sex talk and sundry amatory advances of men and coquetries of women are commonplace in the factory, and among office workers. See also Gary S. Page, 'Social Nudism: The Social Organization of Southern Ontario Nudist Camps,' in W. E. Mann (ed.), *Social Deviance in Canada,* The Copp Clark Publishing Company, 1971, 390-405.

Norms may also be situational. Some evidence suggests that while group norms are influential in the conduct of the members of boys' gangs, they are also tenuous and situational. The loose criteria for membership in the gangs tend to reinforce this. There are no norms that require, much less constrain fighting of all gang members, even under the most provocative conditions.[18]

Clarity in the rules is also an important problem. Rules refer to classes of events; as such they are difficult to apply to particular situations, and seldom can they specify in detail what behavior is desired. In order to do their job, rules must specify the expectations, obligations, and boundaries to social interaction. When persons are forewarned of the required conduct it helps guide their behavior. But rules and their meanings are often vague. The broad parental prescriptions, 'Be a good girl at the party', or 'Be careful with the car' are not likely altogether clear to many of today's teenagers. Yet these are precisely the gross indicators used by parents to guide their children. Does the prescription, 'Be a good girl at the party' mean that a girl should not hold hands with her boy friend, dance closely, kiss good night, practise different types of kissing and physical intimacy? What does the rule *really* mean? Are there qualifications to the rule? Under what conditions is the rule applicable?

Perhaps it is by probing the limits of propriety and sometimes other rules that an individual learns of his deviance. Many cases of premarital pregnancy among young people may be the result of experimentation in an area where the informal rules are in flux. Similarly, the radical student who confronts the university president with an obscene name to his face may find the president hamstrung, unable to act, because the rules are foggy. Has a deviant act occurred? But the student who steals the president's confidential files from his private office may soon find himself in court charged with theft. Here the rules (in this case the law) are clear. The president may act.

The broad definition of delinquency in the law often increases the difficulty of establishing the status of a youth's acts. Although the criminal code is considerably more specific, it, too, is influenced by time and place. Laws grow outdated yet remain on the statute books, and can therefore be enforced at any time. Laws may also fall short of clarity; for example, the criminal law explicitly forbids unauthorized possession of marijuana, but the meaning of possession within the law is unclear. Recently a lower-court

---

18    James F. Short, Jr., and Fred L. Strodbeck, *Group Process and Gang Delinquency*, Chicago: The University of Chicago Press, 1965, 206.

judge found that traces of marijuana in the accused's pipe was insufficient evidence of possession, and he was acquitted. On the other hand, although a law may be clear, the conduct in question is open to interpretation. Stripping is legal in some areas, but whether what transpires on stage is obscene or too suggestive is a matter of interpretation. The interpretation of the law often depends on the whims of the law enforcement officials, and in some cases the contribution of tourist revenue to the local economy. While the law requires relatively circumspect performances, the local police may tolerate lewd performances and flashing (lowering a G-string from time to time), if this meets favor with conventioners and the tourist trade. Similarly, the law may forbid stripping and allow exotic dancing only, but local officials may take a permissive approach and stripping may occur.[19]

The protective nature of rules is nicely exemplified in the norms governing the game of cruising for the one-night stand among homosexuals. These include: avoiding the exchange of biographical data; watching out for teenagers (they may be dangerous); never forcing your intentions on anyone; not criticizing a sex partner and never backing down on trade agreements.[20] Among strippers norms serve as protection from her audience. For example, she is not to allow the customer to 'cop a feel'; if he does it costs him money. Other norms govern her relationships with other strippers: a stripper should not make a play for another stripper's husband; she should not steal another girl's gimmick; she must not imitate another stripper's wardrobe.[21]

There are still more complicated networks of rules. Goffman remains the authority on the intricate controls that govern our social conduct in public places in everyday life.[22] There are rules against picking the nose, teeth, or any part of the face, scratching oneself or combing the hair in public, applying make-up in restau-

---

19  Jacqueline Boles and A. P. Garbin, 'Stripping for a Living: An Occupational Study of the Night Club Stripper' in Clifton D. Bryant, *Deviant Behavior: Occupational and Organizational Bases,* Chicago: Rand McNally Publishing Company, 1974, 271; Marilyn Salutin, 'Stripper Morality,' in Craig L. Boydell, Carl F. Grindstaff and Paul C. Whitehead (eds.), *Deviant Behaviour and Societal Reaction,* Toronto: Holt, Rinehart and Winston of Canada, 1972, 532-545.

20  Laud Humphreys, *Tearoom Trade,* Chicago: Aldine Publishing Company, 1970, 47.

21  Boles and Garbin, *op. cit.,* 324

22  Erving Goffman, *Encounters: Two Studies in the Sociology of Interaction,* The Bobbs-Merrill Company, Inc., 1961; Erving Goffman, *The Presentation of Self in Everyday Life,* Edinburgh: University of Edinburgh Social Sciences Research Centre, 1958.

rants, or muttering or talking to oneself.[23] There are rules against staring at others, or away from others when in their presence; against wearing dark glasses when talking to someone without any; that influence how we present the body in public;[24] against staring at the basket contents of others in supermarkets, and against eating other than small morsels of food on the street; and there is the complexity of rules which guides our conduct in the bedroom with subtle variations for the stranger, friend, mistress, or wife. There are even rules against alerting others to their improprieties, and rules limiting the punishment of those who do.

Thus, the course of our action is influenced by the fact that we judge our own conduct and the conduct of others according to rules. Whether the behavior is legal or illegal, deviant or conforming, secret or public, whether it is the conduct of judges, junkies, prostitutes or nuns, it is subject to rules. Despite the fact that rules are undergoing rapid transformation and are often less than clear resulting in some degree of moral chaos, there is not sufficient reason to doubt the importance of them in social conduct, or to abandon their examination in the study of deviance.

# The Function of Norms

A certain amount of conformity is essential if a social system is to maintain itself. If people are to get along together and do business with each other, there must be *some* common agreement about what they want, and how they are to go about getting it. In effect, these are the rules (however arbitrary) according to which the games (social activities) will be played. People could not cheat their friends, collaborate with their enemies or blackmail their employers without some common understandings or system of rules operating. However adaptable we may be, it seems unlikely that we can improvise our way through every social situation in which we participate. Yet we should be prepared to encounter

---

23 Erving Goffman, *Behaviour in Public Places*, New York: The Free Press, 1963, 72-73.

24 A major service of one's apparel is to hide what is underneath, but not completely! One of the functions of very tight blue jeans worn by young and not-so-young men is to outline their genital apparatus. Prior to leaving the washroom, after washing the hands and combing the hair, a final adjustment is made so that everything is obviously displayed to its best advantage. In another context, such rules may interfere with a woman's engaging in certain sports. In playing pool certain shots may require a woman to lean over the pool table; depending whether she wears a skirt or slacks, this position will involve displaying her legs or buttocks which women often find embarrassing. See Polsky, *op. cit.*, 39.

seemingly contradictory demands in conduct, attitudes, and values in much of our social interaction. The need for us to adapt and adjust (sometimes full circle), and our ability to cope with a reality that often makes conventional conformity especially difficult, will likely vary with the social worlds in which we live.[25]

At the same time some system of order and security must be maintained if people are to interact without fear of attack or plunder. Protection from mental discomfort and verbal aggression is also important, and is evident in many of society's formal rules, e.g., the laws against criminal libel, offensive odors, loud noises and disturbances of the peace. Without rules, families, secret societies, political parties, prisons, brothels, and universities could no longer operate.

This does not mean that rules must circumscribe man's every action. Every social system can withstand a certain quota of ambiguity, confusion, deviance, and mistrust. Most viable systems are organized to handle precisely these kinds of problems. Man's individuality requires some degree of freedom for his actions. He must at least *feel* that he is doing his own thing. Rules must never be so detailed as to suffocate man's efforts at cooperation or stifle his attempts at creativity. The essential degree of tolerance in any system of rules allows for unanticipated events, confusion, and errors. However, notwithstanding the good intentions of men, the risk to society is too great not to have some rules that set limits to our discretion and inclinations.[26]

In this regard rules govern the degree of one's participation in an enterprise. The extent of a person's participation in an activity will depend largely on the proportionate payoffs and rewards that are forthcoming for his efforts. However, unlimited participation and total devotion to an enterprise cannot mean unlimited rewards. Normative rules govern the demands that participants may make for their total participation. Such rules help reduce the strain and anxiety of others who are less committed to the enterprise, and give them time to engage in other spheres of activity. Thus the rules which govern the internal operations of one enterprise enable the operation of other spheres of endeavor.[27]

Persons do not likely conform to rules solely through a sense of duty, or obligation, or fear of punishment. Admittedly it is often

---

25  James F. Short, Jr., and Fred L. Strodbeck, *op. cit.,* 227-229.

26  Some of the ideas that follow are taken from Albert K. Cohen, *Deviance and Control,* Englewood Cliffs, New Jersey: Prentice-Hall, Inc., 1966, 3-4.

27  Notes taken in a class given by Professor Albert K. Cohen at Indiana University.

easier to conform. However, it seems to be true that the majority of people in society conform to its rules because for the most part they approve of the rules, and take them seriously. When rules are not taken seriously they are seldom obeyed. Often a pool hall will have displayed a list of rules for the conduct of its patrons, e.g., no foul language, no spitting on the floor, no sitting on the tables, no drinking of alcoholic beverages, etc. These rules are broken regularly, but they are symbolically functional since they create the impression to the police that the establishment is upholding the law.[28]

One reason that the crime rate is not higher is likely that people conform through a sense of decency and morality. Some degree of internalization of the rules likely occurs—especially of the important rules; persons take these rules seriously—through conviction, not by force. Cognition of the rules is sufficient, perhaps, for conformity to technological rules like driving on the right hand side of the road, but it is probably not sufficient for moral matters.[29] Since it is impossible to secure conformity through coercion (except in the short run), it simplifies matters if people believe in the rules that they are expected to obey. In most cases they do. At some point the 'demands of others must become demands which persons place upon themselves.'[30] Generally people find it gratifying to conform, embarrassing to deviate.[31] Moreover, it pays off in the respect that they obtain from their 'significant others'—persons whom they respect, and whose opinions they value. Obedience to the rules helps us convince ourselves and others that we are good citizens and decent fellows.

No rule is self-sustaining, and obedience to rules is never automatic. Conformity requires some effort which implies that the conformity of others should not be taken for granted. Nor can we

---

28  Lorna Roth, 'The Olympic Player: A Study of Pool Hall Regulars,' in H. Taylor Buckner (ed.), *Urban Life Styles: St. Catherine Street—Friday Night,* unpublished collection of papers, Dept. of Sociology, Concordia University, 1972.

29  It has been suggested that most of us do not act customarily on the basis of a deeply internalized set of values. Rather, we are likely to interpret values in accordance with particular situations, and we use counter rationalizations which allow us to deviate under certain conditions. See Howard S. Becker's review of Mary Owen Cameron, 'The Booster and the Snitch: Department Store Shoplifting,' in *The American Journal of Sociology,* Vol. 70, March, 1965, 635-36, and Short and Strodbeck, *op. cit.,* 228.

30  Gresham M. Sykes, *Crime and Society,* New York: Random House, 1956, 19.

31  Conformity is not always easy. Young men in nudist camps who spend much of their time sunbathing (on their stomachs) are, in fact, attempting to control an otherwise (i.e., were they on their backs) deviant and embarrassing state of affairs.

be certain that our conformity will be rewarded. In one way or another all social action is costly. For example, some subcultures refuse to condone hard work; premium value is given to the 'maximum use of mental agility and a minimum use of physical effort.' In the lower-class street corner world, hustling women, gambling, con games, pushing dope, and begging are highly valued activities.[32] Moreover, obedience to the rules can sometimes be a nuisance; violation of the rules may be a quicker, more efficient, less troublesome method of reaching one's goals. In many instances theft is a quicker means of making a dollar than working a forty hour week. 'There are always temptations . . . to cut corners, or otherwise to violate the understandings. Every rule, then, creates a potential for deviance.'[33]

The question is what to do about persons who cut corners and violate rules. Participation in a social event, for example, a marriage, an examination in sociology, or a business deal, carries the presumption that the conduct of others will follow prescribed lines of action. However, to permit spontaneous reaction against those who deviate would jeopardize the system. Thus, there are rules that govern the reactions of others against those who deviate. These not only limit those who may legitimately take action against the deviant, but they also govern the kinds of measures that may be applied. Therefore, rules lessen the effectiveness of deviance control by limiting the wholesale application of the means of control. In some countries a man may lose his hand if convicted of theft. Elsewhere he may be placed on probation or be sent to penitentiary. In either case rules apply. Even in La Cosa Nostra, rules function to limit the punishment of offenders. The murder of debtors is discouraged by usurers. They may break your legs and crack your skull, but seldom will they kill the 'goose that lays the golden egg'. However, these rules mean that our responses to deviance may themselves be deviant, as happens when police officers torture those whom they arrest.[34]

In spite of organizational complexity and cultural variability, different versions of morality, and behavioral and normative in-

---

32  Walter B. Miller, 'Lower Class Culture as a Generating Milieu of Gang Delinquency,' *Journal of Social Issues,* Vol. 14, No. 3, 1958, 5-19.

33  Cohen, *op. cit.,* 4.

34  A number of allegations by victims of police brutality by members of the Toronto police force are reported in *The Globe and Mail,* Wed., October 16, 1974, and *The Toronto Star,* Tues., October 15, 1974. See also Alan Barth, *The Price of Liberty,* New York: The Viking Press, 1961, 35-51; Albert K. Cohen, 'The Sociology of the Deviant Act: Anomie Theory and Beyond,' *American Sociological Review,* Vol. 30, 1965, 5-14.

consistency, we persist in thinking only of a law-abiding normative system in society. It is equally important to recognize the existence of a rule-violating normative system. Indeed, it is precisely because our kind of society openly encourages the pursuit and organization of different moral perspectives that there exist competing and conflicting moral standards.[35] More than one rule-violating normative system is likely operating. This suggests that a premium is placed on perpetuating deviance and refraining from deviance. Deception, guile, trickery, mendacity, pilfering, sponging, malingering, cutting corners, double-crossing, sharp practices, and graft are not the adventitious acts of a regrettable minority of persons or institutions in society. They seem to be an endemic ingredient of our daily activities and relationships. A rule-violating normative system is more than the widespread practice of deviance, or the predominance of crime and delinquency among certain social segments in society. It is somthing more than 'putting on the brakes' among workers[36] or the 'patterned evasion of the law'.[37] It is the idea that our daily life is characterized by rule violation of one form or another, and that deviance occurs in everyday respectable contexts. In this sense normal, respectable people not only experience deviant impulses, evil thoughts, and obscene fantasies, but also engage in criminal acts.[38] Moreover, it is seldom difficult to recruit some others who will encourage,

---

35   John Lofland, *Deviance and Identity*, Englewood Cliffs, New Jersey: Prentice-Hall, Inc., 1969, 95-96.

36   See Everett C. Hughes, 'The Sociological Study of Work: An Editorial Forward', *The American Journal of Sociology*, Vol. 57, March, 1952, 423-426. The phrase 'putting on the brakes' belongs to Max Weber; see footnote 1, page 425 of the editorial.

37   Robin M. Williams, *American Society*, New York: Alfred A. Knopf, 1960, 372-391. Walter Lippman writes that law breaking is so pervasive an ingredient of American Life 'that scrupulous respect for all the laws and a refusal to accept favours is almost everywhere regarded as priggishness. The few men I have ever known who were really scrupulous have often wondered whether they were not suffering from some form of compulsion neuroses.' Walter Lippman, *op. cit.*, 66.

38   See, for example, Mary Owen Cameron, *The Booster and the Snitch*, New York: The Free Press of Glencoe, 1964; Richard Quinney, 'Occupational Structure and Criminal Behavior; Prescription Violation by Retail Pharmacists', *Social Problems*, Vol. 11, Fall, 1963, 179-185; Marshall B. Clinard and Richard Quinney (eds.), *Criminal Behavior Systems*, New York: Holt, Rinehart and Winston, Inc., 1967, esp. 130-169. In professional sports many forms of illegal tactics are widely institutionalized. Among professional hockey players varying kinds of violence and assault are highly instrumental in the achievement of role confidence, and in gaining appreciative recognition from colleagues. See Robert R. Faulkner, *Violence, Camaraderie, and Occupational Character in Hockey*, Department of Sociology, University of Massachusetts, unpublished paper, 1971.

promote, and reward us, as we do them, for breaking rules.

It is important to emphasize the inevitability of learning about deviance, and its widespread practice in society. The most obvious reason why people fail to conform to the rules is that they have not been properly trained to do so. Conversely, a major reason why people violate the rules is because they have learned to do so, and anticipate the rewards from so doing. Of course, one of these rewards is money and the things that money can buy, and in our kind of society it is far, far better to be rich than to be poor. Moreover, since success is a cardinal Canadian value, money goes a long way towards symbolizing its achievement.

It is impossible to isolate, much less teach, knowledge that is useful for legitimate activities only. However careful may be the instruction (formal or informal), however exemplary the methods and wholesome the environment, the learning of facts, attitudes, and rationalizations suitable for deviance cannot be avoided. Indeed, the importance of rule violation is spotlighted early in the socialization of children. Moreover, the early realization of the ways in which deviance pays off seems to fortify our temptations. We not only become sensitive to deviant ways and alert to short cuts in obeying rules and achieving objectives, but we soon learn the benefits of evil—the social, psychological, material, and aesthetic rewards from doing wrong. This tends to support the temptation for deviance that the creation of every rules provides. And since a prominent ingredient in the socialization of children (especially of middle and upper-class youths) is the control of emotional display, we learn soon how to blanket our deviant performances behind a mask of innocence.

Nor do the principal socializing agents (family, school, church, peer group, etc.) always agree about what should be taught or how best to teach it. Schools and families do not always agree, the church often feels left out, and the worlds of teenagers seem to remain a mystery to everyone, including themselves at times. However secure the situation, legitimate acts are sometimes the source of deviant attitudes and sentiments, as they would be for the prison inmate who learned about alarm systems by taking an electrical course in prison.[39] Whatever can be had legitimately in our kind of society is very likely obtainable through illegitimate means as well; moreover, someone is apt to have been there before us. Thus the news tends to spread, the culture is transmitted, a heritage is born.

---

39  Peter Letkemann, *Crime as Work,* Englewood Cliffs,New Jersey: Prentice-Hall, Inc., 1973, 127.

The 'defective nature of human surveillance' highlights opportunities (the back alley, darkened room, unlocked automobile, gullible spouse) for us, and facilitates deviant enterprise through subterfuge. Simultaneously, it reflects the utter impossibility of total vigilance in the larger society, and in conducting our personal relationships. The inordinate cost in time, energy, money, and social organization would drastically impair the overall operation of the system. Under such conditions the adhesive element of trust assumes cardinal significance in our daily affairs. As a major ingredient in the apparatus of social control it allows personal relationships and institutions (deviant and non-deviant) to endure without constant surveillance. Many of the operations of organized crime are necessarily based on trust among its participants. The definition of trust violation as a major form of deviance reflects the importance of trust in the control of social relations in society, while the possession of trustworthiness as a personal quality is especially valued.

The rewarding responses, and when required, the easy collusion of others help spotlight a rule-violating normative system, as do the unhesitating cooperation of institutions such as hotels and restaurants in providing false receipts for clients, the improper use of grant monies by university professors and their deceptive methods of gathering data from respondents,[40] the ease with which we pocket objects that do not belong to us,[41] the expected participation in trickery, guile, false advertising and fraud at every level

---

40  As in other professions deviance is widespread among university professors; there are professors who regularly begin lectures ten minutes late and finish five minutes early; others cancel classes with little justification, while others, instead of giving lectures, have students run discussion groups. Also, however else they may justify their use, objective, machine-corrected examinations are likely highly correlated with large classes. There are also professors who beg off administrative duties because of their research—which never seems to get completed.

41  See Cameron, *op. cit.,* 1964; Erwin O. Smigel and H. Laurence Ross, (eds.), *Crimes Against Bureaucracy,* New York: Van Nostrand Reinhold Co., 1970. Some years ago the writer used to play in a swing band. Regularly after a job one of the penniless musicians would walk about casually lifting knives, forks and spoons from the tables to bring home to his wife. Also, I am told that some university students steal their meals weeks in advance. By purchasing special parka jackets with the extra large inside pockets they can surreptitiously fill them with steaks, chops and assorted cold cuts. Others who work at the L.C.B.O. during the Christmas vacation are able to pass out cartons of liquor to their friends during the Christmas rush, when the stores are crowded, and surveillance is almost impossible.

of business,[42] and the institutionalization of kickbacks as a way of doing business.[43] The same system is reflected in the tolerant, but functional attitude of priests towards upper-class adultery,[44] our multi-functional use of the words 'I love you', the emotional pretense of spouses who share the same bed, our secret means of sexual pleasure[45] and the ease with which we lie our way through social interaction,[46] e.g., in church we confess our sins—selectively. How easily we accept the illicit means used by high school or university coaches in recruiting players,[47] or secretly envy those who can successfully bribe the traffic cop[48] or tip the head waiter for a previously 'reserved' table! These are a few of the more commonplace ways of every man and woman.

42 Of course deception is not restricted to the business world. A bartender once remarked to me, 'You have no idea the number of people who will try and do anything for a free drink. Any bartender will tell you. They complain that there is no scotch in the glass, or even, for Christ's sake, that the scotch is bad!' Yet pouring-short is widely institutionalized among bartenders. Should a customer complain the bartender categorically denies the act. To highlight the absurdity of the complaint he will give the customer a drink with double or triple the quantity of liquor. Also, bars often use two kinds of orange juice, pure and 'bar mix' made from powder and water. The bar mix is used in cocktails for lounge patrons; the pure orange juice is served to patrons seated at the bar. The same price is charged for both drinks. Again, beverage rooms and cocktail lounges are licensed legally to seat a specific number of customers; often an extra 25-50 chairs are available in the room.

43 Recently four former salesmen for large pharmaceutical companies testified before a subcommittee on health, that pharmacists and physicians who bought their companies' drugs were rewarded with gifts, ranging from golf tees to color television sets. Senator Edward Kennedy charged that the practice smacks of payola and that it is influencing doctors to prescribe drugs 'irrationally.' Witnesses told of some doctors who sold free samples to their patients and traded samples to pharmacists in return for cologne for their wives. The *Kitchener-Waterloo Record,* Saturday, March 9, 1974.

44 Lois B. DeFleur, *Delinquency in Argentina,* Washington State University Press, 1970, 77.

45 Arthur H. Lewis, *Carnival,* New York: The Trident Press, 1970, 50, also 216-227.

46 The generic character of a rule-violating normative system is captured best by Tennessee Williams, when he has one of his characters talk about the inevitability of having to live with lies and pretenses—one form of rule violation. Tennessee Williams, *Cat on a Hot Tin Roof,* New York: The New American Library, Inc., 1955, 8081. David Matza and Gresham M. Sykes, 'Juvenile Delinquency and Subterranean Values,' *American Sociological Review,* Vol. 26, No. 5, 1961, 712-719.

47 Recently a high school basketball star player in the United States reported that one college coach offered him '$1,000,000 under the table' to sign with his college. The *Kitchener-Waterloo Record,* Monday June 24, 1974.

48 Some Montreal cabdrivers used to keep a folded five dollar bill next to their driving license in their wallets. If stopped for some traffic infraction, the routine manner in which the driver presented the closed wallet to the police officer precluded the accusation of bribery. Sometimes the wallet was returned minus the five dollar bill, and the officer would walk away. Of course such tactics are not limited to taxi drivers.

Admittedly, we get our kicks from doing what is right, but few would deny that they also derive some pleasure from doing what is wrong. All motivation is a mixed bag, and recourse to the plethora of culturally current rationalizations and justifications for our acts helps us to blissfully eclipse the cost of remorse of our deviant ways. In a world infused with deviance, to be deviant helps establish oneself as human.

## Institutionalization of Norms

Normative complexity characterizes every social system. There is a wide variety of norms in a system, and the degree to which they receive moral support is variable. Many common practices fail to receive widespread moral support. For example, petty theft, gambling, cribbing on examinations, and unmarried couples living together are relatively common activities, but they are not institutionalized in society. Rules that are institutionalized always have reference to a particular social system. The system may consist of merely two persons; thus the ritual of Saturday night sex may be institutionalized between a middle-aged married couple; a Friday night poker game may be institutionalized among five members of a twenty member Sociology department—a slightly larger social system. The rational and inexorable use of murder in the world of organized crime reflects the institutionalization of violence. Institutionalized rules often (but not necessarily) deal with matters that are considered strategic or morally important for the system. Acts that are considered 'wrongs in themselves' (*mala in se*) are often proscribed by institutionalized rules, as are incest, robbery and sexual assault. Of course, what is morally forbidden today may be morally acceptable tomorrow.

When the validity and authority of rules are unquestioned they are institutionalized. Institutionalized rules have the moral consensus of a relatively large segment of the system; people take the rules seriously and believe that everyone should obey them. Moreover, norms that are institutionalized usually receive protection through sanctions that are actually enforceable. However, the legislation of rules is no guarantee of wholesale moral support. Laws that protect the person and his belongings, for example, against burglary, assault, murder, and rape, are strongly institutionalized and receive almost total moral backing. Their violation is strongly condemned. Traffic laws, Sunday 'blue laws' and the laws against vagrancy, public drunkenness, and the use of pinball machines[49] receive considerably less moral support; they are con-

---

49  Pinball machines are illegal in Kitchener-Waterloo, Ontario and regional
    morality police officers are enforcing the Criminal Code. However, students at

21

sidered much less reprehensible and their violation is not severely condemned. It is also true that people feel much less compunction about stealing from large bureaucracies, especially the government.[50] On the other hand, the informal, unwritten rule which says that 'you should not break your mother's heart' is strongly institutionalized.

Perfect institutionalization is an ideal. Cultural diversity and social differentiation are endemic features of modern societies, and help generate social distance, suspicion, and exploitation among men. Since a democratic, pluralistic society encourages the pursuit of private interests and moral preferences, there are always competing, and sometimes antithetical perspectives on good and evil, and on what is considered important in society. This precludes the perfect institutionalization of norms, and makes the task of reaching consensus at the ground-level of social conduct very difficult. This is the function of the social organization of men—to reach accord in the operationalization of everyday acts that have reference to abstract principles.[51] There is also the problem of the institutionalization of contradictory moral tenets. Robert S. Lynd has pointed to the following statements as creating dilemmas for people in America; they apply equally well to Canada: 'Honesty is the best policy,' but 'Business is business . . . ;' 'Education is a fine thing,' but 'It is practical men who get things done;' "Religion and 'the finer things of life' are our ultimate values . . . ," but 'A man owes it to himself and to his family to make as much money as he can;' 'Everyone should try to be successful,' but 'The kind of person you are is more important than how successful you are.'[52] Especially during a period of rapid social change, these difficulties may highlight the 'realisation of the contingent, tentative, and even arbitrary character of all definitions of action.'[53] However, at any time they mark the variability in the institutionalization of norms.

This means that there is an absence of agreement about what activities and moral principles are to be given 'compliance priority'. This expanding area of uncertainty and ambiguity allows,

the University of Waterloo and Sir Wilfrid Laurier University are launching an appeal to the regional board. The *Kitchener-Waterloo Record,* December 29, 1973.

50  Erwin O. Smigel and H. Laurence Ross, *Crimes Against Bureaucracy,* New York: Van Nostrand Reinhold Co., 1970, 28.

51  John Lofland, *op. cit.,* 92-100.

52  Robert S. Lynd, *Knowledge For What?,* New York: Grove Press, Inc., 1964, 60-62.

53  Lofland, *op. cit.,* 100.

and implicitly legitimates, personal discretion and latitude in the ranking of activities and the judgment of their moral status. Thus, a vast range of deviant acts may be defined as subjectively available and relatively moral. Swinging, key parties, other forms of sexual amusement, collective sabotage, student demonstrations, stage nudity and vivid sexual displays on the cinema screen are cases in point.[54] Similarly, discretion continues to be a major criterion and justification among those who smoke pot and consider its use a relatively pleasurable pursuit.

To further complicate matters there are always persons who will question the legitimacy, validity and authority of rules. It is typical of nonconformists to question the existing rules, and to wish to replace them with rules which they believe to be morally superior. However, unlike the revolutionary, the nonconformist need not deny the moral authority of the overall normative structure. The revolutionary does precisely this; he does not recognize the legitimacy of persons in power, and he denies the authority according to which the system of rules claims validity. In doing so, he severs moral bonds with those other than his own revolutionary group. This means that rights and legitimations are always associated with groups and social positions, and these must always be specified.

Yet persons do not always question nor repudiate the rules that they violate. The vast majority of criminals fall into this category. Motivated largely by self interest, they go about their business violating laws and trying to avoid detection and/or conviction.[55] As a 34-year-old career burglar remarked, 'You might laugh . . . but I'm for law and order. What I do is my business. I don't hurt anyone, anyway most of the people who lose stuff are insured, and I could tell you about the way they inflate their losses. But this mugging on the streets and the rapes and the way they have to coddle these creeps makes me sick.'[56] The criminal worlds are not a repudiation of the larger legitimate cultural system. Indeed most criminals agree with the rules, accept the right of others to apprehend and penalize them for their wrongdoing, and expect them to do so. This element of reciprocity is per-

---

54 See Robert R. Bell, *Social Deviance*, Homewood, Illinois: The Dorsey Press, 1971, 63-88.

55 Peter Letkemann, *op. cit.*, 30.

56 Nikolas Pileggi, 'The Year of The Burglar' in Clifton D. Bryant, *Deviant Behavior: Occupational and Organizational Bases*, Chicago: Rand McNally College Publishing Co., 1974, 396.

haps the essential ingredient of institutionalization.[57]

Notwithstanding the imperfect institutionalization of rules in a system, there is usually some set of rules that is dominant, that enjoys more respectability than do other rules. These are rules that are publicly recognized, by which the man on the street conducts his daily affairs.[58] Such rules comprise the common sense of the solid citizen and the normative backbone of the community. People firmly believe in such rules and try to adhere to them. Violators are frowned upon, disapproved, considered odd or different.[59] Sometimes it is sufficient to merely dispute the rules to be defined an outsider.[60] Conscientious objectors during wartime, homosexuals who publicize the 'naturalness' of their conduct, conscientious atheists, proponents of free love, and some extreme political groups are among such persons. Their attitudes, sentiments and values, (like those of the parents who named their child america spelled with a lower case 'a' attempting to show their disenchantment with society) and their daily routines run against the main grain of Canadian or American society. However, not everyone in the system needs to internalize the norm for it to be institutionalized. What is important is that persons closely associated with the practice are aware of and sensitive to the norm, and the requirements connected with it. For example, among prostitutes orgasm is discouraged; emotional pretense is the norm. Most prostitutes likely subscribe to the norm, but while orgasm with a John is infrequent, it is not unknown.[61]

We began this section by referring to the normative complexity of a society. This does not imply that the concept 'deviance' is any less important because there is less than perfect institutionalization in a system. Notwithstanding the degree of institutionalization, people will continue to define those who break rules as deviant. Moreover, the sociologist must attempt to explain the occurrence of the behavior, however it is defined.[62] Finally, it is always crucial to specify the social system to which a particular

---

57 Alvin W. Gouldner, 'The Norm of Reprocity: A Preliminary Statement,' *American Sociological Review,* Vol. 25, No. 2, 1960, 161-178; Harry Johnson, *Sociology: A Systematic Introduction,* New York: Harcourt, Brace & World, Inc., 1960, 15-47; Albert K. Cohen, *Deviance and Control,* 19-21.

58 Cohen, *Deviance and Control,* 20.

59 *Ibid.,* 20.

60 Howard S. Becker, *Outsiders: Studies in the Sociology of Deviance,* New York: The Free Press of Glencoe, 1963, 1-18.

61 James H. Bryan, 'Apprenticeships in Prostitution', *Social Problems,* Vol. 12, 1965, 287-297.

62 Cohen, *op. cit.,* 20-21.

norm applies, whose conception of the norm is being dealt with, and the degree to which persons consent to have designated others sanction them for norm violation. Only then can we establish whether a norm has been violated, and whether the offender considers his conduct deviant.

# Deviance

**3**

Deviant behavior is behavior that violates rules, but the breach of any rule does not necessarily qualify as deviant conduct. Deviance is behavior that violates the normative rules of a social system of action, the institutionalized expectations and understandings that are respected and considered legitimate. However, to say that deviance is the violation of institutionalized rules is insufficient. The larger society is not a perfectly homogeneous, culturally integrated, social system; rather it is breathtakingly complicated, a complex configuration of multi-varied social worlds. And the cultural coherence, normative integration, and moral consensus of each world are always variable. Most of us possess scanty knowledge of these worlds, and our images of them are vague and unstructured. Other persons are their inhabitants, and are immersed in them as we are not; they are committed to their roles as we cannot be, and abide by rules which have little meaning for us. This means that it is imperative to establish the frame of reference of deviance, the particular system of normative expectations in which the violation transpires. Only in this manner can we attempt to establish the normative complexion of the system, the variable institutionalization of its norms, and their differential distribution throughout the particular system. But the degree of institutionalization of expectations and understandings required to determine deviance is always difficult to establish, since 'the criteria of institutionalisation are themselves multiple and to some extent vary independently.'[1]

Deviant conduct is not only a departure from some statistical norm; it is not merely the frequency of an act, but its undesirability that matters. Deviance also includes 'secret deviance', and deviance that is visible only to small groups of insiders.[2] The deviant acts of kings and queens, presidents and prime ministers, judges and the police are cases in point.

Much sociological research has concerned itself with the study of offenses against the law, e.g., crime and juvenile delinquency; however, it is important to realize that legal norms constitute only one kind of norm and their violation only a single kind of deviant behavior. There are many other types of norms from which deviance is possible, e.g., rules of courtesy, folkways, mores, professional ethics and religious commandments.[3] Laughing at a person who stutters is a deviant act; the possession of heroin is both a deviant act and a violation of the criminal law. Among most persons who smoke pot (and thereby violate the law), and who question the propriety of the law, there are informal rules that influence their own use of the drug; for example, the solitary use of marijuana is rare and often considered wasteful. Similarly, failure to demonstrate the appropriate attitude and appreciation when using pot at a party may be defined deviant by the participants.

We have noted that rules are necessary for any social system; this means that deviance can and does occur in systems as diverse as a family, a criminal gang, or a church service. The criteria for establishing deviance and conformity in a particular social system are always difficult to establish. Sometimes the rules by which persons conduct their affairs are fuzzy; if rules are unwritten it can be especially difficult to establish their precise meaning and significance. Also, the meanings of rules undergo change, and with differential emphasis move from one group to another; in time the rules may disappear. Furthermore, there are fashion swings to deviance; ten years ago smoking pot was 'out'; today it is consid-

---

1  Albert K. Cohen, *Deviance and Control,* Englewood Cliffs, New Jersey: Prentice-Hall, Inc., 1966, 150.

2  Albert K. Cohen, "Stability and Change in Deviance", in Bernard Barber and Alex Inkeles (eds.), *Stability and Change,* Boston: Little, Brown and Company, 1971, 285-310.

3  For an extremely informative account of folkways, mores and law see the classic by William Graham Sumner, *Folkways,* New York: Dover Publications, 1959.

ered 'in'. Among some groups key parties and swinging are popular forms of sexual change;[4] tomorrow, other forms may be fashionable. The routine use of four-letter words by young girls is audibly fashionable among some groups. Under these circumstances the status of an act is uncertain; it may be deviant, conforming, or variable.[5] Perhaps at any time the stability of meaning of a social act is an ideal.

One criterion used in establishing whether a deviant act has occurred is the willingness of others to apply sanctions against the offender. Since there are still many persons who condemn abortion, marijuana use, and young unmarried couples living together, this is testimony that serious rules are being breached. However, the declining extent of condemnation reflects a decrease in the moral reprehensibility of such activities.

Deviant behavior refers to the activities in which people participate, not to the kinds of people they are or the personalities they possess. We all break rules; those who violate the serious rules include a motley assortment of personality types, but no more or less so than those few, if any, who abstain. The pathology of a person's personality is judged according to clinical criteria; it has special relevance for, and is to be understood according to, the personality system of the individual. To a very large extent, this is the specialized work of clinical psychologists, psychiatrists, and psychoanalysts. Deviant conduct is not established according to clinical criteria, but has relevance to the particular system of rules in which the action transpires. There is nothing untenable, unnatural, or psychologically abnormal about forging cheques, stealing for a living, pimping, prostitution or passing counterfeit bills. Large numbers of people are successfully engaged in these activities every day.[6] The less successful merely reflect that occupational hazards are characteristic of all business enterprises, whether legal or illegal. There is no reason to believe that such persons are any less happy, or any more maladjusted than the thousands of workers who, we are told, are disenchanted, alienated and generally fed-up with their lot. Maladjusted personalities and deviant behavior have very little in common; to believe that the majority of deviance in society is conducted by sick personali-

---

4   Robert R. Bell, *Social Deviance,* 63-88.

5   John Lofland, *op. cit.;* David Matza, *Delinquency and Drift,* New York: John Wiley & Sons, Inc., 1964, 33-152.

6   Two million dollars in phoney bills were seized by the R.C.M.P. in 1973; the *Kitchener-Waterloo Record,* Saturday, January 12, 1974. The $50.00 Canadian bills are of such good quality and so numerous that the acceptability of a $50.00 bill whether good or bad has been seriously undermined. The *Kitchener-Waterloo Record,* Saturday, December 29, 1973.

ties is wrong thinking, and has little basis in social scientific fact. The problems that generate deviance are very seldom located only in the characteristics of the deviating persons.

Clinically normal people produce most of the deviant behavior in society. Are the increasingly large numbers of young persons who smoke marijuana disturbed personalities? Consider the prostitutes and their clients, the shoplifters, grifters, grafters and chiselers; consider the persons who cheat on their income taxes, and in organizations, occupations and professions—does it make sense to consider these persons sick or unhappy personalities? Is it possible to think of a single type of work where the opportunity does not exist for some kind of deviance? For example, the role of housewife provides an excellent opportunity for occupying the joint role, prostitute-wife. Some better class prostitutes are happily married, suburban housewives with families, whose supplementary earnings contribute to the family budget.[7]

Unquestionably there are maladjusted persons who break the law. But there is no necessary correlation between deviant behavior and abnormal personalities. Clinically defective personalities are very likely too ill to participate in much deviant conduct. Albert K. Cohen has written, ' . . . many clinically abnormal people, confronted by sexual temptation and opportunity to which many normal people would succumb, are incapable, in consequence of their pathological anxieties concerning sex of anything but virtue.'[8] In any case the relationship between rule-violating behavior and clinically defective personalities is an empirical one.

# Deviance and Roles

There must always be some set of rules operating to guide people's behavior, and a certain segment of the group must agree that these rules are valid and ought to be obeyed. This is mirrored, for example, in the laws against abortion, keeping a gambling house, and the possession of marijuana, with which a considerable segment

---

7    Much deviance originates from the routine conventional settings where we spend most of our time. For example, recently two Canadian customs officers were arrested for having sexual relations (in an office at the port of entry) with newly arrived immigrants, as a requirement for permission to enter the country. Similarly, some years ago in London, England, a minister was found having regular sexual relations with his female parishioners in the vestry of his church. More recently, five Roman Catholic priests and a layman were sentenced to jail terms for indecent assaults on children in an institution for the socially maladjusted. *The Globe and Mail,* Saturday, May 3, 1975, 2.

8    Albert K. Cohen, "The Study of Social Disorganisation and Deviant Behaviour" in Robert K. Merton, Leonard Broom and Leonard S. Cottrell, Jr., (eds.), *Sociology Today,* New York: Basic Books, 1959, 463.

of the population is still in agreement. To claim membership in a group means to become subject to its rules regardless of how one feels about them. The person must try to conform or be sanctioned, perhaps forfeiting the claim to group membership. Since the majority of the population very likely agree with the laws regulating abortion, drug use, gambling and prostitution, and because these people are seldom in circumstances conducive to their violation, they experience little trouble in conforming to the laws.

Rules are not only intimately associated with groups, but also with the social roles that people occupy in them. Institutionalized rules define the role expectations and obligations to which one becomes subject when joining a group. This means that deviance is relative to the groups to which one belongs, and to the social roles that one holds. To occupy the roles of Canadian citizen and medical doctor is to be subject to the laws that govern the society, and to the rules that regulate the medical profession respectively. Similarly, to be an habitué of the underworld, or an insider in the 'gay world' is to be privy to the secrets, the relationships that develop, and the events that transpire therein. It means also knowing the *modus operandi* of their typical activities, and the rules by which they are conducted. To be knowledgeable of the world of poolroom hustlers is to know their methods of deception—the technical expertise that is required in order to feign less competence than the hustler really possesses[9]—and the rules that govern their relationships with opponents.[10] On the other hand, unless one is actively homosexual one is not subject to the informal system of rules that articulates homosexual activities and relationships.

It is also true that not all groups are concerned with obtaining conformity only from their members. For example, a temperance organization usually tries to apply its rules to people outside the organization, those whom they consider deviant because they drink alcoholic beverages.

We all belong to a number of groups (e.g., a family, a profession, a political party, a golf club), and occupy a variety of social roles (e.g., father, dentist, lesbian, friend, petty thief). To lay claim to a role, be it formal or informal, means that we wish to assume a certain identity and wish others to define us as a particular kind

---

9   Perhaps there is a little of the hustler in all of us, especially in social situations. Do we not size up the situation, evaluate others, feign less confidence and knowledge than we actually possess before we commit ourselves and put our best foot forward—and then only when it serves us best?

10   Ned Polsky, *Hustlers, Beats, and Others,* New York: Doubleday Anchor Books, 1969, 52-68.

of person. However the roles that we admire and the pictures of ourselves that we secretly cherish are culturally limited. The groups of which we are periodically members, especially the sub-cultures—social worlds—in which we participate and the roles that we claim, limit the kinds of person we may be, and the attitudes, sentiments and behavioral postures that we may assume. For example, the sexual preferences and repertory of the homosexual who has been 'out' for a number of years are very likely different from those of his initial experiences.[11] Claiming the role of teenager among boys in the middle-class youth culture requires active participation in heterosexual activities such as dances, parties and sports events. It means the cultivation of social skills and a social personality, and requires sophistication rather than aggressive masculinity in 'making out' with girls.[12] Social roles are, therefore, a very important mechanism of social control. To successfully claim a role means at least to try to conform to the expectations of those others with whom one typically interacts as role occupant. Failure to do so produces strain and usually elicits the disapproval (sanctions) of others.

But in the midst of rapid social and cultural transformation in society the appropriation of clearcut roles and tenured group membership is sometimes difficult. As major institutions undergo change, we are constantly alerted to the realignment, and sometimes gradual erosion of the groups and affiliations to which we belong. Thus we are forced to seek new alliances for social and psychological comfort. Moreover, our claims to particular roles are no longer certain. It is no longer fashionable to claim the role of university dropout, and the role of student radical no longer requires organizing sit-ins, strikes, and the destruction of property. In other cases it is increasingly difficult to be absolutely certain of the expectations and obligations of the roles that we occupy. Notwithstanding the phalanx of 'experts', the mass media, and paperback books prescribed as sources of clarification, in many areas there remains little agreement concerning appropriate role conduct. For example, the role obligations of adolescent, especially in the middle and upper-middle classes, remain unclear; similar-

---

11  Martin Hoffman, *The Gay World,* New York: Basic Books, Inc., 1968, 37; Barry M. Dank, "Coming Out in the Gay World," in James R. McIntosh (ed.), *Perspectives on Marginality,* Boston: Allyn and Beacon, Inc., 1974, 81-98. For recent Canadian material see Peter Sawchuk, "Becoming a Homosexual," in Jack Haas and Bill Shaffir (eds.), *Decency & Deviance,* Toronto: McClelland and Stewart Limited, 1974, 233-245.

12  Edmund W. Vaz, "Middle Class Adolescents: Self-Reported Delinquency and Youth Culture," *The Canadian Review of Sociology and Anthropology,* Vol. 2, No. 1, 1956, 52-70.

ly, the traditional role of mother is beginning to wear thin. With the rapidly growing practice of enrolling children (sometimes babies) at all-day care centers, the role of mother may soon give way to the role of 'weekend mother'.[13] Here role expectations and obligations are more in accord with current behavioral practices. It is therefore imperative that we be knowledgeable about a particular role, its rights and obligations, and the groups of which it is part, before any reliable judgment of deviance-conformity is made.

If a person does not hold membership in a group or claim any of the roles contained within the group, whatever his behavior it cannot be deviant. Moreover if a person's conduct does not fall within the jurisdiction of the rules of the group, his behavior cannot be deviant.[14]

# Deviant Roles

It is one thing to break a rule or violate a law—to tell a lie, to steal money, commit murder or bigamy, or engage in a homosexual act. It is something else to have others think of us as a liar, a thief, a murderer, a bigamist or a homosexual. These are social roles—socially recognized categories of persons. As Matza has written, 'To be signified a thief is to lose the blissful identity of one who among other things happens to have committed a theft.'[15] Perhaps the main function of a social role is that it enables others to categorize a person, which makes it easier to deal with him. It makes for anticipated, consistent conduct. A social role is a kind of reputation, and people then know what to expect of the role occupant and how best to act towards him.

All social roles include names, terms or labels, and these are part of the language that we use in classifying people. Depending on our knowledge of the role, the terms have relatively precise meanings for us; the roles of father, mother, actor or convict are well known. But the role of 'twinkie' is perhaps best known in

---

13   At one time some parents enrolled their young children (usually sons) at their universities, presumably because they were proud of their schools and wished the best for their children. Today parents enrol their prospective babies at all-day care centers, presumably because the law requires the care of babies and parents wish the best for themselves.

14   Albert K. Cohen, *Deviance and Control,* Englewood Cliffs, New Jersey: Prentice-Hall, Inc., 1966, 13.

15   David Matza, *Becoming Deviant,* Englewood Cliffs,New Jersey: Prentice-Hall Inc., 1969, 156.

homosexual circles,[16] that of 'plunger-boy' among gamblers,[17] 'Pete man' among safe crackers,[18] 'cowboy' among Montreal cab-drivers,[19] and 'pothead' and 'mellow dude' among some drug users.[20]

The terms that we employ in categorizing others suggest that they are certain kinds of people. To be known as a con man, habitual criminal, pimp or broken-down hooker implies certain things; it suggests that one possesses a special kind of character, that one *is* that kind of person, possessed of certain deviant quali-ties that distinguish him (or her) from others. It also says that one's attitudes, sentiments and values befit the label; in other words, the terms that we use suggest something about the person's self. How a person thinks about himself is closely associated with the social roles that he occupies, and the saliency of these roles for him. The extent to which the person identifies with the role, and orients his everyday life about it will strongly influence his self conception. Marilyn Salutin has informed us that strippers in Toronto see themselves as strippers primarily because they have seldom aspired to become anything else. Although they may ver-bally upgrade their work, they reveal no shame about their occu-pation. Their definition of stripping as 'socially useful', legitimate entertainment reflects their effort to protect their vested interest in the work as it is.[21] Similarly, if a person earns a successful livelihood from burglarizing other people's homes, and has done so successfully for some time, he is very apt to think of himself in such terms—as a house burglar, and a successful one to boot! To the extent that we occupy roles, those with whom we interact will anticipate that we conduct ourselves in accordance with the role expectations. The more we identify with a role, and the great-er our emotional investment in the role, the more strongly this

---

16  A "twinkie" is a boyish, sexually desirable young man. Martin Hoffman, *op. cit.*, 68-70.

17  A 'plunger' is a gambler who lays big bets, someone who takes a 'plunge'.

18  A 'Pete man' is a dying breed of thief who uses nitroglycerin in cracking safes. See Bill Chambliss (ed.), *Box Man,* New York: Harper & Row, 1972, 9; Peter Letkemann, *Crime as Work,* 35.

19  A 'cowboy' is a reckless cabdriver. See Edmund W. Vaz, *The Metropolitan Taxi Driver: His Work and Self Conception,* Unpublished Master's thesis, Department of Sociology, McGill University, 1955.

20  Alan G. Sutter, "Worlds of Drug Use on the Street Scene," in Donald R. Cressey and David A. Ward (eds.), *Delinquency, Crime and Social Process,* New York: Harper & Row, 1969, 802-829.

21  Marilyn Salutin, "Stripper Morality" in Craig L. Boydell, Carl F. Grindstaff and Paul C. Whitehead (eds.), *Deviant Behaviour and Societal Reaction,* Toronto: Holt, Rinehart and Winston of Canada, Ltd., 1972, 532-545.

will govern our self conceptions, and constitute the social lens through which our versions of morality are defined. However, at no time does a particular role call forth the totality of a person's behavioral and attitudinal baggage. Role requirements are associated with particular social situations; a pickpocket is not apt to operate at his own wedding, but his occupational colleagues might.

Whenever we refer to social roles (deviant or otherwise) we must always consider the role criteria according to which persons may legitimately claim and be granted a particular role. For example, we can ask when a woman may legitimately claim the role of prostitute. Is it sufficient to accept 'favors' (how many?), money (how much?), be apprenticed, or work in a brothel? What are the operating criteria according to which her claims are judged? What are the criteria operating for claiming the role of 'Box man' among safe crackers? How many safes must a thief crack? Does the quality and neatness of his work count?[22] Are reliability and loyalty relevant qualities? What are the operating criteria for the role of cat among black drug addicts? Among jazz musicians? Of course, these questions can be asked as well of non-deviant roles. Can the person who writes unpublished novels claim the role of writer? How many novels or stories must he publish before others will legitimately grant his role claims? Must he earn his livelihood from his writing? Does the quality of his work make a difference? Role criteria are also variable and depend on the groups to which we belong.

For every social role there are culturally, and often subculturally, established signs which reflect role or group membership. Signs are the visible indices which suggest possible membership in a social role and they may be variously public. Since almost anything may be a sign of a social role (a uniform, insignia, membership card, etc.), the more knowledgeable we are of the social worlds in which people live, the more reliable will be our interpretations, and efforts at classifying those whom we encounter. It is often on the basis of signs that members of deviant groups identify each other; lesbians and homosexuals are knowledgeable and especially sensitive to their own particular role signs. The cruising homosexual is not distinguished from non-homosexuals by his physical characteristics, but by the behavioral gestures which indicate the role; these include use of the eyes, prolonged searching looks of the other man's entire body, and glancing backward at the person.[23] Perhaps one's sex is the most obvious sign of a gener-

---

22  Chambliss, *op. cit.*, 1-24.

23  Hoffman, *op. cit.*, 47.

al social role; the apparel[24] (e.g., denims, overalls, a buttoned-down or turned-around collar, or being well-dressed—the conventional sign of respectability and trustworthiness) is often an immediate and helpful sign in categorizing people; a wedding band, an open top button on a pilot's tunic,[25] the smell of petrol on a person's breath,[26] and a person's accent, posture, physical build and a full range of facial habits and expressions are also signs. For example, the cauliflower ear of the wrestler or boxer, the usually red, scarred fingers of the butcher, the slightly puffed lip of the trumpeter, the loose catlike gait of the novice lightweight—all are signs of role and group membership. It is also true that our religious beliefs, aesthetic standards, political views and forms of etiquette are often selected on the basis of the demands of the roles to which we lay claim. With the gang boy it is the strut that counts; it proclaims his group membership and his claim to leadership.

> Someday I come walking down the street they all look at me
> with respect and say. "There goes a cold killer. Here comes
> Duke Custis. He a cold killer." Then everybody pay attention—
> an listen when I talk . . . I keep movin. Some time I wave a
> hand to em. The coolies look at me . . . It make em mad to see
> me when I strut. Screw them. Aint no place for coolies in this
> world. Keep walkin. My rumble strut. Everybody know
> somethin is cookin. Here comes Duke. He got a rep Man. Man
> he got heart. I swinging with the gang tonight. They all waiting
> for *me*. Duke Custis. The War Lord of the Royal Crocadiles.[27]

Signs are usually found in clusters: the role of butch in women's prisons requires short hair, no makeup, unshaven legs and a mas-

---

24  For the importance of clothing in the work world see William H. Form and Gregory P. Stone, *The Social Significance of Clothing in Occupational Life,* East Lansing: Michigan State College Agricultural Experiment Station, Technical Bulletin 217, June 1955, 1-53; also relevant is Bernard Barber, *Social Stratification: A Comparative Analysis of Structure and Process,* New York: Harcourt, Brace and Company, 1957, 146-151.

25  Although it was against regulations, wearing an open top button on a tunic indicated a fighter pilot in the Battle of Britain.

26  An unfortunate but telling sign of the dying street occupation of the 'fire-eater'; see Ernest Hemingway, *A Moveable Feast,* New York: Bantam Books, 1965, 156.

27  Warren Miller, *Cool World,* Greenwich, Connecticut: Fawcett Publications, 1964, 12. Copyright ©1959 by Warren Miller, by permission of Little, Brown and Co.

culine walk;[28] that of the punch drunk boxer demands an ambling gait, thickened speech and misshapen nose. An English barrister wears a wig and gown; the fashion model is characterized by the slim figure, tall walk, tote bag and makeup case; and a drop-out major in poetry may be found in a dimly-lit coffee house carrying a copy of John Donne and wearing dark glasses and sandals. Anything may be a sign to a person to the degree that it enables him to reliably categorize others. Sometimes the absence of signs is equally revealing; no makeup, no jewelery and no bra likely denote, these days, a so-called liberated woman. 'The way a man stands, moves his hands, hunches his shoulders or smiles while talking can reveal a great deal to his listeners.'[29] Yet some roles possess relatively low visibility. The transient and the unemployed are often difficult to spot; their signs are best discernible against a special part of the city, for example, the park bench, train yard, or third-rate tavern. Perhaps the ambiguity of such roles serves as a suitable cover for certain kinds of criminal acts.

Most social interaction is very likely initiated on the basis of signs. Our easy recognition of signs often evokes in us feelings of security in our surroundings and confidence in our transactions with others. But the inability to recognize signs can be very discomfiting. One reason why rural persons sometimes feel lost in large cities is their inability to recognize and interpret the variety of subtle and not-so-subtle signs that surround them. Their preference for 'life on the farm' reflects partly their easy familiarity with the less dynamic signs of rural living.

We may, and often do, misinterpret signs, and this can have differential consequences for the flow of interaction. For example, women who appear shapely may be found to be otherwise; lower-class boys who wear the 'right' clothes and effect a tough, defiant posture may, in fact, lack 'heart', be 'weak', without any 'guts.' The female drinker in a tavern who uses foul language, tells dirty stories and makes insinuating gestures may not, in fact, 'put out'.[30] Of course, one may impersonate a role occupant and wear the signs falsely, as do the spinster who wears a wedding band because she prefers to be considered married, the occupational novice who continuously uses jargon in an effort to be defined a 'veteran', and

---

28 Robert R. Bell, *Social Deviance*, Homewood, Illinois: The Dorsey Press, 1971, 351.

29 Thomas Kochman, "Rapping in the Black Ghetto", *Transaction*, Vol. 6, No. 4, 1969.

30 See Mennachem Amir, "Patterns of Forcible Rape," in Marshall B. Clinard And Richard Quinney (eds.), *Criminal Behavior Systems*, New York: Holt, Rinehart and Winston, Inc., 1967, 68-69.

the person in a first-class restaurant who carefully, slowly, and seemingly knowledgeably sips the profferred sample of wine with a tongue burned from cigarettes and habituated to soft drinks. Detectives often initiate action on the basis of signs—long hair, skin color, beards, a flashed bank roll—only to find that their suspect is the wrong man. In nineteenth century England, youths would substitute their clothes for rags, then beg for clothes from passing pedestrians.[31] In some cases persons may legitimately possess the signs, yet the criteria may undergo periodic change. On some bomber squadrons during World War II nothing short of a tour of operations was sufficient to be considered a 'veteran'.[32] But when posted to another squadron, air crews who had almost completed their second 'tour of ops' were regarded with considerable awe—now *they* were the veterans. Two tours had become the criterion.

Whenever we employ a label or term referring to others it usually evokes certain images in our mind of what kinds of person fill the role. These images may be sketchy or detailed depending on the popularity of the role and our knowledge of it. For example, the pictures evoked by the terms physician, minister or prostitute are much clearer than those produced by terms such as 'rounder',[33] 'wire'[34] or 'Bankroll man',[35] because these roles are relatively esoteric, parts of closely knit subcultures, and are not widely known in society. The mere fact that a large number of people engage in similar kinds of conduct does not inevitably generate a clearcut image of their role. The term social drinker does not

---

31  J.J. Tobias, *Crime and Industrial Society in the Nineteenth Century,* Middlesex: Penguin Books Ltd., 1972, 68-69.

32  The public sign of having completed a tour of operations was a small pair of bronze wings worn on the tunic. Innumerable measures were taken to avoid being considered a novice. For example, a well worn uniform signified a lot of 'time' in service; some airmen would sew their old, dirty wings on their new uniforms, while still others took measures to have the fluff removed from their new uniforms. Some signs carried more impact and told more of a story than others, for example, the pilot who always wore a cap with a bullet hole and powder markings clearly visible.

33  To be a 'rounder' is to be committed to an illegitimate style of life. It means to be reliable in one's world, to be committed to one's task and to execute the job with planning and organization.

34  A 'wire' is the member of a team of pickpockets who extracts the billfold from the mark's pocket. Synonyms are 'tool', 'instrument', or 'hook'. See Edwin H. Sutherland, *The Professional Thief,* Chicago: The University of Chicago Press, 1937, 44-48; Mary McIntosh, "Changes in the Organization of Thieving" in Stanley Cohen (ed.), *Images of Deviance,* Middlesex, England: Penguin Books Ltd., 1971, 104-109.

35  A 'Bankroll man' is one who finances a gambling scheme. A near equivalent role in the legitimate world is that of 'Angel', the person who finances a musical show.

easily call to mind a clear picture of the role occupant. The expectations associated with the role are very general, and the increasingly large number of people who take a drink seems to preclude a public image from emerging. Drinking socially is likely becoming part of the general expectations of 'socializing', and such conduct is defined as neither more nor less important than attending a movie. Consider the role of adultress. Hawthorn's literary character Hester Prynne, a known adultress, was required to wear a scarlet 'A' embroidered on her garment when she walked in public.[36] The label evoked a clear image of the woman in the minds of others. What has happened to the image? The behavior prevails; married women continue to take lovers, but there is no longer a public image of the adultress. Perhaps this means that violation of the rule is considered less serious, and that adultery is becoming increasingly widespread. On the other hand, as we learn more about the relatively closed subcultures in which drugs are used, the terms 'junkie' and 'pusher' take on more meaning for us, the images grow sharper, and the kinds of conduct expected of such persons become publicly known. Also, our imagery is culturally variable. For example, the term 'political criminal' will evoke different images in communist and non-communist countries.

It is true also that roles demand of us both conduct and emotion, i.e., we are expected to perform behaviorally in an appropriate manner, according to role expectations, but we are obliged also to display the proper emotions at the proper time. This is not as difficult as it sounds. Unless one occupies a role 'at a distance', with little or no commitment, one soon begins to experience ('really feel') the expected kinds of sentiments. For example, the newly crowned beauty queen almost invariably expresses joy chokingly, with tears; similarly, the retiring superstar leaves the game tearfully.[37] The hoodlum feels tougher with a gun in his fist, the professor feels wise as he pontificates in class, and it is easy to feel sophisticated when dining at Maxim's. Again, an excellent remedy for feeling blue is a shave, shower and shampoo. But Berger says it

---

36 Sculley Bradley, Richmond Croom Beatty and E. Hudson Long (eds.), *Nathaniel Hawthorne, The Scarlet Letter: An Annotated Text, Backgrounds and Sources Essays in Criticism,* New York: W. W. Norton and Co., 1962, 43.

37 The range of emotional display is, of course, culturally variable. Edson Arantes Do Nascimento, commonly known as Pele, and regarded by many as the greatest soccer player of all time "suddenly . . . dropped to his knees" and "knelt on the pitch with tears streaming down his face. As he slowly turned to the four sides of the arena, still kneeling but arms raised in a last farewell, a roar of 'Pele, Pele' rose from the 30,000 fans . . . . Slowly, rising to his feet, Pele . . . removed for the last time his black and white striped No. 10 Santos shirt . . . ." The *Kitchener-Waterloo Record,* Thursday, Oct. 3, 1974.

best: 'One feels more ardent by kissing, more humble by kneeling and more angry by shaking one's fist.'[38] Under such conditions it would be psychologically unbearable to pretend for very long in our daily affairs. Others give short shrift to inconsistency, and our allotted degrees of freedom are limited. Moreover, we tend to concentrate our attention, our consciousness, and our emotions on a single role and identity at a time. Other roles and identities are recruited, and we switch roles at a moment's notice, to fit the circumstances. For example, one moment Team Canada players stand erect, heads bowed, filled with emotion listening to their national anthem; the next moment armed with wooden weapons, they do battle violently—but in vain—against their Soviet opponents. As soon as the battle is over they assume new roles; like puppets they shake hands with their opponents, their heads bobbing up and down as they leave the ice. Again the circumstances change, and they become tourists sightseeing through the streets of Moscow. 'Normally, one becomes what one plays at.'[39] It is also true that there are worlds and roles about which we know almost nothing like the 'tearoom' world—the world of speedy sex encounters.[40] In this world roles may be standardized, but their occupancy may be temporary, and demand speed and secrecy. Participants in these 'tearoom encounters' must be able to step in and out of these roles at will. The 'exigencies of these encounters demand a great deal of role flexibility.'[41] Similarly, in one of Montreal's most notorious gay bars, members crowd together in a row at the 'meat rack' and hands reach out to touch and evaluate thighs, genitals and backsides. Fellatio can and does transpire without so much as a 'swift glance between partners.'[42]

But there is more to the matter. Attributes of moral character are also part of socially defined role expectations and obligations, and not inborn qualities of persons, and they are integrally related to the social organization of the worlds in which we live. For example, the attributes of responsibility and self-control regarding the role of a young person are sometimes hard to come by. We are skeptical occasionally, of the ability of young people to satis-

---

38   Peter L. Berger. *Invitation to Sociology,* Garden City, New York: Doubleday and Company, Inc., 1963, 96. This is a gem of a book.

39   Berger, *Ibid.,* 98.

40   Laud Humphreys, *op. cit.*

41   Humphreys, *op. cit.,* 45-58.

42   Richard Bass, "Montreal's Homosexual Community: Why It is Different," in H. Taylor Buckner (ed.), *Urban Life Styles: St. Catherine Street - Friday Night,* unpublished collection of papers, Dept. of Sociology, Concordia University, 1972.

factorily police their own conduct especially in heterosexual matters, and consequently we watch them accordingly. However, distinctions regarding the attributes of responsibility are a built-in feature of the business world. The relative absence of supervision over managerial positions implies expectations of responsibility and trustworthiness. This is not so with unskilled and semi-skilled positions which require almost continuous supervision. Similarly, methods of pay in the work world reflect role expectations of responsibility and self-control. Upper echelon positions are paid by cheque on a monthly basis, the implication being that role occupants can satisfactorily manage their finances throughout this lengthy period. Lower-ranked positions—waitresses, truck drivers, bellhops, cabdrivers and bartenders—persons who are often perched on the fringes of the conventional world—are usually paid on a weekly or fortnightly basis; the implication here is that role holders are less responsible, less able to manage their affairs, and require more frequent payments.

Scott has shown us that the attributes of courage, integrity and cool are socially defined role expectations of jockeys, and are generated by the social organization of their world.[43] Among jockeys, gallantry is defined as the capacity to follow rules when it is costly to do so, as the jockey does who hands his whip to a rider who dropped his during the race, and then resumes a hand race to a winning finish. Similarly, moral character is to possess 'cool' in risky situations. A jockey demonstrates his 'cool' when he waits far back in the pack risking the possibility that once his horse has been passed he will not get started again. Similarly, the ability to endure pain is highly valued among professional football players and an implicit role expectation. In *Mad Ducks and Bears,* George Plimpton reports the following conversation between two defense coaches. "Also he could play hurt," Sandusky said. "That's another attribute—to have a great pain tolerance. Donovan could play with a broken bone. I remember one day we asked him about an injury he had; did it hurt? And he said, 'Yeah, in between plays.' "

"Unitas has that quality," Bullough said. "He's been hurt for years, and right now he's playing off that Achilles tendon injury. You know it hurts him, but when you ask him how he feels, it's

---

43  Marvin B. Scott, *The Racing Game,* Chicago: Aldine Publishing Company, 1968, 336-355. Besides the more general quality of 'character', similar qualities are occupationally defined role expectations of professional hockey players. See the excellent unpublished paper by Robert R. Faulkner entitled, *"Violence, Camaraderie, and Occupational Character in Hockey",* Department of Sociology, University of Massachusetts, 1971.

'fine!' like he's never had an injury."[44] Among handicappers an important norm is the ability to 'eat a loss.' Under such circumstances his esteem among peers depends on his 'stay[ing] loose'.[45] On the other hand, it is difficult to occupy the roles of drug addict or alcoholic in our society and continue to possess the qualities of control and reliability. These socially defined expectations are simply not accorded to such roles. In the worlds of crime the 'hype' and 'alkie' are considered unreliable, poor partners for crime.[46]

Finally, not all social roles are of equal rank in society. Each social role has assigned to it a certain quantum of prestige or approval by the larger community. This means that every social role evokes some judgment on our part concerning its rank relative to other social roles. This is its status, and has relevance for the role only, not the incumbent. In the larger society deviant roles are the least prestigious. For example, the deviant roles of thief, liar or defector rank lower than the devalued, non-deviant roles of gambler, alcoholic or stripper. However, it should be understood that the status of roles is subculturally variable; among criminals the sneak thief ranks low, but the role of con-artist holds considerable status. Similarly, the role of swinger is not likely devalued among those who enjoy such sport.

Perhaps our use of the concept of role has created a false image of the flow of social action. In no way do we deny social process, nor do we wish to convey the impression that social action is a concatenation of static acts. To isolate an act from the

---

44  George Plimpton, *Mad Ducks and Bears,* New York: Bantam Books, 1974, 304. Of course athletes (especially professionals) are not remarkable for their ability to play with pain. The expectation that players participate in spite of injury and pain is widely institutionalized in the sports world. In the world of organized hockey, socialization begins as early as nine or ten years of age, and the expectations are made very clear to the youngster. At this stage the coach encourages the player who is injured not to cry, to be a man and to get back in the nets. This socialization continues throughout a player's career and becomes internalized as a value and an indelible part of the role expectations of a hockey player. By the time a player reaches the senior leagues he may be 'carried bleeding from the ice' on Friday night and be 'confined to a wheelchair in hospital as late as 1 p.m. Saturday, but by 8 p.m. that night he (will be) back on the ice.' Moreover, his return will elicit a 'standing ovation.' See the *Kitchener-Waterloo Record,* Monday, April 28, 1975, for the almost blow-by-blow account of the violence-ridden series between the Barrie Flyers and the St. John's Capitals in 'the game of hockey.'

45  A handicapper is a person who reads the racing programme and obtains other relevant data on the horses, and on the basis of all accumulated information he places a bet. See Iris Lowsky, 'C'est Un Depart', in H. Taylor Buckner (ed.), *Urban Life Styles: Observations in Montreal - '72,* unpublished collection of papers, Department of Sociology, Concordia University, 1972.

46  Letkemann, *op. cit.,* 24-26; also Chambliss, *op. cit.,* 77.

flow of social conduct precludes our full understanding of its significance in the sequence of events. However, to understand the give and take of social interaction, it is fruitful to explore the roles that persons occupy and the role requirements and rules by which the transaction is carried on.

# Social Definitions of Deviance

# 4

The inevitability and importance of rules for the government of men's conduct do not make them appear automatically. The problem of knowing which activities to regulate by what kinds of rules continually challenges society. How do we distinguish acts that will contribute to the welfare of society from those that will not? What criteria do we use to condemn one form of conduct and encourage another? How do we best enforce morality in a highly differentiated society—a society of countless groups each vigorously encouraging and promoting its own version of reality, morality and virtue? Under such conditions, whose morals do we enforce?

One criterion that is employed is to try to equate deviance with what is defined as dangerous for the society, i.e., to proscribe those activities and customs that are considered damaging to the wellbeing of people. Admittedly, there must be some rules to preserve the security and public order in the community; there must also be rules to regulate the acquisition, use, and distribution of goods and services. There must be provision for the distribution of property and sexual favors, and every society needs some kind of arrangement for the replacement, training, and care of its new members. Moreover, the large majority of people believe it reasonable to legislate against treason and the indiscriminate killing of others, and to prohibit practices that endanger the health of the community. In the long run, wholesale violation of such rules might seriously disrupt the daily operations of society and ultimately jeopardize its survival. However, it is extremely difficult to equate deviance with the danger that it presents for society. The institutionalization of the cocktail party, for example, is an excellent way of generating alcoholism.[1] To confuse matters there are some activities that include in their practice a high risk of serious injury or death. Rather than forbid them, we organize ceremonies for their performance, and train our children to become expert in them. Moreover, we encourage our children to actively socialize with members of the opposite sex, which, under many contemporary conditions, is highly conducive to extreme forms of sexual intimacy of which many groups in society still strongly disapprove.[2] The rub is that each of us believes that he knows what practices are dangerous and damaging and ought to be prohibited, but to establish what practices are really dangerous is a more difficult and troublesome problem.

In fact, there is no scientifically proven way of establishing the best policy for prohibiting a particular kind of conduct. If we could establish objectively which practices and activities were absolutely damaging and disruptive to society and which were not, matters might be easier, but it seems we can never know enough about this in advance. Sometimes we have too much faith in the efficacy of rules, and we believe that they can effectively prohibit any kind of activity. Yet many people are asking whether the enforcement of morality through the criminal law (a formally designed set of rules) is the best policy. Are these rules not unenforceable? Do these laws not generate more human suffering than the practices they are designed to prohibit? There is considerable evidence to attest to the ineffectuality of such laws. Moreover, the recreational use of marijuana is not so important a social problem

---

1    See Sanford H. Kadish, "Overcriminalization" in Leon Radzinowicz and Marvin E. Wolfgang (eds.), *The Criminal in Society,* (Vol. 1 of Crime and Society), New York: Basic Books, Inc., 1971, 56-71; Herbert L. Packer, *The Limits of the Criminal Sanction,* Stanford, California: Stanford University Press, 1968, 301-312. Concerning drugs see Alfred R. Lindesmith, *The Addict and the Law,* Bloomington: Indiana University Press, 1965.

2    See William Westley and Frederick Elkin, "The Protective Environment and Adolescent Socialization", *Social Forces,* Vol. 35, 1957; John R. Seeley, R. Alexander Sim and Elizabeth W. Loosley, *Crestwood Heights,* New York: Basic Books, Inc., 1956, 159-292.

that it requires prohibition by criminal law. To do so makes criminals of persons who enjoy pot in much the same way that most of us enjoy a cocktail. What about prostitution, the hardiest of society's institutions? Must we make criminals of the relatively few women who, for whatever reasons, elect to earn their livelihood in this manner? However evil they may be considered, prostitution, drug use, abortion and homosexuality have been around for a long time; recently they have been called 'crimes without victims.' The rationale behind such laws is that the activity is considered immoral; but what was defined as immoral in the past may be considered less so today. As social conditions undergo change so do the morals and norms which govern men's activities. By criminalizing abortion, vagrancy, gambling, prostitution, public drunkenness and similar forms of societally innocuous activities we run against the established practices of people; it makes criminals of socially harmless persons, and only the naïve would assert that we are a more moral society than another. For many people these laws are out of date and costly, moral support for them is divided, and they likely do more harm than good for society, because they seem to foster crime and other forms of criminal activity.[3] There is a growing belief that such matters be removed from legal concern.

It is clear that some activities are forbidden notwithstanding their innocuous practice; society strongly endorses other activities despite the obvious threat they pose to the lives of its members. How might we account for this? On balance it seems that society considers some forms of conduct to be excessively costly, and it cannot tolerate this. Yet not everyone is convinced that society is quite so rational and calculating in the legislation of its laws. Some theorists suggest that modern society is a highly specialized, socially differentiated, multi-grouped organization, with each group possessing its own values, customs and vested interests. Thus, there exists a conflict of interests and perspectives. In a pluralistic kind of society there is apt to be a kind of 'moral politics' going on where competing blocs are continually struggling for power, and negotiating for the enactment of laws to protect their particular interests, and standards of decency and morality.[4]

---

3   Edmund W. Vaz, *A Sociological Interpretation of Middle-Class Juvenile Delinquency,* unpublished Ph.D. dissertation, Indiana University, 1965.

4   Stanton Wheeler, "Deviant Behavior", in Neil J. Smelser (ed.), *Sociology: an Introduction,* New York: John Wiley & Sons, Inc., 1967, 614. We have relied on Wheeler for certain parts of this section.

Under these conditions, laws are legislated by the most powerful groups in society who have an interest in a particular piece of legislation, can influence others as to the urgency of the legislation, and make their views prevail over the objections of competing interests.

As society undergoes further specialization and differentiation so do the characteristics of the relevant powerful interest groups. This is evident in the particular groups in Canada and the United States that exercise influence over the content of the criminal laws. For example, psychiatrists exert considerable influence in determining the types of offenses that will be defined as criminal, [5] and the conditions under which a person should be considered insane.[6] Law enforcement agencies also have special interests in the kinds of law that are enacted. Because the police are considered highly knowledgeable in understanding and explaining criminality in society, they exert a role in determining what criminal rules they will enforce. It is not surprising that sometimes they advocate laws that are easy to enforce.[7]

The foregoing suggests that much of what is considered deviant in society (e.g., types of mental illness, prostitution, abortion, drug addiction, vagrancy, etc.) represents little more than the special brand of morality of the prevailing power holders in the society. This view is especially evident in the history of prohibition in the United States and narcotics legislation in Canada during the years 1908 to 1923.

---

5   William B. Chambliss and Robert B. Seidman, *Law, Order and Power,* Reading, Massachusetts: Addison-Wesley Publishing Co., 1971, 63-73; Fred Desroches, "Regional Psychiatric Centres: A Myopic View?", *Canadian Journal of Criminology and Corrections,* Vol. 15, 1973, 3-21.

6   Gwynn Nettler, *Explaining Crime,* New York: McGraw-Hill Book Company, 1974, 23-32.

7   Chambliss and Seidman, *op. cit.,* 68-70. There is good reason to believe that the use of marijuana is here to stay. Moreover, it is likely that many police officers (especially younger men) consider the majority of arrests for possession of marijuana relatively unimportant, and they would favor a relaxation in the marijuana laws. This attitude is congruent with the considerable change in public opinion towards the use of marijuana. However, although hard-drug legislation does not appear to work, the police are not likely to favor the softening of hard-drug legislation. This would run against the vast majority of public opinion; besides, the police themselves are likely to disfavor the use of hard drugs.

# Canadian Narcotics Legislation: An Example

In her historically-oriented discussion Shirley Cook[8] emphasizes three prominent groups involved with drugs at the time: the medical profession, whose members were commonly prescribing medications containing opiates, the Chinese pedlars of opium, and the general public among whom there was widespread use of medicines containing opiates. Admittedly the Patent and Proprietary Medicines Act was introduced to control the indiscriminate use of harmful drugs by physicians and others, but the penalties for violation of this Act were much less drastic than those for violation of the Opium and Narcotic Drug Act. In the end it was the Chinese who were the losers; they rather than the physicians were designated deviants. Cook suggests that the decision to consider narcotic users as criminals clearly reflects the stratification order and power differential between groups at the time.

Secondly, the moral reformers 'had the arena of social legislation-making to themselves.'[9] Because it was largely a 'hidden type conflict', there were no opposing views, their moralistic testimonials and writings went unchallenged, and there was no need to arouse public opinion. They encouraged belief in the 'dope fiend' image of the drug user, they condemned the use of drugs which they said encouraged the 'natural depravity of man', and they strongly advocated protection for the moral fiber of the citizenry. It is noteworthy that these views were 'espoused by the superordinate group who made and enforced the rule,' and that the absence of public debate successfully neutralized any objection.

Another factor was the long-standing hate and hostility directed against Asian immigrants, especially the Chinese and Japanese, in Canada. In the 1922 narcotics debates, the 'moral ruin of innocent young people' was attributed to the 'foreign inferior race,'[10] an allegation which heightened the moral indignation of the legislators and led to stiffer penalties. Had this racial hatred been non-existent, Cook suggests that the moral indignation against drug users and stringent law enforcement would have waned, as they had against the manufacturers of tobacco and al-

---

8  Shirley J. Cook, "Canadian Narcotics Legislation, 1908-1923: A Conflict Model Interpretation", *The Canadian Review of Sociology and Anthropology,* Vol. 6, No. 1, 1969; for a brief account of the American narcotics legislation see Edward M. Brecher and the Editors of the Consumers Reports, *Licit and Illicit Drugs,* Mount Vernon, New York: Consumers Union, 1972, 42-63.

9  Cook, *op. cit.,* 40.

10  Cook, *op. cit.,* 43.

cohol, many of whom were of British ancestry. Their high social standing helped immunize them from the kind of intense vilification that was directed against the Chinese. Until after World War II, the Chinese remained a despised social group because of immigration restrictions, their occupational skills, and their 'high social visibility'.

The evidence makes quite clear that the Canadian Narcotics Legislation was engineered by groups of resourceful 'moral entrepreneurs'. Neither rationality nor the opinions or sentiments of the majority were evidently involved. The positions of power held by the crusaders, their freedom from countervailing views, and their intense hatred of Asians greatly influenced the content of the legislation.

At this point we might emphasize that the efficacy of a repressive law depends largely on the conduct it is meant to control. One reason for the ineffectiveness of laws in satisfactorily controlling vice—drug use, gambling, prostitution and other forms of sexual deviance—is that the private and consensual nature of the conduct makes law enforcement extremely difficult. But the damaging side effects in criminalizing these activities ought not to be overlooked. For example, ineffective enforcement of the law tends to contradict the 'moral message communicated by the law,' and the paucity of prosecutions reflects poorly on law enforcement in general. Moreover, the use of the criminal law in this fashion 'invite[s] discriminatory enforcement against persons selected for prosecution on grounds unrelated to the evil against which these laws are purportedly addressed . . . .'[11] Admittedly, other countries have some criminal legislation affecting these practices, but often we seem bogged down in a morass of morality; in our fervor to create a so-called better society our laws succeed also in creating a higher criminal population.[12]

Informal controls and social definitions of conduct are no less important in regulating many of the social activities of men. Most of our conduct and choice of activities is independent of legal status. For example, it is not the illegality of prostitution that deters so many young women from its practice; nor is it the fear of prison that deters us from murder, or social disgrace that diverts us from treason, incest or armed robbery. The mere thought of such acts is revolting to us, and violates our sense of decency.

---

11 Kadish, *op. cit.*, 59.

12 For some general observations on the problems involved in morals legislation see Louis B. Schwartz, "Morals and the Model Penal Code," in Leon Radzinowicz and Marvin E. Wolfgang (eds.), *The Criminal in Society,* 71-76.

'Shooting smack', popping pills, or sniffing glue turn us off; we have neither the interest nor appetite for these kinds of activity. It has already been noted that some forms of conduct should be legally forbidden. But to 'decriminalize' other activities is not to announce the outright approval of their practice, nor will it automatically open the floodgates for the abuse of such activities. Indeed, that the vast majority of society strongly disapproves of prostitution, drug use and varying forms of sexual exchange is itself a functional control deterring persons from their practice.[13]

Despite increasing arrests, prosecutions and convictions, and the threats of severe punishment for drug use, and notwithstanding the varied and ingenious tactics used by the police in their efforts at law enforcement, the evidence is perfectly clear; the demand for narcotics continues unabated, and the sources of supply, while irregularly curtailed, are unsuppressed. In a business-oriented society, wherever there exists a large demand for goods and services be they licit or illicit, there will likely emerge some business group to meet the demand. But the provision of drugs, like the provision of prostitution, gambling and loan sharking, is illegal; however, there is a relatively low risk of arrest, and a high margin of profit. Thus the setting is ripe for illicit business groups to enter the market to seek profits by organizing the supply of illegal goods and services. However, since these goods and services are unavailable legally, and there is risk (from occasional vigorous police enforcement) and stigma attached to the operation, the laws tend to limit the supply without necessarily reducing the demand. There are always people willing to pay for their pleasures and vices; for those willing to take the risks, the traffic in drugs provides the opportunity for high profits, and 'the more vigorous the enforcement, the greater the profits.'[14] The penalties for trafficking in addictive drugs are extremely severe, which likely contributes

---

13  Packer, *op. cit.*, 301-312. Also, recently (1973) the state of Oregon revised its marijuana laws; possession of small amounts of marijuana was decriminalized. One year later (1974) a series of interviews was conducted with a cross section of Oregon residents. Despite a year without criminal penalties only 9 percent reported that they were current marijuana smokers, and almost all of these respondents reported that they had begun smoking prior to the change in the marijuana laws. "Most nonusers of marijuana in short, had enough persuasive reasons for not using it without the need to buttress their decisions with fear of criminal penalties." This was reported in *Consumer Reports*, Mount Vernon, N.Y.: Consumers Union, Vol. 40, No. 4, 1975, 265-266.

14  Read Albert K. Cohen, "Deviant Behavior and Its Control," in Talcott Parsons (ed.), *American Sociology*, New York: Basic Books, Publishers, 1968, 231-243; for an interesting discussion of the economics of the black market in heroin see Edward M. Brecher and the Editors of the Consumers Reports, *Licit and Illicit Drugs*, 90-100.

to the exorbitant cost of drugs. Unless the addict is wealthy, the cost forces him to steal in order to support his habit. It makes a criminal of an otherwise law-abiding citizen, and the cost in human suffering is incalculable.

Moreover the cost of using the criminal law in controlling men's vices cannot be gainsaid. Our 'zeal in attempting to stamp out nonconforming behavior by criminal legislation' has not helped solve the narcotics problem in society. Instead it has aggravated the issue. It tends to transform relatively harmless behavior into crime; it spawns large-scale business enterprises organized for the production and provision of illicit products, ultimately leading these groups to diversify their operations and expand their criminal activities; and finally it has multiplied the intractable difficulties of enforcing the law.[15] The cost to law enforcement agencies in time, energy, and frustration defies estimate. The regulation of men's vices through the use of criminal legislation has clearly resulted in an increase in crime statistics, and the further social degradation and suffering of an increasing number of persons.

One of the most interesting perspectives on the problem of defining deviance was suggested by the great French sociologist, Emile Durkheim. He believed that deviant behavior does more than disrupt the stability of society; it exerts a positive effect on it. A breach of the serious rules, especially violation of the criminal code, reinforces social cohesion among men. As persons come together to express their anger and indignation, and to bear witness against the offender, the rate of their social interaction increases. In the process they articulate shared sentiments and common concerns, exchange mutual assurances, and the absence of criticism and objection strengthens the bonds of solidarity and the sense of mutuality among them. In this manner crime alerts people to their common interests, it welds individual consciences into a shared sense of morality, and highlights the 'collective conscience' of the society. Crime breeds unity among men.[16]

An implication of this perspective is that in order to preserve its stability and remain operationally viable, society requires a certain quantum of deviance. Perhaps society functions so as to

---

15   Kadish, *op. cit.,* 62.

16   Emile Durkheim, *The Division of Labor,* (Trans. by George Simpson), Glencoe: The Free Press, 1949, 102-103.

generate the volume of crime that it 'needs'.[17] Are not penitentiaries, jails, reformatories, and mental hospitals, institutions of higher learning in crime, delinquency and other kinds of deviance? Do not these institutions return large numbers of highly trained graduates to the community each year?[18] To some extent these institutions help guarantee and keep constant a certain amount of crime, delinquency and deviance in society.[19]

But there is more to the matter. Modern society is highly specialized and fragmented along social class, ethnic, religious and occupational lines. Since each of these groups possesses its own customs, interests and loyalties, the institutionalization of common values and sentiments among them is always problematic. Do acts of crime ordinarily evoke a collective outrage among such diverse groups? Is there collective concern about crime? Do criminal acts create uniform resentment that binds people together? Except for the local sex crime, widespread acts of crime breed suspicion and fear among men, and uneasiness within society.[20]

Witness the marijuana issue in society. Instead of breeding social cohesion in society, it has inflamed controversy, divided families and bred dissension. The conflict in attitudes and values

---

17  An excellent study by Erikson shows that the crime rates in colonial New England tended to remain relatively stable over an extended period. Kai T. Erikson, *Wayward Puritans: A Study in the Sociology of Deviance,* New York: John Wiley and Sons, Inc., 1966.

18  D. F. Cousineau and J. E. Veevers, "Incarceration as a Response to Crime: The Utilization of Canadian Prisons," *The Canadian Journal of Corrections,* Vol. 14, No. 1, 1972, 10-31.

19  Erikson, *op. cit.,* 1966. See also Peter Letkemann, *Crime as Work,* Englewood Cliffs, New Jersey: Prentice-Hall Inc., 1973, 121-128. However, the constancy in the amount of deviance detected, and in the number of deviants produced in a society will be influenced by the kinds of control mechanisms operating. For example, the degree to which the control apparatus is organized, the methods employed in detecting and prosecuting deviance, and the extent of interest in the apprehension of deviants are variables to be considered. Walter D. Connor, "The Manufacture of Deviance: The Case of the Soviet Purge, 1936-1938," *American Sociological Review,* Vol. 37, 1972, 403-413.

20  Donald R. Cressey (ed.), *Crime and Criminal Justice,* Chicago: Quadrangle Books, 1971, 4-17. John Barron Mays, *Crime and the Social Structure,* London: Faber and Faber, Ltd., 1963, 69-78. Of course deviance is functional also in other ways. For example, deviance often helps cut through bureaucratic red tape; sometimes it spotlights the benefits of virtue, and it also occasions the re-thinking and re-evaluation of our social and normative structures. Read Albert K. Cohen, *Deviance and Control,* Englewood Cliffs, New Jersey: Prentice-Hall, Inc., 1966, 6-11; Kingsley Davis, "Prostitution" in Robert K. Merton and Robert A. Nisbet (eds.), *Contemporary Social Problems* New York: Harcourt, Brace and World, Inc., 1961, 262-288.

has perhaps widened the generation gap. Sometimes under such conditions formal agencies of control are recruited for assistance. Law courts often function to reduce ambiguity in the meaning of the rules, and reaffirm confidence in the normative order. In this instance the government appointed enquiry into the nonmedical use of drugs is designed to help clarify the issue and generate a common understanding to the problem. Durkheim's ideas are obviously exciting and challenging, but only a considerable amount of research can establish their empirical value.

There is no agreement about how society decides what forms of conduct to consider deviant. Moreover, as Wheeler writes, 'Some forms of conduct appear to be proscribed in just about every society; some forms show the work of special interest groups; and no society has yet managed to eliminate deviant behavior.'[21]

---

21   Wheeler, *op. cit.,* 615.

# Socialization
# and Deviance

5

If a social system (legal or illegal, deviant or non-deviant) is to persist for an appreciable period of time, it is essential that its members learn what tasks and duties must be performed. In other words, they must learn the requirements of the formal and informal roles that they occupy. Socialization is the term used for this learning process.[1] What persons learn while being socialized is culture. This learning of culture (values, norms, attitudes, knowledge and sentiments) is usually associated with the basic configuration of roles, and the more prominent values of the larger system. The socializing process makes persons into system members, and thereby prepares them for role occupancy; the content of the learning will depend on the system in which the person participates. Whether it is a legitimate endeavor such as medicine, business or teaching, or an illegal pursuit such as picking pockets,[2]

---

1  For a very clear account of the socialization process see Alfred R. Lindesmith and Anselm L. Strauss, *Social Psychology,* New York: Holt, Rinehart and Winston, 1968, 233-363; Harry M. Johnson, *Sociology: A Systematic Introduction,* New York: Harcourt, Brace & World, Inc., 1960, 110-144.

2  Edwin H. Sutherland, *The Professional Thief,* Chicago, The University of Chicago Press, 1937, 44-48; Bill Chambliss (ed.), *Box Man,* New York: Harper and Row, Publishers, 1972, 70-96; David W. Maurer, *Whiz Mob,* New Haven, Conn.: College and University Press, 1964.

prostitution[3] or homosexuality,[4] the process of socialization will include the learning of skills, attitudes, norms and values, i.e., the rights and obligations of the particular roles.

The patterned processes of socialization as they are located throughout the system, and the social structures that produce them, are of particular sociological interest. One task is to locate and to describe in detail the various forms of socialization. Another is to establish the association between differential socioeconomic location and socialization patterns. How are different forms of socialization conducive to varying kinds of deviance, e.g., juvenile theft, acts of violence or drug-taking activities? What are the forms of learning whereby respectable members of the community become involved in white-collar crime? How significant are 'deviant others'—reference groups and role models—in learning deviant conduct, and how is their distribution a function of the social structure? How does the social structure generate systematic vocabularies of motives (i.e. rationalizations and justifications that occur prior to the act) for particular forms of criminal behavior like 'compulsive crimes'?[5]

Usually one thinks of socialization as beginning at birth and occurring mainly in the family. However, a family is not an isolated set of relationships, but can be plotted according to its socioeconomic position in society. In this respect the family is a social unit much like others similarly located. This is why it makes sense to refer to upper-class families, lower-class families and families of the middle class, while recognizing that variations in family patterns exist at each level. Furthermore, what transpires within the family is influenced by, and has consequences for, the larger social structure. The family and other major institutions tend to take on much of the general culture typical of their socioeconomic position. This suggests that we can expect noticeable differences in socialization patterns among socioeconomic strata.

In some cases early socialization may have tragic consequences for the persons involved. It has been suggested that the social disability of lower-class black gang boys in their interpersonal relationships has its roots in their early family socialization.[6]

---

3   John H. Gagnon and William Simon (eds.), *Sexual Deviance,* New York: Harper & Row, 1967, 105-146; "The Business of Sex", in Donald R. Cressey and David A. Ward, *Delinquency, Crime, and Social Process,* New York: Harper & Row, 1969, 973-985.

4   Laud Humphreys, *Tearoom Trade,* Chicago: Aldine Publishing Company, 1970.

5   Frank E. Hartung, *Crime Law and Society,* Detroit: Wayne State University Press, 1966, 136-166.

6   James F. Short, Jr. and Fred L. Strodbeck, *Group Process and Gang Delinquency,* Chicago: The University of Chicago Press, 1965, 217-247.

There are data which reveal that as early as four or five years of age black children are 'less able to maintain non-aggressive close physical body contact with their age mates than are children from middle-class homes.'[7] This disability impairs these youths in their later social contacts. Moreover, the relatively narrow range of experiences of these gang boys which restricts their role-playing opportunities, likely aggravates the problem, and handicaps them later for adult role occupancy and success in the work world.

In contrast, relatively little is left to chance in the socialization of young people in the middle and upper classes. Social status and expertise in handling interpersonal relationships are highly valued. At each stage in the socialization process the appropriate opportunities in the form of adult regulated associations are provided, and careful attention is paid to the cultivation of social skills and proper social contacts.[8] At the very upper levels of society the private school exercises a major influence in the social refinement of young people. According to C. Wright Mills, 'The one deep experience that distinguishes the social rich from the merely rich and those below is their schooling, and with it all the associations, the sense and sensibility, to which this educational routine leads throughout their lives.'[9] The final product of this private school experience is a person who 'will always know what to do even if one is sometimes puzzled', who is the possessor of an 'easy dignity' that can arise only from an 'inner certainty that one's being is a definitely established fact of one's world, from which one cannot be excluded, ignored, snubbed, or paid off.'[10]

However, we should not believe that early family socialization in the lower class is an inevitable condition of juvenile or adult crime, or that socialization in the middle and upper classes is a sufficient safeguard against participation in illegality. The important explanatory variables that may help to account for the large majority of adult crime and much of juvenile delinquency are apt to be found in the role-relationships, social structural strains, institutional networks, and value systems outside the family. At the same time wise research will examine the relationship between the

---

7   *Ibid.,* 234-247.

8   A brilliant study of an upper middle-class Canadian community is by John R. Seeley, R. Alexander and Elizabeth W. Loosley, *Crestwood Heights,* New York: Basic Books, Inc., Publishers, 1956; William A. Westley and Frederick Elkin, "The Protective Environment and Adolescent Socialisation," *Social Forces,* Vol. 35, 1957, 243-249.

9   C. Wright Mills, *The Power Elite,* New York: Oxford University Press, 1957, 63; E. Digby Baltzell, *An American Business Aristocracy,* New York, N.Y., Collier Books, 1962, 327-371.

10   Mills, *op. cit.,* 67.

family and these kinds of variables. Early mismanaged family relationships are not likely responsible for the prevalence and distribution in society of income tax evasion, white-collar crime, prostitution, bribery, adultery, embezzlement, political corruption and abortion among other forms of deviance.[11] Nor is the bulk of delinquency an inevitable outcome of disturbed family relationships.[12] For example, a recent government enquiry in Canada estimated that approximately 215,000 high school and university students use marijuana. There is also an unknown, large number of non-student users.[13] Are we to assume that such widespread use of pot is attributable to wretched family contacts? Some limited research among Canadian youths suggests that middle-class delinquency is attributable to active participation in *legitimate* youth culture activities.[14]

It is true that a child's conduct reflects partly his socioeconomic position and family socialization, and that his experiences in the family help hone the lens through which he 'perceives, interprets and evaluates the world outside.' But it is equally true that one's learning is obviously not limited to the family setting, and that the socialization process continues throughout life. Once the child decides to leave home and school he will have to grapple with a kaleidoscope of rules, roles, moralities and definitions of reality that differ markedly from his own, and it is questionable whether his early family training is adequate preparation for this task. Much of a person's socialization occurs once he leaves the family milieu, when he joins new groups, enters the complex worlds of work, assumes adult roles and participates in a multiplicity of new relationships. Admittedly, part of this later learning

---

11  Admittedly there is little research to support this contention since the bulk of research has been conducted on juvenile delinquents.

12  Recent discussions of research dealing with the family and juvenile delinquency are to be found in Stephen Schafer and Richard D. Knudten, *Juvenile Delinquency: An Introduction,* New York: Random House, 1970, 191-199; Sophia M. Robison, *Juvenile Delinquency: Its Nature and Control,* New York: Holt, Rinehart and Winston, 1960, 108-120. See also a recent study by Winton A. Ahlstrom and Robert J. Havighurst, *400 Losers,* San Francisco: Jossey-Bass Inc., Publishers, 1971.

13  *Interim Report of the Commission of Inquiry into the Non-Medical Use of Drugs,* Ottawa, Queen's Printer for Canada, 1970, 142. A more recent study of marijuana use at a major university in Ontario found that 53 percent of a random sample of all students had tried pot. Forthcoming is a report by M. Nawaz, Department of Sociology, University of Waterloo.

14  Edmund W. Vaz, "Middle-Class Adolescents: Self-Reported Delinquency and Youth Culture," *The Canadian Review of Sociology and Anthropology,* Vol. 2, 1965, 52-70; also Edmund W. Vaz, "Juvenile Delinquency in the Middle-Class Youth Culture" in Cressey and Ward, *Delinquency, Crime and Social Process,* 361-375.

overlaps with, and reinforces, some of the content that he has already internalized, and conformity to these norms and customs lends continuity to the established patterns in the worlds in which he lives.[15]

But the socialization of adults is not always an easy matter especially when it involves the learning of technical skills, when role responsibilities are particularly onerous, or when it includes learning norms, attitudes and values contrary to those already internalized.[16] This is a major reason why it is so difficult to rehabilitate the long-time professional criminal; the task is analagous to trying to resocialize the professional physician, lawyer or business executive. Intelligent money would bet against it.

One qualification of the socialization process is whether the person (young or old) is being socialized alone or as a member of a group. For example, in school, children are socialized in what has been called a 'collective serial relationship'. On other occasions persons are first trained in large collectivities, then as members of closely-knit groups. In World War II, air crew personnel—navigators, radio operators, pilots, air gunners, etc.—were initially trained at different technical schools where they were taught the theoretical requirements of their special roles. Once they reached Operational Training Units they were formed into bomber crews, and thereafter their training was experienced as a bomber unit. In a totally different context, the mutual socialization of spouses is an instance of each learning from and training the other. Finally, the apprentice Box man occupies the role of thief while he learns the required skills for blowing safes from his partner in crime.

> **I worked for Dick for three years as an apprentice. My job was to go steal the dynamite and cook it up; which, incidentally gives you a terrific headache if you smell its fumes while you're cooking it . . . . I would also lay on the joints [places they were going to burglarize] that he picked out. It was my job to watch the joint for three or four nights and see when the door-shaker**

---

15 Socialization is seldom a smooth course of learning. Invariably it involves gains as well as losses. Sometimes new learning conflicts with already established attitudes, values and knowledge; sometimes the socialization into new roles means abandonning old roles, and the gradually learned commitment to one role often precludes alternative courses of conduct. See Theodore Caplow, *Principles of Organization,* New York: Harcourt, Brace and World, Inc., 1964, 169-200.

16 Our guide in part of this section has been Orville G. Brim, Jr., and Stanton Wheeler, *Socialization After Childhood: Two Essays,* New York: John Wiley & Sons, 1966.

[night watchman] or the policeman would come by; what time they closed the place up; what time they opened in the morning . . . . I did all the work and he was the brains . . . Denver Dick was a past master at shooting a box. He could lift that door right off and sit it right where he wanted . . . . I worked for him three years before he even let me shoot a box . . . . I eventually learned how to open boxes by talking to him . . . . He wanted me to learn so he would take me with him . . . . I eventually learned all the different makes of safes. Some of them you could take a gut shot and open it up easy and other safes you couldn't. You could blow the door all to hell and still it wouldn't take a gut shot. So you would have to use a jam shot. He taught me all about the different safes and how they operated. Mostly I learned in conversation.[17]

Although the call girl doesn't have much to learn, some teaching does occur as she immerses herself in the world of prostitutes. Much of what she learns is imitation although some explicit instruction takes place. Of primary concern is securing and maintaining a lucrative clientele. She also learns a few sexual techniques and responses, and she might learn how to control orgasm. She is taught how to guard against venereal disease and how to avoid detection and arrest. Also important is how to treat her customers; for example, she sees to their anonymity, she will give no sign of recognition outside, and she will not likely overcharge.[18]

The process of socializing adults seldom requires the person to assume the more formal role of learner, although exceptions are common, some being the resocialization of prison inmates in correctional institutions, or the training of army recruits, and of young business executives to be 'company men'. In crime, 'Formal teacher-student relationships are rare: partners in crimes, whether experienced or inexperienced, tend to be equals.'[19]

The kind of relationships in which the socializing occurs is ordinarily closely associated with the degree of formality in which the process transpires. In an institutionalized setting the socialization occurs in a formal organization such as a university, army

---

17  Chambliss, *op. cit.,* 9-11.

18  James H. Bryan, "Apprenticeships in Prostitution, "*Social Problems,* Vol. 12, 1965, 287-297; Robert R. Bell, *Social Deviance,* Homewood Illinois: The Dorsey Press, 1971, 226-247; Gagnon and Simon, *op. cit.,* 105-164; and Clive L. Copeland and Norris A. McDonald, "Prostitutes are Human Beings: An Unorganized Counter Institution," in H. Taylor Buckner, *Deviance, Reality, and Change,* New York: Random House, 1971, 261-269.

19  Peter Letkemann, *Crime as Work,* Englewood Cliffs, N.J.: Prentice-Hall, Inc., 1973, 136.

camp or penitentiary. For example, where school or vocational training is available at correctional institutions inmates will often enroll to acquire skills or experience that may be used in legitimate employment after release. In a recent Canadian study 38 percent of 'dischargees' and 58 percent of parolees attended classes.[20] In these situations relationships tend to be impersonal; there are well defined roles and established status differences between teacher and learner, and the process is confined largely to a specific learning situation.[21]

However, socialization also occurs in informal settings, e.g., the family, a boy's gang, hanging on street corners, in the yard of a penitentiary, or regular meetings at a drive-in-restaurant— situations where persons undergo recurrent sets of experiences, where relationships are relaxed, and participants are perhaps more emotionally involved with each other. On the streets of high delinquency areas in large cities, it is sometimes difficult for youths to avoid learning about crime in considerable detail. Here they are taught how to steal from department stores and trucks and how to get rid of the goods; they learn also how to roll drunks. This training includes what performances to employ when they are caught, when to cry and when not to cry, and how to lie to adults.[22] In the following example, the informality of the socialization process is captured as the 'jack roller' relates how he learned to steal while working in tandem with his older brother.

> He taught me how to be mischievous; how to cheat the rag
> peddler when he weighed up our rags. He would distract the
> peddler's attention while I would steal a bag of rags off the
> wagon. We would sell the rags back to the victimized peddler.
> He ... would direct me to steal from the counter while he
> waited at the door .... In the street car William would give me
> orders on what to steal and how to go about it. I listened to
> him with interest and always carried out his orders. He had me
> in the palm of his hand, so to speak .... He instructed me on
> how to evade peddlers and merchants if they gazed at me while
> I was stealing. After arriving at the market, William would lay

---

20  Irvin Waller, *Men Released From Prison,* Toronto, University of Toronto Press, 1974, 66.

21  Of course what is learned in these institutions is not limited to what is taught in vocational classes. See Waller, *op. cit.,* 65-66, also Letkemann, *op.cit.,* 117-130.

22  Donald R. Cressey, "Delinquent and Criminal Structures", in Robert K. Merton and Robert Nisbet (eds.), *Contemporary Social Problems,* New York: Harcourt Brace Jovanovich, Inc., 1971, 160.

**out the plan of action and stand guard while I did the stealing.**[23]

In a more obvious way jails, penitentiaries, detention quarters, lock-ups and mental hospitals provide ideal settings for an informal education in crime, delinquency and the development of deviant roles. Housed under such conditions people who have initially been given the same public label are now provided the time and opportunity to contaminate one another. And they often do. Informal relationships and friendship patterns provide the communication channels through which the learning occurs.[24] Experiences are shared, anti-social attitudes are strengthened, techniques are improved and transmitted, new skills are devised and qualities of responsibility and loyalty are developed and tested.[25] Through mutual reinforcement of attitudes and values, the inmates strengthen one another's alienation from the remainder of society.

In these kinds of informal circumstances one also learns the special vocabularies, the marginal, but crucial variation in gestures, and the colorful nuances and subtleties of conduct so essential for adequate role performance[26] and for the adornment and tutored presentation of self. These are the social ingredients, which along with the knowledge, attitudes and values, often comprise the grist, and therefore influence the consequences, of social interaction.

# Deviance and Motives

To ask the question 'Why do people deviate (or conform)?', is to enquire about the motives for their conduct. It suggests too that motives are individual inventions. Admittedly a person may have personal motives for his conduct; in some instances his motives may be largely physiological; in others he may be unaware of his motives.[27] But if his conduct closely resembles the conduct of oth-

---

23  Clifford R. Shaw, *The Jack-Roller: A Delinquent Boy's Own Story,* Chicago: The University of Chicago Press, 1966, 52-53.Copyright 1930 by the University of Chicago.

24  Letkemann, *op. cit.,* 122-123.

25  Letkemann, *op. cit.,* 125.

26  See the fine work by Gerald D. Suttles, *The Social Order of the Slum,* Chicago: The University of Chicago Press, 1968, esp. 61-93.

27  One trouble with motives that are 'unconscious' is that they are difficult to evaluate and test. One doesn't know where to look first. It is also true that the term 'drive' is often used to refer to the physiological energy which underlies all human action.

ers who are similarly circumstanced, we should expect there to be common social sources to their motivation.

For a long time the motivation for men's conduct was thought to be associated with the so-called primary or basic 'needs'. However, we know now that the knowledge of men's basic needs tells us relatively little about their social conduct. For instance, we do not eat three meals a day plus a late evening snack because of our fundamental need for food. The reasons that Frenchmen drink wine and Canadians water with their meals have little to do with their need for liquid. Nor does the 'secondary (derived) need' for money explain why some persons embezzle it, others gamble for it, steal it at the point of a gun, or work a forty hour week for it. Similarly, only the most gullible would believe that our sexual activities are closely related to our basic need for sex. The fact is, in our society a person possesses almost complete control over his sexual energies.[28] The rates and patterns of our sexual conduct do not reflect so much our need for sex, as they do the norms, customs and values that we learn concerning sex. It is also true that our sexual patterns are partly linked to the occupational structure; if husbands work nights and their wives are employed days, the opportunities for sexual congress are likely to arise at times and under conditions that others might regard a trifle odd. Similarly, our attitudes towards sex and our sexual styles are associated with our socioeconomic position. In the middle and upper sectors of society the phrase, 'Variety is the spice of life' is apt to be more of a joke than a fact of life regarding one's sexual behavior. But among some lower-class, street corner men, there exists the firm belief that it is the 'dog' in man which impels him to seek a variety of sexual partners, which in turn allegedly heightens his sexual performance. As Elliot Liebow states, the following standard joke is told among these men more as a fact of life than as a subject of humor:

> **An old man and his wife were sitting on their porch, rocking slowly and watching a rooster mount one hen, then another. When the rooster had repeated this performance several times, the old woman turned to her husband and said, "Why can't you be like that rooster?"**
>
> **"If you look close", the old man said, "You'll see that that rooster ain't knockin' off the same hen each time. If he had to**

---

28 This is much less the case in some Latin American countries. Role expectations imply much less control over sexual impulses, and chaperones are therefore required to supervise heterosexual relationships among young people from the upper social strata.

**stick with the same one, he wouldn't do no better than me."[29]**

It is the patterned variation in social behavior that requires explanation, and it is difficult to account for the differential rates and various patterns of social conduct according to the same basic need. Invariably we must examine the properties of social systems (the social worlds, the structures and the cultural contents) in which people live if we are going to understand the forms and rates of their conduct. Here, individuals learn the kinds of conformity and forms of deviance that are tolerated, the social relationships to foster, the attitudes, beliefs and values to espouse, besides the variety, frequency and style of the sex that they want.

# Reference Groups and Motivation

Cohen has suggested that much of our conduct is oriented to the maintenance and improvement of our self-conception, and that the images we have of ourselves are intimately associated with the roles that we occupy.[30] However, not all our conduct (deviant or otherwise) results from a strongly internalized set of beliefs, standards and values. Seldom are we so confident about the rightness of our daily conduct that we do not welcome some sign that others approve of our actions. Their approval gives us confidence and our acts, validity. Actually we are constantly alert to the discrepancies between our own conduct and attitudes, and the conduct and attitudes of others. Although it is true that we want others to approve of our acts, the source of the approval is also important. To a large extent our beliefs and attitudes and our notions of what is right and wrong depend on those groups whom we respect and whose opinions we value. Since we are in daily contact with a variety of groups, the term *normative reference group* is reserved for those groups whose standards and perspectives are authoritative for us in establishing the meaning and rightness of our conduct.[31]

This has implications for the motivation of social behavior. Since we are unable to 'go it alone,' i.e., to proceed without *some*

---

29  See the sensitive study by Elliott Liebow, *Tally's Corner,* Boston: Little, Brown and Company, 1967, 123.

30  Albert K. Cohen, "Juvenile Delinquency," in Robert K. Merton and Robert A. Nisbet (eds.), *Contemporary Social Problems,* New York: Harcourt, Brace and World, Inc., 1961, 98. See also Robert K. Merton, *Social Theory and Social Structure,* (revised edition), New York: The Free Press, 1967, chaps. 8 and 9; Harry M. Johnson, *Sociology: A Systematic Introduction,* New York: Harcourt, Brace & World, Inc., 1960, 39-46.

31  Cohen, *op. cit.,* 101.

form of social support for our acts, we are not likely to overlook the current standards, values and perspectives in our normative reference groups. Thus, the roles we select, and the identities we exhibit are strongly influenced by the standards and perspectives of those groups to whom we look for guidance. For example, if young girls, who are often initially ambivalent about engaging in sexual relations, can rationalize their proposed behavior by looking to their peers (normative reference group) from whose perspective their behavior is acceptable, it will greatly help them to overcome their ambivalence and organize their conduct so that they may proceed with clearer consciences. Facilitating this process is the operational vocabulary of motives which the person employs—'I really love him,' 'I'm old enough,' 'I know I won't get pregnant' or 'He'll be careful.'

Since most of our everyday conduct is carried on in public, it is to others that we look for social recognition, admiration and acceptance—social status. It is worth noting that the extent to which we accept ourselves, i.e., are relatively happy with who we are and what we are, depends on the degree of acceptance that we receive from those groups whom we admire. Groups from whom we desire recognition and approval are called *status reference groups*. Because social status is highly desired (and there is never enough to go around), and since the course of our conduct is influenced by our status reference groups, we are disposed to look to their standards and opinions in selecting our roles and identities. For example, among 'socially-oriented' middle-class youths, the teenager who claims to be sophisticated must place a premium on cultivating social skills and a 'social personality', and active participation in social events. Rough, aggressive behavior is taboo. When the Pittsburgh Pirates of the National Baseball League, the first team to wear doubleknit uniforms, began the practice, many minor league teams insisted on wearing identically knit outfits. Similarly, in minor hockey and baseball leagues, teams often pattern their warm-up sessions after the top teams in the league.[32]

Cohen suggests that our 'Normative and status reference groups are likely to be identical, but they are not necessarily so.'[33] When we are young the family usually serves as both our status and normative reference group. But as peers consume more of our

32  These examples are taken from Brian Messerschmidt, "Sociological Analysis of the Rostick Juvenile Fastball Team," term paper submitted for Sociology 101 course, Dept. of Sociology, University of Waterloo, April, 1975.

33  Cohen, *op. cit.*, 101.

time, and we form new allegiances and widen our group membership, the 'status and normative-conferring functions' are sometimes performed by different groups. A businessman may look to
his occupational colleagues for status, but if he is a God-fearing
man he may turn to the church for guidance as to the morality
of his proposed behavior, and refrain from 'fixing prices'. What
seems clear is that our status and normative reference groups perform major functions in the motivation of social conduct.

# Vocabularies of Motives

Motives ought not to be thought of as 'subjective springs', or
starters of action; nor should they be considered elements located
'in individuals'.[34] A helpful way to think of motives is to consider
them 'distinctively linguistic products'—everyday vocabularies
that persons use which enable, encourage and influence them to
act in one way or another. Motives are socio-cultural products;
they emerge, develop, are modified, and rendered differentially
complex as the interaction of men undergoes change and assumes
varying degrees of organizational complexity. Mills writes that
motives as vocabularies, 'stand for anticipated situational consequences of questioned conduct.' They are the names for 'consequential situations, and surrogates for actions leading to them.'[35]
This means that our vocabularies—the daily terminologies that
we use—help us evoke images of the future, and we likely select
the course of action that we consider best in the face of multiple
alternatives. In this way our vocabularies of motives help us to
rationalize and organize our prospective courses of conduct prior
to, not after the act.[36]

To a considerable extent it is in terms of our everyday
vocabularies, for example, poolroom, business, political or private
club rhetorics, that we make sense of the worlds in which we live.
It is according to such terms that we select alternative forms of
conduct, make decisions, and choose relationships that are meaningful. However, these views of the world are not realities, but

---

34  Our notion of motives is taken from among others, C. Wright Mills, "Situated
    Actions and Vocabularies of Motive," in Irving Louis Horowitz (ed.), *Power,
    Politics and People,* New York: Oxford University Press, 1963, 439-452;
    Kenneth Burke, *Permanence and Change,* Indianapolis: The Bobbs-Merrill
    Company, Inc., 1965, and Donald R. Cressey, *Other People's Money,* Glencoe,
    Illinois: The Free Press, 1953.

35  Mills, *Situated Actions and Vocabularies of Motive,* 441.

36  The commonplace notion of rationalization is that it occurs after the act. For
    example, a student goes to a dance during the week, and rationalizes
    afterwards that he needed a rest from his studies.

interpretations of reality,[37] which suggests that different verbal orientations and interpretations will mirror different definitions of reality. Thus the plausibility to others of the motives for our conduct will depend largely on their comprehending, indeed sharing, the meanings of the terms that we employ in recounting our experiences. To the extent that others comprehend the meanings of our vocabularies our accounts will make sense and be acceptable to them; it will help them understand our definitions and selection of the options ('consequential situations') that we encounter. If they reject the vocabularies that we use, i.e., if they do not share with us a common vocabulary of terms, it increases the difficulty of their understanding our accounts. When lower-class boys report that they 'played chicken' at 120 mph along the highway 'just for kicks' they may be using the only terms, i.e., vocabulary of motives, they possess to explain their behavior. Failure of the police officer or upper middle-class psychiatrist to make sense of these accounts does not deny the youths' veracity, but reflects the adults' failure to understand the meanings of the terms used by the youths. When delinquents report that homosexuals are not 'natural', that society is best rid of them, and that 'They had it coming to them', they are using the daily terms and phrases according to which they define reality, and justify their activities, in this case 'beating up' on homosexuals.

Like most things that are social, vocabularies of motives are not uniformly available to everyone. Some attitudes, beliefs, slogans and terminologies are relatively widespread;[38] others relate more specifically to smaller groups and social sectors in society. Their socioeconomic location, social organization, and special content are a function of the structure of the larger system. Nor are vocabularies of motives necessarily codified, neatly coherent systems of terms with crystal clear meanings. Vocabularies of motives are more likely to include tangentially related slogans, terms and phrases that comprise a configuration of motives in linguistic terms. Perhaps it is only in structurally stable subcultures with long achieved consensus among members, and institutionalization

---

37  Burke, *op. cit.,* 35.

38  Different vocabularies of motives are applicable to different groups and situations. When professional and junior hockey players sign large-salaried contracts with National Hockey League teams, they do so for the money, because the opportunity is there (for the money), or because they realize that a hockey career is short. However, when they are selected to represent the nation and play for Team Canada against the Russians suddenly their vocabularies change; now they play for 'pride' and 'honor.' The *Globe and Mail,* August 10, 1974; the *Kitchener-Waterloo Record,* Tuesday, September 3, 1974.

of attitudes and customs, that a vocabulary of motives is apt to be well established. For instance, among the professions, members are strongly motivated, indeed obligated, to consider the interests of others, e.g., patients, clients, students or parishioners whom they serve, rather than their self interest.[39] In such cases the motivation is an integral part of the role of professional, and is learned as one is socialized into the role and culture of the profession. Part of the ideology expressed by 'serious thieves' in Toronto is that 'everybody else steals too.' As West writes, "If stealing is 'the only game in town' one is justified in playing it".[40] On the other hand, the beliefs, sentiments and rationalizations common to the 'delinquent subculture' are neither codified, nor systematic,[41] yet to some extent they are still likely to influence the conduct of delinquent youths. In any case, different social sectors and groups will generate their own relatively distinct common cores of motivation, with their accompanying vocabularies of rationalizations and justifications for conduct.

It is more likely that the larger culture is the optimum source of general information about deviance, prevailing images of deviants, and contemporary rationalizations for deviant acts. We have noted already that our daily lives are infused with deviance, and that it is especially difficult to avoid noticing its practice in a society socially fragmented into a variety of social categories, each with its own moral priorities and conceptions of what is good and evil. Moreover, the mass media (a veritable storehouse of knowledge on deviance) contribute colorfully to our daily appreciation of deviance, and often highlight the social and material rewards from crime. Everyday reports about the widespread crookedness, deception and sharp practices among repair shops, retail stores, garages, political parties, and the world of corporate business must certainly assist a person in adopting rationalizations for deviant acts.[42] Slogans such as 'Everyone has a racket,' 'Only suckers work,' 'Everyone is an operator,' and 'Smart guys always skim

---

39  For example, see Talcott Parsons, *Essays in Sociological Theory Pure and Applied*, Glencoe, Ill.: The Free Press, 1949, 200-217.

40  William Gordon West, *Serious Thieves: Lower-Class Adolescent Males in a Short-Term Deviant Occupation*, unpublished Ph.D. Dissertation, Department of Sociology, Northwestern University, 1974, 275.

41  See David Matza, *Delinquency and Drift*, New York: John Wiley & Sons, Inc., 1964, esp. chap. 3.

42  For example, see the Reader's Digest test report that found 63 percent of mechanics charged for repairs they didn't make, that 65 percent of radio repair shops and 49 percent of watch repair men "lied, overcharged and gave false diagnoses," reported in Paul Goodman, *Growing Up Absurd*, New York: Vintage Books, Random House, 1960, 20. See also Frank Gibney, *The Operators*, New York: Harper & Brothers, Publishers, 1960, 35-39.

[something] off the top' are statements from the general culture easily applied as justifications prior to a person's behavior. The statements 'Busines is business,' and 'Everybody in business does it' are prevailing rationalizations for countless forms of shady deals, illegal transactions and off-color business acts. In the top echelons of business executives there are not likely many officers who would apply to themselves the statement that 'All business-men are crooks.' However, the notion that a 'company man' is one who 'goes along with his superiors and finds balm for his conscience in additional comforts and the security of his place in the corporate setup' is likely a meaningful rationalization for an executive faced with alternative courses of action.[43]

Moreover, the 'Moralization or neutralization of acts on the ground of their not hurting others', i.e., the denial of injury, is a rationalization for deviant conduct that is well embedded in the larger culture.[44] The variable definitions of and arguments for and against such acts as homosexuality, gambling, drug use, suicide and abortion help spawn slogans and terms like 'crimes without victims', that are easily employed as rationalizations for a person's acts. Once the person can 'break the relation between what he did and its consequences' for others, it helps him to define himself and his acts in something less than disreputable terms.[45]

The society is generous also in propounding social definitions and special circumstances for special kinds of deviance. Youthful acts that are defined as vandalism or merely good clean fun depend on the time, place, and circumstances. Overturning out-houses or farm wagons on Hallowe'en is one thing; overturning an automobile on a city side street is considered the malicious destruction of property. Similarly the costly widespread destruc-tion of property by university students at homecoming football games on Canadian and American college campuses is often con-sidered acceptable, little more than pranks. Were such behavior perpetrated by non-university youths of the town there would be an immediate outcry for a stricter enforcement of the law.[46] In such instances, it is the social definition and, therefore, the hypothesized consequences of such acts that provide much of the motivation for their undertaking.

---

43 Throughout this section we have relied also on the work of Frank E. Hartung, *Crime, Law and Society,* Detroit: Wayne State University Press, 1966, esp. 63-84.

44 John Lofland, *Deviance and Identity,* Englewood Cliffs, New Jersey: Prentice-Hall, Inc., 1969, 96.

45 Hartung, *op. cit.,* 72.

46 *Ibid.,* 72-73.

Among many juvenile court personnel, social workers, probation officers, judges, police officers and some psychiatrists, the view is still held that a patient/client is not responsible for his behavior, especially his deviant conduct. Responsibility for the behavior is often placed on unconscious conflicts, the environment, society, poor parental upbringing or other social circumstances. In particular, this notion applies to the conduct of children, and has been reinforced by the existing philosophy of the juvenile court, and some of the social scientific theories of human conduct proposed by psychiatry and sociology. Although delinquents often attempt to con and manipulate any adult representing the lawful world, some professionals take these youths at their word and confirm their rationalizations, 'They're just picking on me', and 'Everybody's against me.'[47] Moreover, there are professionals and semi-professionals who seem to accept uncritically the delinquents' own notions of the circumstances surrounding their depredations. Later, in discussions and publicly held meetings, they report on the injustice perpetrated against the poor, and the existence of two classes of justice—one for the rich, another for the poor. Unintentionally, they are providing youths with meaningful rationalizations for their delinquent conduct, e.g., 'The cops are always picking on me.' It is not surprising that when a child comes from a badly disturbed home where the father might be an alcoholic and unemployed and the mother is unable to hold a job, he is seldom held responsible for his delinquency. In this arena of professionals there is often the 'continual tendency for reasons to be used as excuses and justifications' for the deviant conduct. When a culture is so rich with explanations of delinquency, it should not surprise us that delinquent youths appropriate the definitions, phrases and explanations used by juvenile court personnel, and employ them as vocabularies of motives for their own conduct.

There is no paucity of information concerning the use of violence in our society. It is a widely recognized notion that aggression is a major criterion of masculinity and toughness. 'The ability to take it and hand it out, to defend one's right and one's reputation with force, to prove one's manhood by hardiness and physical courage—all are widespread in [Canadian] culture.'[48] Admittedly not all sectors of society subscribe wholeheartedly to this standard, but it is equally likely that seldom, if ever, does a father rear

---

47   *Ibid.*, 79.

48   David Matza and Gresham M. Sykes, "Delinquency and Subterranean Values," *American Sociological Review,* Vol. 26, 1961, 717.

his son to be a 'sissy'. A middle-class youth who challenges an antagonist to knock the match stick from his shoulder issues a well known invitation to violence. Such customs and the terms that accompany them are easily learned by young people.

This suggests, at the very least, that in a highly differentiated society like that in Canada, there is no lack of familiarity with deviance, images of deviants, and piecemeal yet serviceable rationalizations for wrong doing. A society characterized by considerable confusion and ambiguity concerning its moral directives provides the person of two minds about committing a deviant act with a plethora of rationalizations which can justify his choice of a course of action. Besides, the overall culture provides easy access to long established, publicly known terms, statements, and slogans—a veritable language of motivation—that facilitate the rationalization of deviant conduct.

However, it is insufficient that the general culture contain an assortment of unrelated terms, definitions, and rhetorics potentially usable as a vocabulary of motives for deviant behavior. Unless the actor is immersed in a subculture, has internalized, and is continually using, a vocabulary of terms, he must employ and appropriate a 'personalized version' of the more general definitions and rationalizations in the public domain, and define them as applicable to his specific case.[49] The application of general rules and definitions to a specific case is what George H. Mead has referred to as taking the role of the 'Generalised Other'. Here the actor stands apart mentally, and thereby observes and defines himself from another person's perspective. 'By indicating to himself the probable reactions of others to himself he observes himself as an object.'[50] In this case, the actor envisages the hypothesized reactions of others to one or another set of terms and rationalizations that he uses. Throughout the process his choice of terms, definitions, and rationalizations is part of the conception that he holds of himself; that is, his selection of terms must be congruent with his self-conception. For example, the 'honest' embezzler might state, "My immediate use of real estate deposits is 'ordinary business' " or "My intent is only to use this money temporarily so I am 'borrowing', not 'stealing' ".[51] As Cressey writes in his study of embezzlers, "The hypothesized reactions to 'borrowing' . . . are much different from the hypothesized reactions to

---

49   This process is elaborated in the case of embezzlers by Cressey, *Other People's Money*, 93-102.

50   Hartung, *op. cit.*, 156.

51   Cressey, *Other People's Money*, 96.

'stealing.' "[52] Moreover, his use of terms and rationalizations helps the actor adjust any conflicting values and attitudes that he might possess. It is through the continued use and internalization of language that he both informs and 'verbally manipulates' or convinces himself that his future deviant conduct is acceptable. It seems clear that how the actor thinks he appears to others, and the hypothesized reactions to a particular use of terms, strongly control his course of action.[53]

More systematized vocabularies of motives are available to members of well established groups, social sectors or subcultures in society. Actors who are deeply immersed in these worlds can easily use these terms to help justify their conduct.[54] The extent of a person's active and psychological participation in such worlds, the degree of his role commitment, and the degree of his isolation from competing social influences are major factors in determining the internalization of norms and attitudes and the use of special vocabularies. Under such conditions the actor will more likely conform to established patterns, and embrace the prevailing vocabulary of motives for his own proposed conduct, because of the rationalizations that he shares with others. Not only does this breed consensus from others, but the respect and recognition that he receives help remove any lingering doubt about the validity of his future course of action.

The recent enormous increase in the use of marijuana among young people allows us to examine the appropriation and use of a vocabulary of motives by participating group members, an ex-

---

52  *Ibid.,* 96.

53  It should be noted that the more "acceptable and independently validated the motive" the less likely is the actor, e.g., the juvenile delinquent, to have to contend with his conscience. Because the terms and definitions are constantly being validated by other persons close to him, e.g., his gang, this facilitates his acceptance and internalization of the motives. The respect and encouragement he receives help convince him of the validity of his conduct and remove doubt about its immorality. However, white-collar criminals are not members of gangs; often they engage in relatively solitary conduct. Seldom do they have others who are a constant source of validation and encouragement. Sanctions for their use of terms and for their conduct are neither systematized nor as widely accepted as the delinquent's. Under such conditions when apprehended these persons may experience considerable shame and guilt for their action. See Hartung, *op. cit.,* 135-136.

54  Persons may also have private rhetorics according to which they perceive the world. However, they are likely to act on the basis of public rhetorics that are parts of the groups to which they belong and to which they look for status and support. See the interesting paper by Herman and Julia Schwendinger, "Delinquent Sterotypes of Probable Victims", in Malcolm W. Klein and Barbara G. Myerhoff (eds.), *Juvenile Gangs in Context,* Englewood Cliffs, New Jersey: Prentice-Hall, Inc., 1967, 92-105.

amination which helps account for their deviant conduct.[55] The rationalizations for smoking pot are appropriated from other group members in the social process of learning to smoke, distinguish the effects, and enjoy the sensations. Gradually an operational set of terms and phrases is learned and internalized, and becomes the only one youths employ to describe their experiences meaningfully.

The rhetoric used by youths to recount their experiences with pot reflects their definition of marijuana, and is congruent with its effects and the fun-orientation of their routine activities. For example, they 'smoke a joint,' 'blow grass,' 'smoke pot,' 'get high,' 'take weed' and 'do dope' because, as they say, 'it's fun,' 'it doesn't do anyone any harm,' 'it's no worse than alcohol,' 'I'm doing my own thing,' 'everyone is doing it,' ' I like to', or 'it's just for kicks.'

However, the variety of groups among young persons, especially university students, include 'politically active,' 'socially conscious,' 'intellectual' units such as the so-called 'Maoists', 'Hippies,' Free Thinkers' and 'Bohemians' among many others. Because young people belong to such groups, they identify with the labels, they claim prominent roles and identities in them, and they define themselves in such terms. Moreover, until their claims to such roles are successfully challenged, or until they outgrow the roles, they conduct much of their daily life according to current group norms and beliefs, and rationalize in terms of recent vocabularies. The words and phrases used by these youths to explain their use of pot will mirror their group's special interests and political orientation, yet overlap with the more specific argot of marijuana use. The end product is a rhetoric that enables youths to rationalize their behavior and help justify the ideology and vested practices of the group.

Expectedly they employ terms that are critical, abstract, serious and idealistic, words that have to do with God, values, aesthetics, freedom, equality, justice and mankind. However, distinguishable differences with terms common to the larger culture of youths will be evident. These youths report that they smoke pot because they are 'alienated from society', they are 'searching for God', it facilitates their 'search for peace', they hope for 'inner satisfaction', they are seeking a 'new awareness' or the 'spirit of love'. Some state that they are looking for 'new values'

---

55  The following discussion of marijuana use is based largely on Edmund W. Vaz, "Deviance and Conformity: The Marihuana Issue," in Dennis Forcese and Stephen Richer, *Issues in Canadian Society: An Introduction to Canadian Sociology,* Prentice-Hall of Canada, Ltd., 1975.

and that spontaneity and originality are no longer possible in conventional society,[56] while others report that they are driven to 'search for authentic experience'.

However, the verbalized motivation for action is not necessarily congruent with the actual social conditions under which their drug-taking activities occur. Very seldom in Canadian society do middle and upper-class youths experience status deprivations, nor are they likely burdened excessively with common strains and stresses. Moreover, only a few are apt to resort to pot because they are 'alienated from society', rebelling against their parents or 'rejecting conventional society'. For the vast majority of young people, especially students, piecemeal disenchantment with society, vocal disillusionment with the world of adults, and critical attitudes are role expectations characteristic of a number of typical student roles. To be a 'drop out' or an 'activist', 'socially concerned', a 'radical,' an 'intellectual' or 'politically active' means to assume these kinds of social roles, hold particular attitudes and convictions, espouse certain values, and above all use the appropriate vocabulary of terms to make oneself heard. This helps remove doubt that one's role claims are only flirtatious, and convinces others as well as oneself that one is the kind of person one claims to be. Instead of being 'driven' to marijuana to 'escape from reality', the narrow circumscribed worlds in which these youths live, the temporary roles that they claim, and the fleeting identities that they assume require that they embrace the routine marijuana-smoking reality of which they are part architect.[57]

---

56 Andrew Garvin, "Why They Do It", *Newsweek,* July 24, 1967.
57 Much the same conclusion is found in E. A. Suchman, "The 'Hang-loose' Ethic and the Spirit of Drug Use", *Journal of Health and Social Behavior,* Vol. 9, 1968, 146-155. See also Herbert Blumer, *The World of Youthful Drug Use,* School of Criminology, University of California, Berkeley, California, 1967, 48-52.

# Acquiring a Deviant Self

Who we are and what we are depends largely on the everyday cultures in which we live and on those others with whom we customarily interact. The variety of roles that are culturally provided will greatly influence the kinds of person we can be. One cannot be a cool cat, a swindler, brain surgeon, 'don', or 'capo' unless these roles and identities are present and available to be learned, claimed, appropriated, or labeled with.

As a result of our daily activities with others, the self emerges gradually as a social object so that ultimately we are able to perceive, prepare, and display it symbolically to others much as we do any other object.[1] It is through our relationships with others, our social encounters, and increasing knowledge of other social worlds, that we are continually trying on new roles, consolidating old ones, and shedding those that we feel no longer become us. This means that to some extent we are continually on the lookout for new groups and cordial relationships in which we can feel behaviorally and psychologically at ease. But social action is al-

---

1   To examine the process whereby an individual acquires a deviant self is to ask a psychological question. To ask what the structure or pattern is to the social process of acquiring a deviant self is a sociological question.

ways something of a gamble and we can never be altogether certain of the outcome of our acts. Moreover, not any group or social relationship will suffice us. Some groups are beyond our reach socially and economically; others, perhaps, are intellectually and politically too high-powered for us, while still others fall beneath our standards. Thus, we try to manipulate our environment so as to reinforce those identities and social roles that have paid us dividends in the past, as for example, the academic who changes universities, but remains in his own league instead of trying for the big time (e.g., Harvard, Oxford, Cambridge or the Sorbonne) does. In a similar fashion we tend to select our friends from among those who consider us trustworthy, a 'nice guy', and pleasant to be with, and we are under less strain to 'perform' with those female companions who consider us charming, witty and, if we are lucky, 'great in bed.'

But as we approach new groups, sample different relationships, and appropriate new roles and identities we do so cautiously, in tiny Median-like steps, continuously defining, evaluating, and rationalizing the responses of those who are categorizing our efforts and judging our performances. To claim a role successfully often means that we must try hard to meet its obligations, and thereby convince others that we are the kind of person that becomes the role. In the process we attempt to manipulate their impressions and interpretations by saying the right word, smiling at the proper time and avoiding the wrong moves. In one way or another, and in varying degrees, we attempt to con others into accepting our presentation of self. To help minimize the anxiety and assuage the pain should our efforts fail, we recruit the appropriate rationalizations and 'techniques of neutralization' and apply them when the going gets rough.

Sometimes we only flirt with particular identities, but we are soon turned off. These flirtations often depend more on our personal standards than on the responses of others. The university coed who toys with a 'hip' identity may be thoroughly uncomfortable without a bra, feel no desire to climb into bed with her boyfriend, and be disgusted at the buckshot use of four letter words.

But this does not mean that we are continually trying to 'make friends and influence people.' Some people we despise and we act accordingly; others we feel are hardly worth our attention. However, at no time are we likely to be totally indifferent to the reactions of anyone. Almost everything we do is linked to a particular conception that we hold of ourselves; for example, women inject their breasts with silicone, or wear 'falsies' to improve their figures; men wear a cod-piece; others manage to invariably catch a trouser cuff in their Wellington boots;[2] university professors wear academic gowns in class, or others perform in army boots (invariably half laced), dungarees and hunting shirts. It is only by seeing how others respond—whether they smile approvingly, frown, or criticize and turn us away—that we can ever tell how successful our role claims are. The boy who claims to turn on with pot but refuses to smoke with others will have difficulty validating his claims among 'insiders'. The self-proclaimed tough guy who never accepts a challenge will soon be derided and rejected. The movie actor who gets bit parts only will not be taken seriously by leading players. At some point one must put up behaviorally or switch roles, or otherwise live in a world of one's own making.

One thing that demands much of our attention and that matters greatly to us is our self and its presentation to others. There are three basic components to the self: the self-image—what the actor believes to be true about himself, how he describes himself to himself; the self-demands or self-expectations—what the actor wishes to be, the standards according to which he compares his self-image, and the moral criteria by which he evaluates his self-image; and the actor's self-judgment—how well his daily conduct helps reduce the discrepancy between his self-image and the demands he places on himself.[3] Generally we are prone to learn those

---

2 These are instances of marginal differentiation at gaining status through behavioral innovation on socially acceptable forms of conduct. The means employed by persons in their efforts at gaining some degree of social recognition (however temporary) defy enumeration. Some examples include the student who wears a single ear ring and top hat as he parades about the college town, or the common one, of the student who wears his hat in class. Among pot smokers, roach holders vary from the common 'steamboat' (an empty toilet roll) to the more jewelled holders or elaborately decorated hookah pipes. What begins as marginal differentiation may become an officially established norm. Some years ago professional hockey players introduced a curve to the blades of their hockey sticks; because some players used too much curvature, the league finally passed an official rule limiting the extent of the blade's curvature. Elliot Liebow notes the same behavior when he writes in a footnote, "Sea Cat cuts his pants legs off at the calf and puts a fringe on the raggedy edges. Tonk breaks his "shades" and continues to wear the hornrimmed frames minus the lenses. Richard cultivates a distinctive manner of speech. Lonny gives himself a birthday party. And so on." See his *Tally's Corner*, Boston: Little, Brown and Company, 1967, 61.

3 The best discussion of the social emergence of the self is found in George Herbert Mead, *Mind, Self, and Society*, Chicago: University of Chicago Press, 1934. See also Charles H. Cooley, *Human Nature and the Social Order*, New York: Charles Scribner's Sons, 1902; for a good introduction to the subject see Alfred R. Lindesmith and Anselm L. Strauss, *Social Psychology*, rev. ed., New York: Holt, Rinehart and Winston, 1968, 314-343; Albert K. Cohen & James F. Short, Jr., "Juvenile Delinquency," in Robert K. Merton and Robert A. Nisbet (eds.), *Contemporary Social Problems*, New York: Harcourt, Brace & World, Inc., 98-104.

postures, adopt those demeanors, and employ those behavioral accessories that will support the roles that we are playing, and best illuminate the identities that we risk on display. Deviant behavior readily serves these functions, and is chosen often when it communicates, symbolizes or otherwise spotlights the identity being claimed. Many forms of deviance are efforts at claiming, testing or reinforcing a certain kind of identity. It has been suggested that much stealing among boys is more for kicks than for utilitarian purposes. It is said to be role-expressive behavior. Although stealing may be disapproved of and considered illegal in society, it leaves no doubt about a boy's masculinity. Whatever else it may be, it is expressive of the self-image of the youth who wishes to prove to himself and others that he is all boy.[4] Pool hall regulars in Montreal often try to present images of themselves as 'subterranean rebels' by appropriating special names, 'short cons', certain kinds of dress and aggressive behavior, and their choice of vocabulary is largely expressive. When a young female researcher enquired about learning how to play pool, she was informed that "If you want to learn to play pool you got to learn how to say 'fuck' ".[5] Much of our sexual behavior is motivated not only by role anxiety, but by wanting others to define us as a particular kind of person. Bell writes that,

> " . . . among the more experienced swinging women orgasm is often not a measurement of their sexual satisfaction . . . (it) is often far more important to the man than to the woman. The man often sees her orgasm as a measurement of his ability as a sexual 'artist'. It is common to hear a woman tell how she has mentioned to a man not to worry about her orgasm because it is hard for her to make it. And the man interprets this as a challenge and may try for hours to bring the woman to a climax. This effort doesn't mean that the man is interested in his partner's sexual welfare as much as that he sees it as a measurement of his sexual ability."[6]

In his effort to claim the role of cat, the young black addict struggles to remain cool. He tries to outsmart others with soft talk; he dreams of luxurious living, and dress, music, and his kick are

---

4   Cohen, *op. cit.*, 99-101.

5   Lorna Roth, "The Olympic Player: A Study of Pool Hall Regulars," in H. Taylor Buckner (ed.), *Urban Life Styles: St. Catherine Street - Friday Night*, unpublished collection of papers, Dept. of Sociology, Concordia University, 1972.

6   Robert R. Bell, *Social Deviance*, Homewood, Illinois: The Dorsey Press, 1971, 82.

important in his effort to make his daily life a 'gracious work of art'. However, on the street the cat is a petty thief, pickpocket, pool shark, or is engaged in some other con-like enterprise.[7] His behavior is role-expressive, and cannot help but persuade others that he is a particular sort of person. It also helps him achieve status within the cheerless circumscribed world in which he lives.

To claim a role and an identity is to announce to others that 'I am this kind of person. You can expect these attitudes, loyalties and conduct of me. This is what I really am.' It invites others to buy one's claims. However, every role has its price. Once we get others to accept our claims to being a certain kind of person (be it priest, nun, pimp or hippie), we can more easily offend, disappoint or anger them by violating their expectations of us. Admittedly there are tolerance limits to roles; once we transgress these limits others will soon insist that we be the kind of person that our role performance reflects.[8] And persons do not enjoy being taken in by a 'false bill of goods.' The faculty member who professes to be a colleague, but who manipulates a fellow colleague out of his students violates the expectations that fellow workers have of him. The priest who is caught out of habit getting drunk in a bar invites censure and jeopardizes his position in the eyes of parishioners; the nationalistic flag-waver who has to be conscripted during wartime, or the loving wife who is known to make it with the next door neighbor jeopardize their role claims by deviating from role expectations. Others who make no such claims run no such risks.[9]

---

7   Harold Finestone, "Cats, Kicks, and Color," *Social Problems,* Vol. 5, 1957, 3-13. In the eighteenth century the norm of possessing coolness, courage and being able to keep one's head in an emergency was called having 'Bottom.' Although school boys were whipped each day, the encouragement of Bottom was so effective 'that full-sized rebellions' broke out in a number of Public Schools. In some instances they had to be quelled by the military. See T.H. White, *The Age of Scandal,* Harmondsworth, England: Penguin Books, 1963, 68-82.

8   The moral status of some roles constitutes "virtually a 'license to steal.'" Nuns who steal books at academic meetings and hide them in the folds of their habits are relatively exempt from prosecution. Publishers' representatives are reluctant to take action against them. It would be interesting to know the limits to such normative tolerance. This example is reported in Donald W. Ball, "The Problematics of Respectability," in Jack D. Douglas (ed.), *Deviance and Respectability: The Social Construction of Moral Meanings,* New York: Basic Books, Inc., Publishers, 1970, 356-357.

9   Of course there are different kinds of costs to occupying social roles. The observability of some roles makes life for the role occupant almost intolerable. In order to 'live a little' priests sometimes have standing arrangements with taxi companies to bring them safely back from a night out on the neighboring town. Read Rex A. Lucas, *Minetown, Milltown, Railtown,* Toronto: University of Toronto Press, 1971, 184.

# Stigma: The Labeling Process

To say that activities that are socially discredited are deviant behavior is only half a truth. There is much behavior that is frowned upon and unwelcome that does not violate normative rules and is not considered deviant. Digging ditches, shining shoes, or cleaning toilets are typically disvalued kinds of work and parents seldom rear their children for such jobs. However, these jobs do not violate the normative rules of society. There is apt to be much less agreement among groups in society whether stripping professionally is deviant behavior, or whether the roles of stripper, stutterer or blind person are deviant categories. Sometimes total communities may be stigmatized. In their study of Africville in the city of Halifax, Clairmont and Magill noted that 'The historical processes of external encroachment and neglect, and of internal deprivation and decay resulted in Africville's being defined as a slum and its residents stigmatized.'[10] Deviance carries with it the idea of responsibility but not all behavior is easily classifiable. People who work at disreputable jobs or who are forced to live in slums are considered unfortunate, but we do not hold them responsible for their misfortune. Sanctions are not applied against those whom we feel have no choice in the matter, e.g., the person who is sick with pneumonia. Not so with the deviant—the prostitute, the mugger, the thief or the person who intentionally becomes sick. Society applies sanctions against these persons because they have violated the criminal code and/or the normative rules of conduct. Besides the judicial action taken by the community, we label and brand people, more for having violated our sense of decency and morality than for having broken the law; herein lies the seed of the stigmatization process. Sometimes, a single act is sufficient for the label to take hold; to commit murder or treason (whatever the circumstances) very likely means having to bear the stigma 'murderer' or 'traitor' for some time to come. However, a person may commit adultery a number of times yet escape the opprobrious label.

To be stigmatized is to be marked as a morally disreputable person.[11] Stigmatization is the collective process of attaching tags and labels of moral inferiority to a person. The collective censure of opinion is a crucial part of the process. For example, in the case

---

10  Donald H. Clairmont and Dennis William Magill, *Africville: The Life and Death of a Canadian Black Community,* Toronto: McClelland and Stewart Limited, 1974, 127.

11  For an early statement on the importance of societal reaction to deviance, see the excellent work by Frank Tannenbaum, *Crime and the Community,* New York: Columbia University Press, 1951. Also, Edwin M. Lemert, *Human Deviance, Social Problems, and Social Control,* Englewood Cliffs, New Jersey:

of the prospective delinquent the censure is initially directed against his play activities. But it is a short step to denunciation of the boy himself. Where the pranks are considered a nuisance, the youth is soon defined bad.[12] To what extent the labeling contributes to the youth's subsequent misbehavior is, however, an empirical question, and the answer is apt to be difficult to establish.

The process of labeling others, of investing them with a pejorative label, is a social process. We have already remarked that sometimes it is chance alone that starts the process. Most people break rules and escape unnoticed; nothing more is heard about it. Since there is nothing intrinsic to a person's conduct that must result in his being labeled deviant, it is society's (or social segments thereof) reactions to the behavior that greatly influence the kind of identity that emerges—whether or not the label sticks.

Very often persons and/or official agencies who endeavor to label others are assisted by the images that are currently available in the culture, i.e., the 'pictures in our minds' of the kinds of people who commit certain acts. We have noted already that there exist presently in the culture relatively common images of people who are 'dope fiends', prostitutes, tough guys, homosexuals, alcoholics and strippers. Whether or not these 'pictures in our minds' are a true reflection of the behavior of such persons is an open question. Investing persons with these qualities of deviance, moral inferiority, and personal stigma derived from such images contributes to the overall success of the labeling process. Walter Lippman writes:

> **We do not first see, then define, we define first then see . . . . We are told about the world before we see it. We imagine most things before we experience them. And those preconceptions, unless education has made us acutely aware, govern deeply the whole process of perception. They mark out certain objects as familiar or strange, emphasising the difference, so that the slightly familiar is seen as very familiar, and the somewhat strange as sharply alien.[13]**

---

Prentice-Hall, Inc., 1967, 40-64; Howard S. Becker, *Outsiders: Studies in the Sociology of Deviance,* New York: The Free Press of Glencoe, 1963, 1-39; Edwin M. Schur, *Labeling Deviant Behavior,* New York: Harper & Row, Publishers, 1971, and Erving Goffman, *Stigma: Notes on the Management of Spoiled Identity,* Englewood Cliffs, New Jersey: Prentice-Hall, Inc., 1964.

12  Tannenbaum, *op. cit.,* 17-19.

13  Walter Lippman, *Public Opinion,* New York: The Macmillan Co., 1922, 81, 90.

Lippman is reminding us that the processes of categorizing and classifying others are in the nature of social interaction. This means that the process of labeling others—the definitions we assign to others and their reactions to us—whether they be favorable or unfavorable, encouraging or objectionable, comprise 'absolutely pervasive social phenomena.'[14] This process helps us structure the expectations we have of others and predict their conduct.

But the tyranny of group obligations and the expectations of others do not imprison us in our conduct. No social determinism is advocated here. Man is not an empty vessel tossed hither and thither by the behavioral and attitudinal reactions of others. He does possess some control over his destiny. Admittedly this will vary with the conditions (e.g., socioeconomic location) in which he finds himself, but usually he makes some effort to manipulate the course of his actions. Thus a distinction should be made between applying the label to a person, his acceptance of it, and his internalization of the stigma. Some persons are arrested, judicially processed, sentenced, imprisoned, labeled, but refuse to think of themselves as criminal.[15] Why?

There is nothing inherent in the labeling process that requires a person to believe and to internalize the epithets that others provide, but some persons do. What are the significant variables, (e.g., social role, socioeconomic status, self-confidence, occupational esteem, the availability of supporting others), that determine why some persons and not others internalize the stigmatizing labels directed against them? Are persons who are especially susceptible to successful degradation differentially distributed throughout the system? The person of high social status or high occupational or professional accomplishment is very likely better able to protect his identity against the collective contumely of others. Must there exist in the process a power differential between reactors and suspected deviants?[16] The ability to successfully reject the censure of others (however systematic it may be), is surely related to the availability of strategic resources and the ability to organize them successfully. It would likely include one's skill in sustaining one's prior identity in the face of a derogatory onslaught.[17] This means recruiting and organizing others against the labelers, and having

---

14  Schur, *op. cit.,* 41.

15  Donald R. Cressey, *Other People's Money,* Glencoe, Ill.: The Free Press, 1953, 127.

16  In some cases a physical disability, e.g., blindness, places a person in a subordinate, socially dependent position in most social situations. See Robert A. Scott, *The Making of Blind Men,* New York: Russell Sage, 1969, 32-38.

17  For a brief discussion of the difficulties of establishing and assessing the relevant resources read Schur, *op. cit.,* 148-152.

others systematically spotlight one's own credibility. Also the ability to articulate one's ideas and images to others as well as to oneself, will help guard against self doubt.

What matters also is the person's belief in and cognitive certainty of who he is, i.e., his self-confidence. The person who is psychologically secure in his values, attitudes and knowledge of self, is likely less vulnerable to the destructive censure of others. If his conception of self is weak, vague and ambiguous, he is likely to experience considerable difficulty in discrediting the stigmatizing imputations of others.[18] Of course, no one is so well integrated that he is not vulnerable at some time, in some situation, to some kind of opprobrious attack. Perhaps, it is for such persons that the support of 'significant others' is especially significant. Is it the inability of the suspected deviant to subjectively recruit significant others from whose perspective he can sustain 'ego strength' and maintain personal integrity, that contributes to his acquiring a deviant identity?

The labeling process is seldom a one-sided affair. What happens to the person is, in part, his own doing. Some act, some difference on his part, called forth the reactions of others. However, the reactions of others, and the meaning and influence of their denunciation will partly depend on *his* reactions to the labelers; how well he fights back, how successful his efforts are at challenging, defending, parrying or otherwise rejecting their attacks. Also very important are how true or valid the label being applied is, and how legitimate the labelers' rights are. How long a person can resist such a collective denunciation is difficult to establish.

A major consequence of occupying visible, devalued roles, and of engaging in socially disreputable activities is that one is easily singled out for special attention. Often this is an important ingredient in social encounters. The degree to which social interaction is strained as a result of stigma is problematic, but visible physical defects or social inferiority enter into, and usually complicate, social exchange. For example, a person with an artificial leg might conceal his handicap and social encounters may proceed without incident. But should he decide to use his crutch and 'leave his leg at home' both he and others might experience a certain strain the next time that they meet.[19] Sometimes recurrent experiences of this kind and their social effect leave their mark on the personality of the stigmatized person.

---

18  Perhaps one's self-confidence is related to the occupational structure: the more prestigious one's occupation the greater one's self-confidence.

19  Goffman has discussed the notion of 'passing' admirably; *op. cit.*, 73-91.

In the minicultures of pot users, the cat worlds of black heroin addicts, nudist camps, the gay worlds, carnival worlds and underworlds, places like Yorkville (in the sixties) with its tattered culture of sorts,[20] and the 'tenderloin' areas of major cities inhabited by runners, hustlers, two-bit dealers in vice, and others perfectly at home in the worlds of crime, the inhabitants limit many of their activities to their own cultural networks, and socialize with others like themselves, thus helping to guard against the scarring consequences of stigma.[21]

# The Organizational Web[22]

What kinds of experiences are most likely to quicken the labeling process is not altogether known. However, lengthy public denunciation and formal degradation procedures are especially difficult to counteract.[23] Sometimes, a function of certain official and semi-official agencies and institutions in society is to label and stigmatize those whom they serve.[24] Law enforcement agencies are a good example. The official authority given the law enforcement agencies and the technical skills they can muster in the process make their success at labeling almost irreversible. It is difficult to be officially summoned, arrested, or detained by the police without there remaining, perhaps permanently, a residue of suspicion on one's identity. Official processing by the police magnifies the person in the eyes of the community; often it dramatizes evil[25] and

---

20   Today the area of Yorkville in Toronto has changed. No longer is it the home of hippies, high school and university dropouts and motorcycle gang members, garishly dressed, meandering the streets aimlessly, each trying desperately to do his own thing. Instead, it is an exclusive area of expensive shops and fashionable boutiques, where well-dressed people meander, window shopping more than anything else.

21   However, this is not true of all deviants. The work of robbers requires that they move where the traffic is, because usually the money is where the action is. A robber's work is executed in homes, banks and business places. Read Peter Letkemann, *Crime as Work,* Englewood Cliffs, New Jersey: Prentice-Hall, Inc., 1973, 158-164.

22   Part of our account follows closely the excellent paper by Eliot Friedson, "Disability as Social Deviance" in Marvin Sussman (ed.), *Sociology and Rehabilitation,* American Sociological Association with the Rehabilitation Administration, U.S. Dept. of Health, Education and Welfare, 1965, 71-99.

23   Harold Garfinkel, "Conditions of Successful Degradation Ceremonies", *The American Journal of Sociology,* Vol. 61, No. 5, 1956, 420-424.

24   Friedson, *op.cit.,* 71-99. A good review of some of the literature on the labeling perspective is found in John J. Hagen, "The Labelling Perspective, the Delinquent, and the Police: A Review of the Literature," *The Canadian Journal of Corrections,* Vol. 14, 1972, 150-165.

25   The term is taken from the early book by Tannenbaum, *Crime and the*

establishes a common focus according to which the person is perceived. It may also lead to the acquisition of a certain reputation, and a slight degradation of the person. In this way these institutions serve as status and identity-making bodies.

When institutions such as the police, law courts, psychiatric clinics, and social work agencies are interlocked into a subsystem of referring agencies—a 'deviance corridor'—through which prospective deviants are processed, their labeling and status-making functions are strongly reinforced. Once the prospective deviant is caught in this organizational web, it is difficult to escape without undergoing the complete 'treatment.' Shunted to and fro, the person is diagnosed, described, analysed, defined and redefined until a label gradually emerges; then he is classified, degraded in the process and sometimes institutionally 'fixed'.

At each stage in this process there is a source of control, an authority who commands, pressures and, however gently, manipulates the person. Slowly there develops an image of the individual as a different kind of person. However different he was to begin with, this institutional processing will likely leave its mark. The gradual, but seemingly ineluctable re-education in who and what the person is, is achieved by the relatively uniform vocabulary of words and gestures that is employed, and the common behavioral responses of officials towards the person. Each official—the policeman, the social worker, probation officer, psychologist and psychiatrist—usually adds (intentionally or otherwise) a little more pitch to the darkening picture.

There are a number of different referral subsystems throughout society.[26] Some agencies like the police and the law courts take a 'punitive' approach; others are 'permissive' or 'therapy-oriented'. It likely makes a difference to which one a person is sent initially. Some agencies are prone to accept only persons who are well motivated and anxious for 'treatment'. They are apt to be selectively biased and prefer 'patients' who are white, well educated, upper-middle class, relatively young, who can afford high fees. It is likely true that this type of person makes the therapist's task easier and less time consuming. Such a selective bias is found in other organizations as well. Whether socioeconomic bias operates among the police in dealing with the public, and in referring persons to the courts is not clearly established. Some statistically

*Community,* 1951, 19. His term is the 'dramatization of evil.' Regarding deviant careers read Becker, *op. cit.,* 24-39.

26   Friedson, *op. cit.,* 71-99; also Scott, *op. cit.*

based studies suggest that hardly any bias is operating.[27] However, an observational study of street patrol police officers suggests that factors other than those examined in statistically-oriented research are in operation.[28] In any case, the youth who is picked up, held in detention, questioned by probation officers, referred to clinics, tested by psychologists, examined by psychiatrists, reinvestigated by others, and finally brought before a judge, is never apt to be quite the same person whatever the outcome of his day in court; a certain stigma will likely remain.

Although the labeling process often occurs within a formal system of institutional contacts—each contact possessing potentially stigmatizing consequences for the person—it would be grossly misleading to think that the formal system of control serves only to increase crime and delinquency through the production of deviant careers and criminal identities in those with whom they come in contact. Usually the enthusiasts of the labeling approach focus their attention on the end product of the labeling sequence, i.e., on those cases that have been processed through one or more control agencies, and have developed deviant careers.[29] But what of those persons who have successfully survived encounters with the officials of social control, who have managed to offset the degradation process, who have not developed criminal identities, on whom the labels of inferiority have failed to stick, or who have amended their deviant ways because of their contact with the police?

The decisions made by the police towards persons may either contribute to crime through the growth of criminal careers, or they may dissuade persons from engaging in further crime and delinquency. There is certainly nothing inherent in police operations that necessarily produces crime. Indeed a number of studies suggest quite the contrary—that a very large percentage of juve-

---

27  See Robert M. Terry, *The Screening of Juvenile Offenders: A Study in the Societal Reaction to Deviant Behavior,* unpublished Ph.D. dissertation, University of Southern California, 1963, reported in David J. Bordua, "Recent Trends: Deviant Behavior and Social Control", *The Annals of the American Academy of Political and Social Science,* Vol. 369, 1967, 149-163. After reviewing a number of statistical studies of decision making among the police Bordua writes that, "they add up to what Terry calls a 'legalistic' picture with little or no evidence of socioeconomic bias." See Bordua, *Recent Trends: Deviant Behavior and Social Control,* 158. See also Donald J. Black and Albert J. Reiss, Jr., "Patterns of Behavior in Police and Citizen Transactions," Section 1 of *Studies of Crime and Law Enforcement in Major Metropolitan Areas,* Vol. 11, Washington, D.C.: U.S. Government Printing Office, 1967, 32.

28  Irving Piliavin and Scott Briar, "Police Encounters with Juveniles," *The American Journal of Sociology,* Vol. 70, 1964, 206-214.

29  Bordua, *op. cit.,* 153-154.

niles are returned to the community without court action being taken.[30] In a recent Canadian study 'outright release' of the youth although not an officially acknowledged departmental alternative, was 'a standard practice for which the officers have developed operating procedures that have been elevated to the force of official policy through continued and unquestioned use.'[31] Moreover, official statistics suggest strongly that the deterrent effect of police operations seems to reduce crime and delinquency in the larger society. It may be, as Bordua speculates, that the processes that produce stabilized deviants may be precisely the operations that reduce crime in the larger population.[32] A more balanced view of the societal reaction approach requires that we not only inspect the failures (deviant identities) produced by institutions of formal control, but also that we look at the successes, i.e., the reduction of crime and delinquency resulting from law enforcement procedures.[33]

Formal control agencies are not the only controlling mechanisms in society. Very often the cultures and subcultures (and the roles therein) in which we live, provide us with relatively ready-made responses to different kinds of deviance and to deviant persons. The worlds of God-fearing men, hippies, sophisticates and young people differ to a marked degree in their characteristic attitudes, values, and in their conceptions of reality. Such persons will possess different feelings and respond differently to many forms of deviant behavior. Murder, blackmail and burglary will be widely condemned, but there will be considerably less agreement regarding activities such as gambling, the use of drugs, prostitution, swinging and perhaps communal living.[34] These services,

---

30  See Natham Goldman, *The Differential Selection of Juvenile Offenders for Court Appearance,* National Research and Information Center: National Council on Crime and Delinquency, 1963, 126-128, also more recently, Donald J. Black and Albert J. Reiss, Jr., "Police Control of Juveniles". *American Sociological Review,* Vol. 35, 1970, 68; also see Bordua's comments on the Youth Bureau Operations of the Detroit Police Department, *op. cit.,* 161-163.

31  John M. Gandy, "The Exercise of Discretion By The Police as a Decision-Making Process in the Disposition of Juvenile Offenders", *Osgoode Hall Law Journal,* Vol. 8, 1970, 333.

32  Bordua, *op. cit.,* 161.

33  Bordua, *op. cit.,* 149-163.

34  See, for example, Craig L. Boydell and Carl F. Grindstaff, "Public Attitudes Toward Legal Sanctions for Drug and Abortion Offences", *The Canadian Journal of Corrections,* Vol. 13, 1971, 209-232, also Craig L. Boydell and Carl F. Grindstaff, "Public Opinion and the Criminal Law: An Empirical Test of Public Attitudes Toward Legal Sanctions", in Craig L. Boydell, Carl F. Grindstaff and Paul C. Whitehead, (eds.), *Deviant Behavior and Societal Reaction,* Toronto: Holt, Rinehart and Winston of Canada, 1972, 165-180.

goods and activities are in considerable demand, and people derive pleasure from them. The recipients of such services are beneficiaries, not victims, and attitudes towards these activities will vary widely. In general, young people are likely to be more tolerant of such conduct, others will condemn them immediately, while there are still others who might understand yet disapprove. The clergy, parents, and senior citizens have often taken a firm stand against prostitution, drug use and other forms of sexual congress.

Finally, whether the controlling agencies are formal or informal, groups or individuals, their responses to deviance are not unlimited, and the labels that they apply are never a private matter. Since the labeling process itself transpires in a social system, it is closely circumscribed by rules.[35] How we respond to the deviance of others, who may legitimately sanction or label another, the justification of the label and the severity of the sanctions that are applied are all governed by rules. Moreover the quality of our responses, whether we are tolerant, violent or considerate is influenced by the roles (both formal and informal) that we occupy and their importance to us. As we have stated above, in order to understand deviant behavior, and the reponses to it, e.g., whether *they* are deviant or not, it is essential to examine the rules of conduct.[36]

# Getting Hooked

Persons do not get hooked only on drugs; they also get hooked on social roles and on identities—deviant and non-deviant. At what point in the process of identity development the hook takes hold is not yet known. Lindesmith has taught us that the heroin addict gets hooked when he 'realizes that the discomfort and misery of withdrawal is caused by the absence of the drug and can be dispelled almost magically by another dose of it.'[37] Repetition of the experience brings about a craving for the drug. Once he obtains his shot he feels fine, and reports that the drug is holding him up well. He feels at ease: the strain and discomfort are gone and he is able to function satisfactorily with others. Is there a

---

35  Albert K. Cohen, "Stability and Change in Deviance" in Bernard B. Barber and Alex Inkeles (eds.), *Stability and Social Change,* Boston: Little, Brown and Company, 1971, 285-310. This paper provides a mature perspective towards the place of labeling theory in the general study of deviant behavior.

36  See the insightful article by Albert K. Cohen, "The Sociology of the Deviant Act: Anomie Theory and Beyond," *American Sociological Review,* Vol. 30, 1965, 5-14.

37  Alfred R. Lindesmith, *Opiate Addiction,* Evanston, Illinois: The Principia Press, no date.

similar process in getting hooked on a deviant identity?

It is true that some people actually seek out deviant roles, but not all deviant roles are eagerly cultivated. Some roles we deplore; those of murderer, alcoholic or psychotic we shun altogether. One of the consequences of being cast in a disreputably defined category is that often it has a self-fulfilling character.[38] To successfully defend one's integrity and self image as a non-deviant in the face of massive discrediting experiences is psychologically discomfiting and socially stressful. It is well known that persons under stress are more suggestible than otherwise. Repeatedly we deny the role, but in time self-doubt is apt to set in. The possibility of the denunciation being correct gradually occupies more of one's thinking and imagery.[39] Are the labelers correct? Is it true what my friends say about me? Am I unreliable, untrustworthy, unmanageable? Have I got problems? Do I need treatment? Was I born this way? Am I really bad?

The process of getting hooked on a deviant identity includes overcoming the misery and discomfort created by the daily tensions and problems that arise from the labeling itself—problems of getting a job and keeping it; interpersonal problems of maintaining relationships, sustaining ties with parents, friends and loved ones; problems of paying debts and supporting one's family—in brief, problems of being accepted, and making it successfully as a publicized deviant in a world of non-deviants.[40]

Ultimately these conditions are apt to highlight the difficulties and diminishing returns from trying to maintain a non-deviant identity. Although we deny that the role is a mirror of our true self, acquaintances shut us out, and friends change their manner towards us. Where one was previously trusted, one is now suspect; persons withdraw their friendship, one is less socially acceptable. One now 'becomes in the eyes of his condemners literally a different and *new* person.'[41] The retrospective discrediting (by the labelers) of selective events and acts in the suspected deviant's past accelerates the process.[42] Alternative courses of action appear closed; options appear to run out. Is the effort worth the cost? A

---

38  Stanton Wheeler, "Deviant Behavior," in Neil J. Smelser (ed.), *Sociology: An Introduction,* New York: John Wiley and Sons, Inc., 1967, 636.

39  Thomas J. Scheff, *Being Mentally Ill,* New York: Aldine-Atherton, 1966, 55-104.

40  Read Robert A. Stebbins, *Commitment to Deviance,* Westport, Conn: Greenwood Publishing Corp., 1971.

41  Garfinkel, "Conditions of Successful Degradation Ceremonies," 421.

42  See Edwin M. Schur, *op. cit.,* 52-56. A fine discussion is found in John Lofland, *Deviance and Identity,* Englewood Cliffs, New Jersey: Prentice-Hall, Inc., 1969, 146-173; also Garfinkel, *op. cit.,* 420-424.

gradual awareness emerges of the impossibility of maintaining one's old identity. Friends (who are now rejectors) are reviewed, reassessed, redefined. Reaction and hostility develop; relationships lapse and die; institutional connections are severed.

The stable institutional arrangements of daily living, and the framework of sympathetic others upon which our integrity, self conception and personal performance were nourished, slowly but ineluctably undergo transformation. Our worlds become increasingly restricted, and we are compelled to seek alternative courses of action. Sometimes we look to others like ourselves.[43] New relationships emerge, friendships develop. With others similarly circumstanced, the need for social and psychological intimacy is satisfied. There are new sources of status, new affiliations and new standards of conduct. Increasingly we become committed to new undertakings and obligations, and to the unanticipated consequences thereof.[44] Anguish and conflict are replaced gradually by comfort and satisfaction in one's newly developing role and identity. New support is received for one's conduct, attitudes, sentiments and emotions. Regularity of such experiences is rewarded; confidence is restored, and one is locked into a new system of social relationships. Gradually a new perspective on reality is structured and assumes new meaning. Life is endurable.

The developing identity strengthens as one begins to offset challenges to self claims by defending one's attitudes and activities according to deviant role standards and rationalizations.[45] Perhaps the hook takes hold when one begins to define one's conduct as a moral enterprise. Under such conditions one may undergo hardship and endure pain in order to sustain a particular identity. Indeed, one may attempt to *improve* one's identity according to deviant role criteria. Success now becomes a source of pride and is rewarded by the approval of supporting others. The delinquent takes pride in his gang; the cat feels proud of outsmarting others; the prostitute knows that she is providing an important service for lonely, unloved men; the radical student sets the university building afire for the 'good of society'. In this manner one's identi-

---

43  The significance of social interaction and the reliance on others similarly circumstanced is less evident in some cases of identity change. For example, physician addicts do not participate in a criminal subculture, and stutterers, epileptics, alcoholics and some kinds of sex offenders "do not form groups" according to Lemert. See Edwin M. Lemert, *Human Deviance, Social Problems and Social Control,* 46-48.

44  See Erving Goffman, *Encounters: Two Studies in the Sociology of Interaction,* Indianapolis: The Bobbs-Merrill Co., Inc., 1961, 88-91, also Howard S. Becker, "Notes on the Concept of Commitment," *American Journal of Sociology,* Vol. 66, 1960, 32-40; Becker, *Outsiders: Studies in the Sociology of Deviance,* 27-28.

45  Edwin M. Lemert, *Social Pathology,* New York: McGraw-Hill, 1951, 76.

ty becomes increasingly contingent on doing well in terms of deviant role obligations.[46] One knows who one really is.

But Lemert cautions our overemphasizing the social context. Self-revelation need not 'always [have] immediate antecedents in participant social interaction dramatizing good and evil.'[47] Self-discovery 'may be little more than solitary moments of disenchantment'—the realization that one's 'fabric of rationalizations' is a shambles, a pretense, a lie. Paul Gauguin suddenly decided that he wanted to paint, deserted his family and job, and left for the South Seas; the consistently failing student realizes that he can 'never make it' and drops out in search of more compatible surroundings; the long-retiring hockey star surrounded by upstart youngsters in training camp, suddenly realizes that he can't 'keep up'—that, 'I'm through.' Perhaps, as Lemert states, 'The logic of self-discovery is an inner one.'[48]

However getting hooked is not necessarily a lengthy process;[49] moreover an identity is sometimes short lived. Unlike heroin addicts, who are apt to remain hooked for life,[50] people can and do divest themselves of roles, and shed identities on short notice. Children happily shed their 'kid' roles and become teenagers—some sooner than others. Students who burn down university buildings, and parade with drawn rifles on campuses seldom occupy these roles and identities for very long. Most of them graduate from college, become businessmen, teachers, or social workers and assume 'straight' identities. Most delinquents outgrow their roles and become law-abiding citizens.[51] Some however, move on to heavier action and become robbers.[52] With the coming of the comet Kohoutek, the Children of God sect held a vigil outside the

---

46  It is often the regularity of role occupancy which contributes to role commitment. Goffman writes that "it is left to gallants, one-shot gamblers, and the foolhardy to become committed to a role they do not perform regularly." Goffman, *Encounters: Two Studies in the Sociology of Interaction,* 89.

47  Lemert, *Human Deviance, Social Problems and Social Control,* 52-53.

48  *Ibid.,* 53.

49  Incarceration in a penitentiary or commitment to a mental hospital may be psychologically traumatic for the person, and he may never again see himself as before.

50  See the excellent work by Edward M. Brecher and the Editors of Consumers Reports, *Licit and Illicit Drugs,* Mount Vernon, New York: Consumers Union, 1972, 64-175.

51  The processes whereby some delinquent youths become law-abiding adults while others move on to heavier criminal action are not known well. See Albert K. Cohen and James F. Short, Jr., "Research in Delinquent Subcultures," *The Journal of Social Issues,* Vol. 14, 1958, 27-28.

52  Letkemann, *Crime as Work,* 117-121; Cohen and Short, *Research in Delinquent Subcultures,* 27-28.

United Nations building in New York City. Dressed in red sack-cloth and ashes they proclaimed the comet was a divine signal that the United States would be destroyed on January 31, 1974.[53] The social and psychological dividends from assuming these kinds of roles and espousing affiliated attitudes and identities are usually temporary. However, because they were hooked they kept vigil every night. Many young people have a way of popping in and out of these kinds of roles with almost predictable regularity.

Of course there are differential costs to the shedding of identities. Some are very great indeed. For example, the lower-class gang boy who decides to take the college route will likely forfeit long-standing friends and companionship; the demands of nightly attendance on the street corner soon conflict with the heavy requirements of university work. The prostitute who decides upon marriage may well sacrifice high income for long-term security. Furthermore, the changing of identities is sometimes so stressful that special positions require special assistance. Like a great race horse who must unwind with daily workouts for a few months before being put to stud, so the retiring superstar is eased down from the heights of stardom by being retained temporarily, as a goodwill ambassador (or some other figurehead) of the team.[54]

Some identities are easier to change than others, and the ease with which we can slip into roles and assume new, but affiliated identities may influence the forms of deviance that we practise. For example, the roles of stripper and hooker are parts of closely related worlds, and identity change is not apt to be especially painful; the roles of salesman and 'con artist', model and actress, are in some respects, occupationally kin; the tough guy may easily assume the identity of bodyguard to the established hoodlum.

There are also some identities that are perhaps impossible to change. Occupational role identities often fall into this category. Does the retired medical doctor give up his identity as doctor?[55] Can the long-time criminal who spends his life hustling consider himself otherwise?[56] The role of mother tends to have a lifetime effect on one's identity.

---

53  *The Kitchener-Waterloo Record,* Saturday, December 22, 1973. In this regard read J.L. Simmons, "On Maintaining Deviant Belief Systems", *Social Problems,* Vol.11, No. 3, 1964, 250-256.

54  Not all athletic stars are so fortunate. Janet Lever, "Soccer As a Brazilian Way of Life", in Gregory P. Stone (ed.) *Games, Sport and Power,* Transaction Books, New Brunswick, New Jersey: E.P. Dutton and Company, 1972, 138-159.

55  A disbarred lawyer may be prevented legally from practising law, however, he will open an office and continue to sell legal advice.

56  For example, read Henry Williamson, *Hustler!,* New York: Doubleday and Company, Inc., 1965.

It is also true that some roles are practised secretly, and we must act to prevent others from identifying us as deviants. We manage our lives and identities so as to camouflage what we secretly cherish and practice. A prostitute for example, takes a legitimate job to learn about well-heeled clients; a salesgirl hustles once a month in the neighboring town; a cleaning woman moves the bric-a-brac, and tilts the paintings so that the homeowner will think that she has done a thorough cleaning job; a housewife disguises herself by wearing a wig to meet her lover, or the upper-class girl, with surgical assistance, is able to restore the appearance of virginity.[57] Sometimes this veil of secrecy involves switching roles on short notice in appropriate situations. For instance, one moment in a public restroom a person might engage in a short lived homosexual act and a few minutes later leave the 'tearoom' and resume life as the 'respectable next door neighbour, home-maker, and businessman.'[58] These practices enable people to avoid detection, they facilitate daily interaction and help overcome what otherwise might be embarrassing problems.

---

57   Lois B. DeFleur, *Delinquency in Argentina: A Study of Cordóba's Youth,* Washington State University Press, 1970, 76.

58   Laud Humphreys, *Tearoom Trade,* Chicago: Aldine Publishing Company, 1970.

# The Incidence of Crime: How Much is There?

**7**

The answer to this question is that we suspect that there is a great deal more crime and delinquency than the official evidence reveals. Precisely how much, and of what kind, we can never be certain. There are no easy solutions to getting the facts about the amount and kinds of crime and delinquent acts that are committed.

The ratio of crimes that are known to those that are unknown remains a mystery, and very likely varies with time, place and type of offense. Offenses known to the police remain the best available official indication of the overall amount of crime and delinquency, and they are suspected to be only a small fraction of the total number of offenses committed. Whether an offense known to the police ever becomes statistically recorded depends on a number of variables. We know, for example, that whatever persons or agencies are doing the observing, the counting, and the recording of criminal acts, some degree of bias is operating. The important question is: what are the sources of the bias? Do they operate systematically to foul the official count? Does the manner in which the police force is organized influence the kinds and frequency of criminal acts that are recorded?[1] Does the racial or perhaps bicul-

---

1    See John I. Kitsuse and Aaron V. Cicourel, "A Note on the Uses of Official Statistics," *Social Problems,* Vol. 11, No.2, 1963, 131-139.

tural complexion of the department make a difference? Does political pressure influence the efficiency and skill of police work? For example, police efficiency is apt to increase prior to an election (in order to 'clean up the city'), perhaps during the visits of heads of state, and during periods of crisis. For example, during World War II, many whorehouses including the notorious '312 Ontario' in Montreal, were closed down.

Nettler writes that 'Official criminal statistics not only are imperfect because of *what* they do and do not count, but are also criticized for imperfections in the *accountant*.'[2] However, recent studies of police discretion fail to reveal any marked extra-legal bias in the handling of serious offenders. In 1950 Goldman under-took an analysis of the arrest records of 1,083 juvenile offenders in four American communities near Pittsburg.[3] This study revealed that the majority of police contacts with young people were handled out of court, and that those offenses classified as 'serious' were more frequently referred to the court than were other offenses.[4] The data revealed no discriminatory treatment of girls, but there was an under-representation of young boys (under twelve) and an over-representation of older boys (over fifteen) in the court records.[5] The proportion of arrests referred to the juvenile courts ranged from 18.6 percent to 71.2 percent among the communities.[6] As Bordua writes, 'Looked at in terms of release rather than referral . . . the police departments in Goldman's study let go from 29 percent to 91 percent of the juveniles they took into custody.'[7]

In their 1967 study, Black and Reiss recorded detailed descriptions of the behavior of police officers and citizens.[8] A total of 5,360 situations were observed. They found that in almost three-quarters of encounters with citizens the police officers 'acted in a business-like or routinized way.' The police were 'good-

---

2   Gwynn Nettler, *Explaining Crime,* New York: McGraw-Hill Book Company, 1974, 49.

3   Nathan Goldman, *The Differential Selection of Juvenile Offenders for Court Appearance,* National Research and Information Center: National Council on Crime and Delinquency, 1963.

4   *Ibid.,* 47.

5   *Ibid.,* 47.

6   *Ibid.,* 126.

7   David Bordua, "Recent Trends: Deviant Behavior and Social Control," *The Annals of the American Academy of Political and Social Science,* Vol. 369, 1967, 157.

8   Donald J. Black and Albert J. Reiss, Jr., "Patterns of Behavior in Police and Citizen Transactions," Section 1 of *Studies of Crime and Law Enforcement in Major Metropolitan Areas,* Vol. 11, Washington, D.C.: U.S. Government Printing Office, 1967.

humoured or jovial' in 15 percent of their encounters with citizens, and 'brusque or authoritarian in 4 percent of their encounters.' In one percent of cases the police were 'openly hostile or provocative' and in 3 percent of encounters they were 'belittling'.[9] Overall, the analysis "revealed no striking differences in 'unprofessional' police conduct by race or social class status of citizens."[10] However, they did find what we know to be true of most of us; nastiness is returned by nastiness. According to Black and Reiss, "Officers are a good deal more likely to be hostile and brusque and to ridicule citizens when citizens are antagonistic than when they show more 'respect' ".[11] In a later study of police contacts with juveniles only, Black and Reiss found that most encounters with juveniles arise largely from citizen complaints, and that of the total number of 'encounters patrol officers have with juvenile suspects only 15 percent result in arrest.'[12] The majority of these contacts are of minor legal importance. However, the chances of arrest for juveniles increase with the legal seriousness of the offense. Moreover, arrest rates are related to the presence of a complainant. 'When a complainant explicitly expresses a preference for an arrest . . . the tendency of the police to comply is . . . quite strong.'[13] In not one case did the police arrest a youth when the complainant preferred an informal disposition.[14] This tendency is costly for Negro juveniles since Negro complainants (with whom Negro juveniles most often had encounters) 'are relatively severe in their expressed preference when they are compared to white complainants vis-à-vis white juveniles.'[15]

In 1964 Piliavin and Briar undertook an observational study of discretion among police officers in their contacts with juveniles. They found that the police had little trouble in judging the character of boys who had committed serious offenses, like robbery, homocide, grand theft, aggravated assault, rape, arson or auto theft. The police officers defined these youths as 'confirmed delinquents simply by virtue of their involvement in offenses of this magnitude.'[16] However, in the case of minor offenders, who com-

---

9   *Ibid.*, 30.

10   *Ibid.*, 32.

11   *Ibid.*, 35.

12   Donald J. Black and Albert J. Reiss, Jr., "Police Control of Juveniles," *American Sociological Review,* Vol. 35, 1970, 68.

13   *Ibid.*, 71.

14   *Ibid.*, 71.

15   *Ibid.*, 71.

16   Irving Piliavin and Scott Briar, "Police Encounters with Juveniles," *The American Journal of Sociology,* Vol. 70, No. 2, 1964, 209.

prised over 90 percent of encounters, the violation was relatively unimportant in determining police action. It was the police officer's assessment of the youth's character which strongly influenced his decision. Clues such as a boy's 'group affiliations, age, race, grooming, dress and demeanor' were important. Boys who were rude, stubborn or who appeared nonchalant in encounters with officers were likely to be defined as 'would-be tough guys' or 'punks', who deserved arrest. Others who appeared fearful, contrite and acted in a respectful manner towards the police, were considered 'salvageable' and an informal disposition usually followed.[17]

One thing seems clear: a violation of the law does not automatically result in an arrest. The best evidence suggests that the offenses which are finally included in official statistics are 'the more obvious offenses, the more serious offenses, offenses whose victims have brought complaints, and offenses some of whose victims are dead—those crimes, in short, for which the public put pressure on their police to make arrests.'[18]

Although there is no striking evidence of systematic and consistent bias in the behavior of police officers, this does not deny differential conduct taken by individual officers towards particular groups. For example, the training of the police officer, his socioeconomic background (although there is likely little variation here), and whether he is starting or ending his shift may influence his decision in making an arrest. Where an act occurs may also influence how it is handled by the police. Stinchcombe[19] has suggested recently that whether an area is legally defined private or public will influence the investigation methods of the police. For example, crimes against persons ('crimes of passion') normally occur within 'morally dense small social systems'—within private places. Police learn of such crimes typically through complaints, and since the victim and assailant usually know each other, arrests are easy to make. Yet the conditions that produce easy arrests often make conviction very problematic. Moral responsibility for passion crimes is difficult to produce in court, and complaints are felt to be something of a betrayal of those to whom we are closely tied. Once the complaint is made, personal ties reassert themselves

---

17   *Ibid.*, 209-212.

18   Nettler, *op. cit.*, 57.

19   See the excellent article by Arthur L. Stinchcombe, "Institutions of Privacy in the Determination of Police Administrative Practice," *The American Journal of Sociology,* Vol. 69, No. 2, 150-160. The different location of crimes also provides differential opportunities for illegality by the police. Detecting a couple engaged in a sex act in a parked car, or stopping a taxicab with no other car in sight, are excellent opportunities for the officer to solicit a bribe.

and the 'main source of evidence refuses to testify.' On the other hand crimes against persons in *public* places are usually handled differently. The police officer is more likely to be on the scene and his own information is sufficient for an arrest. Assailants are usually unknown, which increases the difficulty of locating them. However, since assailants are usually unrelated to the victims, once they are located the 'establishment of legal and moral responsibility is easier,' and the complainant is less motivated to drop the case.

In small communities and rural areas a police officer will personally know many of the residents, and will likely exercise more discretion before making an arrest. This is less likely to happen in large cities, characterized by anonymity, where there are much stronger norms about 'deliberately not noticing' the conduct of others, and where 'more behavior is *only* inquired into by the police.'[20]

What is perceived and ultimately reported as a crime by the police is often a complicated matter. For offenses against the person like murder, attempted murder, rape, wounding, and assault, the rule seems to be that one offense is reported for each victim. For offenses against property, like breaking and entering and theft, a single offense is recorded for a single operation; each operation refers to the same time, location and circumstances. When there are multiple offenses during a single incident, for example, when a robber holds-up a liquor store, rifles the till, pistol-whips the attendant, steals the wallet from a customer, and in the process breaks some merchandise, the most serious offense is recorded, the criterion being the maximum legal penalty involved, or if the penalties are the same, the most serious offense as defined by the police.[21]

The range of visibility of an act can vary from only the parties involved to a large number of others. Minimal social visibility characterizes many deviant acts, e.g., illicit sex acts, confidence games, some drug taking and call-girl prostitution. Depending on who witnesses a criminal act, e.g., a friend, stranger, or the police, there will be differential consequences for the offender. A youth who discovers a friend shoplifting may want to join the 'action.' A middle-class girl caught by the next-door neighbor soliciting a man in a night club, may suffer more than if she were spotted by a plainsclothes officer. Depending on the girl, the circumstances surrounding the conduct, and the inclination of the officer,

---

20  Stinchcombe, *op. cit.*, 152.

21  Canada: Statistics Canada, *Police Statistics,* Ottawa: Information Canada, 1971, 8. For a very sound review of many of the problems dealing with reporting, recording and use of official statistics, see Nettler, *op. cit.*, chapter 4.

official action may or may not be taken. However, the neighbor is apt to be an immediate source of gossip.

The visibility of offenders can also vary. Because of their social and physical characteristics, some groups are more visible than others. Negroes, Indians, Eskimos, and members of some immigrant groups in areas not predominantly inhabited by persons of their own nationality, are apt to be more conspicuous when they violate the rules.[22]

But there is more than this. Since it is relatively easy to violate certain criminal laws, as many of us do each day, and go undetected, the police learn more about the criminal acts that are committed than they do about the offenders themselves. 'Persons arrested or summoned' and 'persons prosecuted' provide the best available information for estimating the number of persons engaged in law violation.[23] An act defined as an 'offense known to the police' is one thing; making an arrest, laying a formal charge, bringing the accused to trial and having him convicted is something else. It is a lengthy process involving a number of contingencies, and a considerable reduction in the number of cases occurs at each stage of the process. A similar filtering process occurs when the police are *notified by the victims* of an offense. Notifying the police is no guarantee that they will arrive on the scene. In a recent study the police failed to arrive in 23 percent of the cases to which they were called. In a quarter of the cases in which they did arrive, they did not define the incident as a crime; domestic quarrels, for example, are seldom defined as crimes by the police. And they made an arrest in only 20 percent of the incidents which they defined as crimes; of those arrested only 42 percent were sent to trial, and of these considerably fewer were convicted.[24] Although the police become involved, there exist many possibilities of escaping legal action or of exerting influence, or otherwise neutralizing the legal process. This includes the possibility of making a 'deal' with the police[25] or of having the case 'fixed'.[26] But the probability of getting

---

22   Edwin M. Lemert, *Social Pathology,* New York: McGraw-Hill Book Company, 1951, 52.

23   Nicolas Zay, "Gaps in Available Statistics on Crime and Delinquency in Canada," *Canadian Journal of Economics and Political Science,* Vol. 29, No. 1, 1963, 75-89.

24   P.H. Ennis, "Criminal Victimisation in the United States: A Report of a National Survey," *A Report of a Research Study Submitted to The President's Commission on Law Enforcement and Administration of Justice,* Washington, D.C.: U.S. Government Printing Office, 1967, 48-51.

25   Donald R. Cressey (ed.), *Crime and Criminal Justice,* Chicago: Quadrangle Books, 1971, 3-17; Harvey Blackstock, *Bitter Humour,* Toronto: Burns and MacEachern Ltd., 1967, 177-183.

26   Bill Chambliss (ed.), *Box Man,* New York: Harper & Row, 1972, 2ff.

off the hook likely decreases the more advanced are the proceedings. Presumably it is easier to bribe a police officer than a judge, if only because one is much more accessible than the other.[27]

Yet each stage in the process increases police knowledge of the offender. Cohen writes, "We may think of the successive stages of the legal process as representing, on the whole, increases in clarity and certainty of offender-identification . . . [but] as clarity and certainty increase, the percentage of 'survivors' from the total population of offenders decreases."[28] The lost cases are the price we pay for increased knowledge. Offenses known to the police is a better index of the amount of crime than the arrest rate: the arrest rate is better than the rate of convictions, and since not all those convicted are imprisoned, conviction is a better index than the imprisonment rate. Statistics show that police forces in Canada reported 1,298,551 actual offenses of the Criminal Code in 1973.[29] But the proportion of individual offenses that were cleared varied widely with the offense. For example, in cases of murder and manslaughter a high proportion (85 percent and 91.9 percent respectively) of cases were cleared. Of those offenses about which the police learn considerably less, such as breaking and entering or theft under two hundred dollars, only 23.9 percent and 24.4 percent respectively were cleared.[30]

A new approach to investigating the amount of crime and delinquency is to study the incidence of victimization in the general population. A recent study was conducted for the President's Commission on Law Enforcement and Administration of Justice in the District of Columbia by the Bureau of Social Science Research, reported by Biderman et al. in 1967.[31] Of the 9,993 inci-

---

27  On the other hand one study found that in New York city, 44.7 percent of the indictments against members of organized crime were dismissed at the state supreme court level during the period of 1960-1969, whereas only 11.5 percent of cases against all defendants were dismissed. See John E. Conklin (ed.), *The Crime Establishment*, Englewood Cliffs, New Jersey: Prentice-Hall, Inc., 1973, 23, footnote 60. Also, "The Law" in *Time Magazine*, October 1, 1965.

28  Albert K. Cohen, *Deviance and Control*, Englewood Cliffs, New Jersey: Prentice-Hall, Inc., 1966, 28. See also W.T. McGrath (ed.), *Crime and Its Treatment in Canada*, Toronto: Macmillan of Canada, 1965, 59-90; Zay, *op. cit.*, 75-89.

29  Canada: Statistics Canada, *Crime and Traffic Enforcement Statistics*, Ottawa: Information Canada, 1972-1973.

30  An offense is "cleared by charge" when an information has been laid against at least one person. Sometimes clearances are made otherwise, e.g., when a person confesses to a crime, but subsequently dies, or if the offender is known and sufficient evidence has been gathered, but the complainant refuses to prosecute, or if the person has been committed to a mental institution. Canada: Statistics Canada, *Crime Statistics*, Ottawa: Information Canada, 1971.

31  A.D. Biderman, et al., "Report on a Pilot Study in the District of Columbia on

dents mentioned by victims only 443 were actual offenses known to the police. This difference between victim reports and offenses known to the police varies with the offense. For example, over 23 times as much aggravated assault was reported as was known to the police, and over 30 times as much robbery. It is also the case that 31 instances of criminal homicide were reported, but only one was known to the police. This finding seems almost incredible. However, the rank ordering of the victim reports and offenses known to the police was similar.

Another recent work previously referred to is the National Opinion Research Center study of the President's Commission on Law Enforcement and Administration of Justice.[32] This study leaves little doubt that there is much more crime committed than is recorded. The report says that 'at least twice as much major crime as is reported occurs, and that minor crime is about twice the amount of major crime.'[33] The survey showed that rates based on victim reports and crimes known to the police vary with the type of offense, and that serious crimes such as robbery, burglary, forcible rape, aggravated assault and theft over fifty dollars are all reported by victims more frequently than they are reported to the police. Two exceptions are homicide and vehicle theft. The survey also found that the rank order of the frequency of the serious offenses reported by victims is identical to that of the Uniform Crime Reports, the exception being vehicle theft. This finding agrees with data from the Bureau of Social Research study. Another not unfamiliar finding was that the crime rate declines as one moves from the city center into the suburbs, smaller towns and rural areas. However, the decline is much sharper for crimes against the person than for crimes against property. The rate of violent crime is about five times higher in the city center than in smaller towns and rural areas, but the property crime rate is only twice as high.[34] Finally, the report noted that there was considerable doubt among victims (55 percent) about police effectiveness in response to criminal victimization. Considering the large attri-

---

Victimization and Attitudes Toward Law Enforcement, Field Surveys 1," *President's Commission on Law Enforcement and Administration of Justice,* Washington, D.C.: U.S. Government Printing Office, 1967. For Canadian data see M.C. Courtis, " Victimization in Toronto" in Robert A. Silverman and James J. Teevan, Jr., *Crime in Canadian Society,* Toronto: Butterworth and Co., (Canada) Ltd., 1975, 119-125.

32  Ennis, *op. cit.,* 1967.

33  *Ibid.,* 13-14.

34  *Ibid.,* 20-40.

tion of cases as they are judicially processed, the victims' doubts are perhaps warranted.[35]

In the NORC study, when victims were asked their reasons for not reporting property crimes, the most frequent response was that they were skeptical of police effectiveness. There was little difference between blacks and whites in the extent to which crime was reported to the police, nor was there much difference in their reasons for not doing so. In the survey conducted by the Bureau of Social Science Research, when victims were asked why they had not notified the police, the most frequent response (34 percent) was that they felt 'nothing could be done about the event.'[36] About 17 percent believed that the police did not wish to help, while the remainder gave a variety of reasons.

These victimization studies are new methods of gathering data on the amount of crime that is committed in the community and they warrant careful attention. As Hood and Sparks note, the data from these surveys 'cast doubt on the assumption of a constant ratio of reporting crime in the population.'[37] But these studies are also theoretically serviceable. For example, not all victims are equally specifiable. As Glaser remarks, the data from victim studies make us theoretically sensitive to the category of 'victim', and draw our attention to predatory crimes compared with crimes without victims, 'public disorder crimes' where 'there is no intention to injure a victim and often no clear injury', or 'negligence crimes' such as speeding or reckless driving.[38] Moreover, the data on whether victims notified the police of their victimization are a sound reflection of their attitudes towards the police. Glaser suggests that these data support the idea that, *'the proportion of total crimes that are reported by victims to the police varies directly with the proportion of reported crimes on which the police act effectively.'*[39] Finally, the data from these surveys are not meant to be substituted for police statistics on crime, but as these new techniques are improved, their continued use along with the official records auger well for our increased knowledge of the amount of crime and delinquency in the larger population.

---

35  *Ibid.,* 41-51.

36  A.D. Biderman, et al., *op. cit.,* 153.

37  Roger Hood and Richard Sparks, *Key Issues in Criminology,* New York: World University Library, McGraw-Hill Book Company, 1970, 43. See also their remarks on the methodological problems of victim surveys, 25-32; also Nettler, *Explaining Crime,* 71-73.

38  Daniel Glaser, "Victim Survey Research: Theoretical Implications," in Anthony L. Guenther (ed.), *Criminal Behavior and Social Systems,* Chicago: Rand McNally and Company, 1970, 137.

39  *Ibid.,* 144.

Since it appears that there is considerably more crime committed than the police know about, the question arises: why do persons not report the crimes that they witness, or victims report their victimization? We have noted already that the type of offense affects whether the victim will report it; the more serious the crime the greater the likelihood of it being reported. Among NORC victims '65 percent of aggravated assaults were reported, but only 46 percent of the simple assaults; 60 percent of grand larcenies, but only 37 percent of petty larcenies.'[40] One reason why murder has a high probability of being known to the police is that, like sexual assaults on children and armed robbery, it is considered an especially heinous offense, and people usually report such offenses. Bank robberies are obviously difficult to hide and seldom go unreported. Although forcible rape is considered a serious offense, it is apt to be reported less regularly; besides the difficulty of obtaining convictions in such cases, persons fear the publicity and embarrassment to the victim. Generally there is increased public pressure on the police to do something about the more serious crimes.

Not all offenses are equally undesirable to the public or to the police. For example, neither the vast majority of the public nor the police are apt to view with alarm activities such as fraud, pot smoking, prostitution or public drunkenness. Again, differential toleration of various forms of conduct in communities usually reflects the ideas residents have of acceptable behavior. What is defined as crime in one community might not be perceived as crime in another. Even if the victim perceives the act as criminal he may be talked out of reporting it. Similarly, he may be paid off on the spot. He may fear the reprisals of others, or like the small store owner to whom every sale is precious, he may be too busy and unable to afford the time to take his case to court. Large department stores often fear bad publicity and fail to report shoplifters; businessmen often fear for their lives and limbs, but seldom inform the police of infiltrative attempts by organized criminal groups; sometimes persons are not always aware that they have been burglarized, and their losses are attributed to other causes. There are also crimes without victims; evidence is difficult to obtain in such cases, and police policies vary widely. Whether such acts as the use of illegal drugs, abortion and illicit sexual relations become known to the authorities depends largely on the initiative, organization and efficiency of the police.

Still other methods have been used to assess the number of people who violate or who have violated the law, the kinds of

---

40  Ennis, *op. cit.*, 41.

violations in which they engage, and the frequency of their depredations. These include the long-term observation of youths, and self-reporting anonymous questionnaires. Most of these studies have been conducted on students. However, a study reported in 1947 by James S. Wallerstein and Clement J. Wylie[41] was conducted on adults located in the New York metropolitan area. Questionnaires listing 49 offenses under the penal law of New York State were distributed to a non-random sample of adults. Questionnaires were returned by 1,020 men and 678 women. The results showed that 99 percent admitted committing one or more offenses; 64 percent of men admitted committing a felony (serious offense); and the average number of offenses committed since age sixteen was 18; the average number of offenses reported by adult men ranged from 8.2 for ministers to 20.2 for laborers.

Using anonymous questionnaires on which were listed fifty-five offenses for which children were brought to court, Austin Porterfield examined the behavior of 337 college students in Fort Worth, Texas. His results were 'indicative of the universal prevalence of past delinquency among college men and women.'[42] Porterfield concluded that there were great similarities in the conduct of college students and youths who were reported to the juvenile court.[43]

In the Cambridge-Somerville Youth Study where there was long-term intimate contact with a 'large group of boys throughout their adolescent years', the results revealed a large amount of 'hidden delinquency.' A conservative estimate is that 6,416 offenses were committed by these 101 boys during a five year period, but only 95 (less than 1.5 percent) resulted in legal action. This study showed also that the more serious and more frequent the violations, the higher the risk of becoming an official statistic.[44] These findings leave little doubt of the vast amount of hidden delinquency in a slum area, and strongly suggest that different kinds of minor delinquency may be part and parcel of growing up in urban lower-class areas.

In 1958, Short and Nye, using anonymous self-reporting questionnaires administered in high school classrooms, found that

41   James S. Wallerstein and C.J. Wylie, "Our law-abiding law breakers," *Federal Probation,* Vol. 25, 107-112.

42   Austin L. Porterfield, *Youth in Trouble,* Fort Worth: The Leo Potishman Foundation, 1946, 38.

43   *Ibid.,* 45.

44   Fred J. Murphy, Mary M. Shirley and Helen L. Witmer, "The Incidence of Hidden Delinquency," *American Journal of Orthopsychiatry,* Vol. 16, 1946, 686-695.

delinquency was 'extensive and variable'.[45] Erickson and Empey interviewed four subsamples of boys; (a) a subsample of 50 randomly chosen high school boys, (b) a subsample of 30 randomly selected boys with one court appearance, (c) a subsample of 50 randomly selected repeated offenders, and (d) a subsample of 50 randomly selected institutionalized offenders. The authors report that 'The number of violations which respondents admitted having committed was tremendous,' and for minor offenses 'more than nine times out of ten—almost ten times out of ten—most offenses go undetected and unacted upon.'[46] Although more of the serious offenses were detected and acted upon, 8 out of 10 respondents reported that these violations went undetected, and that 9 out of 10 did not involve any court action.[47] Among the 'serious thieves' studied by West in Toronto varying kinds of illegal acts were widespread.[48] In a study of 850 middle and upper-middle class high school boys from the Hamilton area aged 15 to 19, 62 percent reported driving a car without a license, 66 percent admitted gambling for money, and 67 percent had 'taken little things that did not belong to you'.[49] Similar results have been found in research conducted in England, Norway, Finland and Switzerland.[50]

---

45 James F. Short, Jr., and F. Ivan Nye, "Extent of Unrecorded Juvenile Delinquency: Tentative Conclusions," *The Journal of Criminal Law, Criminology and Police Science,* Vol. 49, No. 4, 1958, 301. No effort is made to review all the studies here. For other research using self-report techniques and reporting a variety of findings see Edmund W. Vaz, "Self-Reported Delinquency and Socio-economic Status," *Canadian Journal of Corrections,* Vol. 8, 1966, 20-27; R.L. Akers, "Socio-economic Status and Delinquent Behavior: A Retest," *Journal of Research on Crime and Delinquency,* Vol. 1, 1964, 38-46; R.A. Dentler and L.J. Monroe, "Social Correlates of Early Adolescent Theft," *American Sociological Review,* Vol. 26, 1961, 733-743. An excellent review of research of "hidden and official delinquency" is found in Hood and Sparks, *Key Issues in Criminology,* 46-80; Nettler, *Explaining Crime,* 73-97.

46 Maynard L. Erickson and Lamar T. Empey, "Court Records, Undetected Delinquency, and Decision-Making," in Donald R. Cressey and David A. Ward (eds.), *Delinquency, Crime and Social Process,* New York: Harper & Row, Publishers, 1969, 140.

47 *Ibid.,* 141.

48 William Gordon West, *Serious Thieves: Lower-Class Adolescent Males in a Short-Term Deviant Occupation,* unpublished Ph.D. Dissertation, Department of Sociology, Northwestern University, 1974, 84-85.

49 Edmund W. Vaz, "Middle-Class Adolescents: Self-Reported Delinquency and Youth Culture Activities," *The Canadian Review of Sociology and Anthropology,* Vol. 2, No. 1, 1965, 52-70.

50 For a review of the English, Norwegian and Finnish studies see Hood and Sparks, *Key Issues in Criminology,* 46-80; John Casparis and Edmund W. Vaz, "Social Class and Self-Reported Delinquent Acts among Swiss Boys," in *International Journal of Comparative Sociology,* Vol. 14, No. 1-2, 1974, 47-58.

What these and other studies reveal is that the 'dark number' of offenses in society is very large. Both adults and juveniles admit to committing major and minor criminal offenses on anonymous questionnaires and in interviews. However, a considerably smaller percentage admit serious offenses. This does not mean that there are no differences between convicted offenders and non-convicted offenders. The evidence suggests that official statistics include a higher proportion of youths who have committed serious offenses, and done so repeatedly, than are found in the larger population.

Of course there are many other forms of deviance (some newer than others) whose incidence is even more difficult to assess. Dishonesty, malingering, the various kinds of leakage of material in the army,[51] cheating on high school and university examinations, extra-marital sexual behavior and swinging are all forms of deviant conduct. But data on their incidence is especially difficult to obtain. It is likely true that extra-marital sexual behavior is increasing, but the appropriate data are not available. Perhaps there have always been swinging couples (especially in large cities), but we can never know this. However, there is some limited evidence that this allegedly new form of entertainment is spreading.[52] The obvious lack of carefully gathered data on deviance in Canada reflects clearly the need for vigorous sociological research.

---

51  See William A. Westley, "The Informal Organization of the Army: A Sociological Memoir," in Howard S. Becker, Blanche Geer, et al., (eds.), *Institutions and the Person,* Chicago: Aldine Publishing Company, 1968, 200-207.

52  Jack Batten, "Marriage is One Man One Woman, One Man One Woman, One Man . . . " in W.E. Mann (ed.), *Social Deviance in Canada,* Toronto: The Copp Clark Publishing Company, 1971, 406-412. See also Robert R. Bell, *Social Deviance,* Homewood, Illinois: The Dorsey Press, 1971, 63-87.

# Socioeconomic Location and Deviance

How does differential socioeconomic location influence the rates and quality of deviance that occur? How do the larger cultural and social systems in which we live affect the configurations and styles of our wrongdoing? What is it about being middle class or lower class that influences the kinds of crime and delinquency that occur? The answers to these questions are not known exactly; nevertheless, we believe them to be important questions. What we do know about the answers pays special attention to the social worlds of people, and to the positions that persons occupy in the social structure, and gives short shrift to the particular characteristics of the persons themselves.

To trace a person's position in the social structure is to locate him according to selected social coordinates such as income, occupation, education, and so forth. Broadly, we look at the kind of work that a person does and the prestige that it carries; the salary that he earns and the quality and level of his education. Furthermore, these facts offer us clues about the person's values, style of life, hopes, possessions, and politics. They tell us whether he works while others sleep, whether he wears a white collar, carries a lunch pail, does shift work, or grubs about from one temporary job to another. They also alert us to the common tensions and problems of those similarly circumstanced—status problems, health problems, problems of identity, of boredom, of alienation, and they may even offer us hunches about the amount and quality of 'happiness' that characterizes his daily life, and the kinds of 'freedom' that prevail. Such information is important because, to a considerable extent, each socioeconomic stratum possesses its own relatively distinct cultural climate. It means also that our view of reality, including the feelings that we enjoy of control over our own destinies, is conditioned by our socioeconomic location in time and space.

The relatively 'sealed handicaps', i.e., differential social locations, under which we live, also create for us differential life chances and varying opportunities for attaining the good things in life, and provide structural and cultural inducement for different kinds and, very likely, different amounts of deviance. However, it is important to emphasize that it is neither socioeconomic location, nor its indicators (income, occupation, education, etc.), that are the causes of crime or delinquency, or other kinds of deviance.

In part, we are sentenced for life to our social locations in society. Being born in a slum deprives us of social status; usually it means growing up tough and poor, and being unable to do very much about it. For kids it means stealing and fighting, having delinquents as friends, and smalltime hoodlums as acquaintances; running with the dropout, the feckless, the unemployed; living where illegal and immoral practices are a daily part of conventional concerns, where prostitution, gambling and fencing are next-door activities. In these areas of poverty, inferior housing, rapid population movement, dependent families, and the presence of adult criminal groups, high delinquency rates are located. Shaw and McKay using juvenile court referrals in 20 cities[1] found this to be true; similar correlations were found in Chilton's study of Indianapolis, Detroit and Baltimore which was based on official statistics.[2] In an early (1929) Canadian study of delinquency in Montreal, Ross concluded, 'In this [high delinquency] area is also found the broken home. Here are bad housing conditions, poverty, and all the accompanying evils. Overcrowding is common.'[3] A more recent Canadian study of Hamilton, Ontario, found that in

---

1  C. R. Shaw and H.D. McKay, *Juvenile Delinquency and Urban Areas,* Chicago: University of Chicago Press, 1942.

2  Roland J. Chilton, "Delinquency area research in Baltimore, Detroit, and Indianapolis," *American Sociological Review,* Vol. 29, 1964, 71-83.

3  Herman R. Ross, *Juvenile Delinquency in Montreal,* Unpublished Master's Thesis, Department of Sociology, McGill University, 1932.

high delinquency rate areas, family incomes are below the city average, that 40 percent of the city's unemployed are residents, and that professional and technical personnel were under-represented.[4] An ecological study of delinquency in a Canadian city found that high delinquency areas were all located relatively near the city center, and that economic poverty (families earning less than $3,000 annually) was the significant variable in account-ing for the rate of delinquency, and for the relationship between delinquency and distance from the city center.[5] More recently, the 'serious thieves' studied by Gordon West resided in a housing project that was poor and heavily populated, with a high percent-age of female-headed households. Located a mile from the center of Toronto, for decades it has been surrounded by the slum dis-trict, skid row, and working-class neighborhoods.[6] A delinquent's own story reveals the kinds of crime that are typical of such areas:

**Stealing in the neighbourhood was a common practice among the children and approved by the parents. Whenever the boys got together they talked about robbing and made more plans for stealing. I hardly knew any boys who did not go robbing. The little fellows went in for petty stealing, breaking into freight cars, and stealing junk. The older guys did big jobs like stick-up, burglary, and stealing autos. The little fellows admired the 'big shots' and longed for the day when they could get into the big racket. Fellows who had 'done time' were big shots and looked up to and gave the little fellows tips on how to get by and pull off big jobs.[7]**

But delinquency in the lower socioeconomic levels of big cit-ies is not all of a piece. Also found typically in these depressed

4   Barbara Nease, "Measuring Juvenile Delinquency in Hamilton," Craig L. Boydell, Carl F. Grindstaff and Paul C. Whitehead (eds.), *Deviant Behaviour and Societal Reaction,* Toronto: Holt, Rinehart and Winston of Canada, Ltd., 1972, 188-189.

5   George K. Jarvis, "The Ecological Analysis of Juvenile Delinquency in a Canadian City," in Boydell, Grindstaff and Whitehead (eds.), *Deviant Behaviour and Societal Reaction,* 195-211.

6   William Gordon West, *Serious Thieves: Lower-Class Adolescent Males in a Short-Term Deviant Occupation,* unpublished Ph.D. Dissertation, Department of Sociology, Northwestern University, 1974, 60-73.

7   Clifford R. Shaw, *The Jack-Roller,* Chicago, Ill.: The University of Chicago Press, 1966, 54. Copyright 1930 by the University of Chicago.

sectors[8] are the worlds of fighting gangs, where occasionally, but less often than is sometimes thought, gang wars break out, and youths sometimes get killed. Few writers have captured the flavor of this kind of conduct as well as Warren Miller:

> The Wolves waiten. A lot of them I don't know how many. I see Angel an maybe 10 guys with him standen by the sand box. I reach in my shirt for the blade. My skin cold an I can feel my heart poundin in there. Cowboy an Rod give the wistle an I tap Saint on the shoulder. "We go." I say. An we runnin in tord them an I see Cowboy an Rod an they men movin in an some Wolves facin us an some turn to face the others.
>
> Then we mixin with them in among them an I hear the swipe an swish of the aireals an guys sayen. "Oh you motheren. Oh you motheren. Oh you motherens. I kill you motheren bastards." An I keep my left arm up for protection an my back all hunched over. I dont see Angel any where. I looken for him. I movin aroun an lookin. I see Foxy layin they with his face laid open. An some guys I dont know weather they Wolves or Crocadiles jus sittin on the ground with the blood runnin down they faces.
>
> "Custis! Duke Custis! I lookin for you." I hear Angel. An then I see him. He standen on top of the sliden bord laughin an lookin at me. The first zip gun go off right behin my head an I drop. They shooten at Angel. He just stand an laugh at them an call my name.
>
> I try to get to him. A Wolf tangle with me an I get him in the shoulder. I see the blood spread on his shirt. "You motheren Crocadile." He say an I bang his head on the ground. Then the Wolves start burnin. One of them got a piece. He fire 2 times an I guess that all the ammo he have. I look up jus in time to see Cowboy goin down. He fall flat on his face the back of head all shot away.
>
> I hear the sirens then an the cop wistles start. Evry body

---

8  The literature is voluminous. For example, see F. M. Thrasher, *The Gang,* Chicago: University of Chicago Press, 1936; *Reaching the Fighting Gang,* New York City Youth Board, 1960; Lewis Yablonsky, *The Violent Gang,* New York: The Macmillan Co., 1962; James F. Short, Jr., and Fred L. Strodbeck, *Group Process and Gang Delinquency,* Chicago: The University of Chicago Press, 1969; Bernard Rosenberg and Harry Silverstein, *The Varieties of Delinquent Experience,* Waltham, Massachusetts: Blaisdell Publishing Co., 1969, and Walter B. Miller, "Violent Crimes in City Gangs," *The Annals of the American Academy of Political and Social Science,* Vol. 364, March, 1966, 96-112. For Canadian material see Kenneth H. Rogers, *Street Gangs in Toronto,* Toronto: The Ryerson Press, 1945.

start to run. Those that can run. Rod an I make it to the
sliding bord together. He musta lost his blade. I see him pick
up some bodys bread knife they have dropped. Angel jump an
take off runnin. He fast Man. I seen him do it befor. Rod an I
take out after him.

We folla him. We follad him between the projeck bildings
an tare after him thru bushes an aroun parked cars. The
projeck guard step out in front of us but when he see the blade
he step out of the way. When we get past him he start blowin
his wistle.

Angel headin for the river first an then he turns. He lost
on the turn. I dont know why he done it. He shoulda know
better than that. Rod right behin him an I watchin Rods legs
not to trip him up. Oh Man I say to my self. Oh Man where
my blade? Because while I running suddenly I relize I musta
drop my blade some where.

Then we come to a place along side one of the bildings
they high green bushes growin with little red berrys on them. It
was right there that Angel stumbled and he moan when he hit
the groun. He half way up when Rod on him an they go twistin
inta the bushes both of them makin cryin noises from they
mouths. I go in after them an Rod got his left arm aroun
Angels neck an they rockin an pullin against each other an then
Rod put on the pressure. An for a second they still. An they
strain against each other. An Rod push the bread knife into
Angels back.

I see Angels face. He closen his eyes real tight. He press
them closed an his mouth pull up. He fall down front wards an
lay without movin talken in Porto Rican. "Sue cio." He say.
"Sue cio. Sue cio. Sue cio."

Then he start moanin. An Rod say. " I tol you I do it an I
do it." Angel moaning. Rod lookin at me. Then he bend down
an pull the blade out. Angel say. "Thank you." An we left him
an took off tord the river.[9]

A number of first-rate studies have arrived at more or less
the same conclusion concerning the sectors in which this kind of
fighting delinquency occurs. Short and Strodbeck stated that versatility characterized the behavior of these youths, and that specialized careers were associated with clique structures rather than

---

9  Warren Miller, *The Cool World,* New York: Fawcett Publications, 1964, 153-
54. Copyright © 1959 by Warren Miller, by permission of Little, Brown and
Co.

with the larger gangs. They also found that lower-class boys were more disadvantaged than middle-class boys, gang boys were more disadvantaged than non-gang boys within the lower class, and that blacks fare less well than do whites in such areas.[10] Rosenberg and Silverstein's study of selected neighborhoods in Chicago, Washington D.C., and New York City found that these areas were predominantly poverty-ridden, and were characterized by poor physical conditions and general disrepair; approximately one-third of all families in each block were receiving public assistance.[11] In Spergel's study of delinquent subcultures the three neighborhoods were all characterized by low annual incomes, relatively low levels of education and relatively low occupational skills, although there was variation among the areas.[12]

The research findings of the studies that rely on official statistics are not without variation. However, the recurrent theme is the indelible impact of economic deprivation and many of its related consequences as major correlates of official delinquency. It is important to emphasize that there is no direct causal relationship between poverty and juvenile crime. Poverty and delinquency are closely associated; however, it is the social and psychological consequences of residing in poverty in modern industrial society that contribute to the high rates of crime and delinquency. Precisely how these social and psychological consequences are interrelated in producing adult and juvenile crime is not fully understood.[13]

But not all delinquency research agrees with the notion that the bulk of delinquency is located in the lower socioeconomic strata. There are a number of recent studies using self-reporting techniques whose results fail to agree with findings based on offi-

---

10  Short and Strodbeck, *op. cit.,* 181.

11  Rosenberg and Silverstein, *op. cit.,* 21-36.

12  Irving Spergel, *Racketville, Slumtown, Haulburg,* Chicago: The University of Chicago Press, 1964, 1-11. Using court records Reiss and Rhodes found the chances of being categorized a serious, petty or truancy offender are greater for blue-collar than white-collar boys, and that the only 'career-oriented' delinquents were 'blue-collar' boys. Read Albert J. Reiss, Jr., and Albert L. Rhodes, "The Distribution of Juvenile Delinquency in the Social Class Structure," *American Sociological Review,* Vol. 26, No. 5, 1961, 720-732.

13  The complicated relationship between poverty and crime has a long history. See J. J. Tobias, *Crime and Industrial Society in the Nineteenth Century,* Harmondsworth: Penguin Books, 1972, 179-232. It should also be emphasized that there is no simple relationship between socioeconomic status and delinquency; the status structure of the high schools, and the general delinquency rates of the residential areas in which youths live are also influential in determining the probability of a youth engaging in delinquency. See Albert J. Reiss, Jr., and Albert Lewis Rhodes, *op. cit.,* 720-732.

cial statistics. For example, Short and Nye used a scale of relatively minor kinds of delinquent acts to rank training-school youths and high school students. They found that almost all of the institutionalized youths were from lower socioeconomic levels, but when they categorized high school students into socioeconomic levels, no relationship was found between delinquency scores and their socioeconomic position.[14] Dentler and Monroe studied 912 seventh and eighth grade students from a middle-class suburb, a rural farm town, and a rural non-farm area. They found that some adolescent youths engaged in serious kinds of theft, that there was no association between occupational level and delinquency, and that serious delinquency was not culturally rooted in these communities.[15] Clark and Wenninger studied a total of 1154 students from grades six through twelve located in four different communities: rural farm, lower urban, industrial city (35,000 pop.) and upper urban. They discovered that the rates of juvenile misconduct increased as one moves from rural farm to upper urban to industrial city to lower urban. The incidence of serious offenses also increases, 'especially in the more serious offenses and in those offenses usually associated with social structures with considerable tolerance for illegal behavior.' But they also found that, with the exception of industrial city, there were no significant class variations in illegal conduct within a community.[16] Arnold's research in six high schools in Lake City did not allow him to reject previous findings by Short and Nye, and Dentler and Monroe.[17] Aker's research findings were not unsimilar; differences among socioeconomic levels in the incidence of relatively minor delinquent acts were not statistically significant.[18] Approximately the same results were found by the writer in his study of high school students in four Canadian communities.[19]

---

14    James F. Short and F. Ivan Nye, "Extent of Unrecorded Juvenile Delinquency," *The Journal of Criminal Law, Criminology and Police Science,* Vol. 49, No. 4, 1958, 296-302.

15    Robert A. Dentler and Lawrence J. Monroe, "Social Correlates of Early Adolescent Theft," *American Sociological Review,* Vol. 26, No. 5, 1961, 733-743.

16    John P. Clark and Eugene P. Wenninger, "Socio-Economic Class and Area as Correlates of Illegal Behavior Among Juveniles" in Donald R. Cressey and David A. Ward (eds.), *Delinquency, Crime, and Social Process,* New York: Harper & Row, 1969, 399.

17    William R. Arnold, "Continuities in Research: Scaling Delinquent Behavior", *Social Problems,* Vol. 13, No. 1, 1965, 65-66.

18    R. Akers, "Socio-economic Status and Delinquent Behavior: a Retest," *Journal of Research in Crime and Delinquency,* Vol. 1, 1964, 38-46.

19    Edmund W. Vaz, "Self-Reported Delinquency and Socioeconomic Status," *Canadian Journal of Corrections,* Vol. 8, 1966, 20-27. Using a small sample

These studies reveal that when you ask samples of high school students to recall and report the number of selected delinquent acts that they have perpetrated, there emerges no regular set of significant differences in the proportion of such acts reported for each socioeconomic level. This means that proportionately no more of these kinds of delinquent acts go on among lower-class youths than among middle or upper-class youths.

But caution should be exercised in the interpretation of data from self-reporting questionnaires. In the first place, many of the selected items used on these questionnaires are relatively minor forms of delinquency; their selection is premised on the assumption that were such activities detected they would elicit legal action. But many of these acts are nothing more than nuisance activities, and it is questionable whether youths would be charged for such offenses. It is also true that these acts differ greatly from the hard core delinquency culturally established in big cities. Secondly, the questionnaire items may be differentially perceived by youths from different socioeconomic strata. 'Stealing little things', 'fist fighting' and 'assault' very likely possess different meanings for respondents from different socioeconomic strata, and this will influence how they respond. Thirdly, the question of reliability plagues the use of self-reporting questionnaires. Can we rely on data from such questionnaires? Are the respondents concealing or exaggerating their responses? There is also the issue of recall; not everyone has an equally reliable memory. Perhaps some respondents can recall most of their deeds, others only a few. Still others will want to forget. We can be certain that, notwithstanding the person's motivation, no one can recall everything, and everyone will likely conceal something. Furthermore, the use of self-reporting, anonymous questionnaires is not the best method of getting at, nor is it the same thing as observing, the tough, bellicose, criminal and delinquent activities that transpire on the streets and back-alleys of big-city slums. No matter how reliable these kinds of data are, they will not tell us much about the deviant worlds and the more challenging kinds of conduct that require explanation. Finally, there is the problem of validity. Nettler is worth quoting here: 'A comparison of a new measure of uncertain validity (self-reports) with old measures of moderate validity (official records) tells us nothing about their relative accuracy *unless there is assurance that both instruments are designed to measure*

---

different results are reported in Stephen Tribble, "Socio-economic Status and Self-reported Juvenile Delinquency", in Robert A. Silverman and James J. Teevan, Jr., *Crime in Canadian Society,* Toronto: Butterworth and Co. (Canada) Ltd., 1975, 95-101.

*the same thing.'*[20] Most self-reporting questionnaires use some terms that are not law violations, and they do not include all items included in the official reports. Finally, many of the studies using self-reporting questionnaires have been conducted in relatively small communities; the social location of the research is important because the meaning and significance of the social variables used to explain the crime and delinquency will vary with the social setting.[21]

Yet a question remains to be answered: does socioeconomic location make a difference in the quality of the crime and delinquency that occurs? The answer is yes. We know that the upper classes comprise a world of graceful living, wealth, and power, where riches shut off the remainder of society, and where exclusiveness is taken for granted. It is the world of private clubs and private schools where families are 'old,' and people are 'somebodies'.[22] Admittedly there are differentials in wealth; the wealthy from a small rural community differ greatly from the wealthy in Toronto. However, very often to be upper class is to feel superior, to look superior, and to be superior. Yet we do not wish to convey the image that upper-class people are a special breed of person. They are not. It is not that upper-class persons do not violate laws,[23] nor that crime and delinquency are somehow endemic to the lower, and not the middle, or upper social strata. The large quota of unofficial crime and delinquency, and secret deviance that are reported suggest otherwise. Because people work in high places, enjoy exalted status, and possess untarnished reputations is not reason enough to doubt their involvement in crime. Bank presidents do not steal cars or hold-up corner stores; corporation executives do not lift wallets; and doctors do not brawl in taverns. However, upper-class work is often corporate work, and upper-class crime is often corporate crime.[24] Although peddlers do not

20  Gwynn Nettler, *Explaining Crime,* New York: McGraw-Hill Book Company, 1974, 94-95.

21  *Ibid.,* 195-97.

22  For example, see C. Wright Mills, *The Power Elite,* New York: Oxford University Press, 1957, 47-117; John Porter, *The Vertical Mosaic,* Toronto: University of Toronto Press, 1965, 303-308.

23  For example, read Gustavus Myers, *History of the Great American Fortunes,* Vol. 1, Chicago: Charles H. Kerr and Co., 1910, 127ff; Mills, *The Power Elite,* 338-361.

24  For example, see Richard Austin Smith, "The Incredible Electrical Conspiracy," in Donald R. Cressey and David A. Ward (eds.), *Delinquency, Crime, and Social Process,* Harper and Row, Publishers, 1969, 884-912; Marshall Clinard, *The Black Market,* New York: Rinehart and Company, 1952; Edwin H. Sutherland, *White-Collar Crime,* New York: Holt, Rinehart and Winston, 1961; Frank Gibney, *The Operators,* New York: Harper & Brothers, 1960.

push their stuff in hospitals, doctors do get hooked on drugs.[25] Attending private schools is no guarantee against delinquency[26] and middle-class delinquency is sometimes aggressive in quality.[27] It is also true that middle-class youths steal cars, get drunk and smoke pot.[28] Some also drop out of school, and become smalltime dealers in hashish. At the same time there is no evidence to suggest that strong-arm tactics, fearlessness and carrying concealed weapons are common among middle and upper-class youths. Admittedly an extreme example, but perhaps more in style, is the account of the teenage gambling casino run by three youths in the basement of an upper middle-class suburban home, where the seventeen year-old host, dressed in white dinner jacket and black tie, provided limousine service for his 'guests'.[29]

No matter how the empirical findings are sliced, as yet there is no substantial body of information to indicate that the same quality of delinquency or crime is proportionately distributed among the social classes. Middle and upper-class boys seldom go about armed with zip guns, nor are they prone to fight with weapons; they do not go armed with iron bars in preparation for gang fights,[30] nor is violence an indelible component of their activities. There are no 'jungles of hunters' among these youths, nor well-armed 'gorillas' ready to do violence to others.[31] Seldom do middle and upper-class boys pimp for prostitutes or hustle women. This is not their style of delinquency, but it is often a pronounced quality of big-city, slum rooted delinquency.

---

25 Charles Winick, "Physician Narcotic Addicts," in Howard S. Becker (ed.), *The Other Side,* New York: The Free Press, 1964, 261-279; Richard M. Hessler, "Junkies in White: Drug Addiction among Physicians", in Clifton D. Bryant, *Deviant Behavior: Occupational and Organizational Bases,* Chicago: Rand McNally Publishing Company, 1974, 146-153.

26 Edmund W. Vaz, "Delinquency and the Youth Culture: Upper and Middle-Class Boys," in *The Journal of Criminal Law, Criminology and Police Science.* Vol. 60, no. 1, 1969, 33-46.

27 Fred J. Shanley, "Middle-Class Delinquency as a Social Problem," *Sociology and Social Research.* Vol. 51, 1965, 185-198.

28 Edmund W. Vaz, "Middle-Class Adolescents: Self-Reported Delinquency and Youth Culture Activities," *The Canadian Review of Sociology and Anthropology.* Vol. 2, No. 1, 1965. See also Reginald G. Smart and David Jackson, "A Preliminary Report on the Attitudes and Behavior of Toronto Students in Relation to Drugs," *Addiction Research Foundation,* 1969; R. G. Smart, Dianne Fejer and Jim White, "The Extent of Drug Use in Metropolitan Toronto Schools: A Study of Changes from 1968-1970," Toronto: *Addiction Research Foundation,* 1971. George Kupfer, *Middle-Class Delinquency in a Canadian City.* Unpublished Ph.D. dissertation, University of Washington, 1966.

29 "Teen Gambling Den Bared," *Detroit Free Press,* Feb. 24, 1965.

30 Personal experience with a gang of English boys in Bethnal Green, London, 1961.

31 Rosenberg and Silverstein, *op. cit.* However, this is not to say that middle-class

# Age

To say that age is correlated with crime and delinquency in society means that specific kinds of illegal behavior are closely associated with specific age levels. Similarly, females are characteristically correlated with certain kinds of crime and delinquency, males with others. This enables us to establish some significant facts and relationships between age, sex, and different forms of illegal conduct. However, age is not a sociological concept, and as an explanatory tool is severely limited. To establish that a specific kind of crime, e.g., crime against the person, peaks recurrently at ages twenty to twenty-four for males and females, or that crimes against property with violence are regularly highest between ages sixteen to twenty-four,[32] or that the largest proportion of delinquencies is committed in the sixteen to seventeen year age group by both boys and girls, are important facts.[33] In fact it seems established that maximum delinquent activity occurs during middle adolescence. However, this fact may not be of much theoretical significance since some research shows that the empirical differences are not great.[34] In any case, it is obviously true that certain delinquent acts cannot be performed by the younger age groups, while other delinquent acts are found to be persistently correlated with older age categories. This fact requires explanation. Age itself cannot do this. For example, if we know the number of fifteen year old boys in a community and we know also the percentage of fifteen year old boys who have been involved in car theft, we can make probability statements predicting the vulnerability of any fifteen year old boy to engage in car theft. We can go still a step further. If we assume that there is nothing about a person's age (e.g., fifteen years) that influences his stealing cars, we may hypothesize a proportionate distribution of car thefts for

---

high school youths do not engage in violence. When they do they sometimes resemble young nazi stormtroopers. See the facial expressions of students attacking a student draft card burner, on the steps of a Boston courthouse; at least six men were attacked by a crowd that included numerous students. *Kitchener-Waterloo Record,* Thursday, March 31, 1966.

32  Canada: Statistics Canada, *95th and 96th Annual Reports of Criminal and Other Offenses,* Ottawa: Information Canada, 1970 and 1971. Based on persons convicted of indictable offences. Data for provinces of Alberta and Quebec excluded.

33  Canada: Statistics Canada, *Juvenile Delinquents,* Ottawa: Information Canada, 1973. Data for provinces of Alberta and Ontario excluded.

34  Travis Hirschi, *Causes of Delinquency,* Los Angeles: University of California Press, 1969, 236.

each age bracket. We must then compare the actual distribution of car thefts for each age category with our theoretical distribution. Should we find proportionately more or less than the expected number of car thefts for any given age bracket, this suggests forcibly that there is something about a specific age bracket, and the circumstances generated within that age bracket, that is distinctly linked to stealing cars. Yet a disproportionate amount of car theft within a single age category does not *necessarily* mean that stealing cars is a 'property' of the kids only in that age bracket. Perhaps older boys provide models, criteria and controls for younger boys who in turn associate with younger boys, etc., thereby providing a transmission belt of delinquent activities, ideas and attitudes. This is one mechanism for maintaining a subculture of delinquency. In this instance car theft is partly a matter of conformity to the models provided by older boys, and not something 'spontaneously generated' by the conditions special to a particular age category.

To illuminate the significance of age for a better sociological understanding of deviant behavior it is essential to examine the social relationships, and the institutional affiliations and controls that are of special importance for a particular age bracket. For example, we know that high school affiliations and academic performance are usually of considerable importance for teenagers. The role and self identity of the academically competent are very likely personally fulfilling, as well as intellectually rewarding. Attachment and commitment to school activities are likely strong. We ought not to be surprised to learn that youths who occupy these roles are less likely than others to be involved in delinquency.[35]

Obviously not all social roles are appropriate for all age groups. Yet the variation in social roles is not limited to adults only. The general roles of teenager and kid carry vastly different obligations and meanings for their respective occupants, and generate different identities, and different kinds of delinquency. These roles are parts of different worlds with complex and variable relationships and normative requirements. For example, the world of younger middle-class boys is largely masculine; girls occupy little of their time, and a particular image of masculinity predominates. At this age adventure, bravado, manliness and muscular prowess loom large, as does their effort to prove that they are all boy. This often leads to particular kinds of delinquency such as vandalism,

---

35  *Ibid.,* 110-130. See also Uldis Kundrats, *Adolescence, Role Commitment and Middle-Class Delinquency,* unpublished M.A. Thesis, Department of Sociology, University of Waterloo, 1975.

fighting and petty theft. However, older adolescent roles require increased participation in youth culture events such as parties, dances, and sports, while cars and girls begin to occupy a larger part of a boy's time. Sophistication replaces toughness, and a premium is placed upon the cultivation of social skills and a social personality. The rougher habits of younger boys are taboo. While the roles of older teenagers call for sophisticated behavior they tend also to generate a more sophisticated brand of delinquency. Drinking, drag-racing, sex, truancy and gambling assume a larger part in the roles of older adolescents.[36]

Age-related roles are also differentially related to social institutions, e.g., the family, high school, church and peer group, and these groups exert variable control over young people. In a period of considerable social change, control agents are often under strain in maintaining and legitimizing their positions of authority. Examination of such affiliations is necessary. We must also explore the range of roles and identities that are culturally available to particular age levels, and the kinds of reward systems that are operating.

What are the role relationships of the academically successful in school? Of the academic failures? Of the athletic star, the 'tough guy' or the 'prestige girls'? What are the variations in life styles of the worlds of which they are part? Are there typical strains and anxieties linked to particular age-related social roles? How are such strains structurally generated, i.e., tied to the changing institutional controls like the eroding controls of the family and school over young people today? Under what social conditions does such institutional transformation lead to subcultural activity, e.g., the profusion of subcultures among young people? How is deviance related to certain kinds of life styles, and how is it functional for certain social roles and role relationships at particular age levels?

# Sex

Given the cultural composition and social organization of Canadian society, it would be surprising if sex did not make a difference in the manner and frequency of deviant behavior. For a long time the values of virtue, goodness and gentleness in society have been associated with femininity. It does not surprise us to learn that males have had consistently higher crime rates and conviction rates than females. Nor is it a surprise that proportionately fewer females than males become involved in crimes of violence, aggres-

---

36  Vaz, *Middle-Class Adolescents: Self-Reported Delinquency and Youth Culture Activities*, 52-70.

sion and the destruction of property. Of course, the disparities between crime rates for males and females will vary with time, place, and the type of crime. For example, in Canada in 1971, the crime rate of males for crimes committed against the person exceeds the rate for females by more than fifteen to one; in particular, the crime rate of males for armed robbery exceeds that for females by more than eighteen to one.[37] It is also true that men more often get arrested for forcible rape. On the other hand, rates of prostitution are expectedly higher for women than for men.

Similar differences are found between the rates of crime for boys and girls in Canada. In 1973 the rate for boys of crimes against property with violence exceeds that of girls by more than seventeen to one. The disparity drops appreciably for crimes without violence. For crimes against property *without* violence the rate for boys exceeds that for girls by approximately four to one; the exception is that the crime rate for boys of auto theft exceeds that for girls by more than seventeen to one.[38] Here is an instance of the differential significance of the automobile for the role performances of boys and girls. For boys the car is something of an extension of self in a way that it is not for girls. It is role expressive. In the words of one boy, 'A car that is souped up, they figure you're like your car. Your character matches it, all fiery and exuberant.'[39]

There is clearly a differential degree of violence and aggressiveness in the crimes committed by males and females. What is it, then, about sex (since it, like age, is not a sociological concept) that influences the types and amounts of crime that are committed? We know that, on the average, males are more aggressive than females, and that this difference in their behavior is fairly general across cultures. Moreover, aggression in behavior cannot be attributed to a biological instinct.[40] Since the forms of crimes which people practise are very largely learned, it is the cultural and social organization of their social worlds which offer the best area for examination.

Until recently cultural prescriptions have encouraged women

37  Canada: Statistics Canada, *96th Annual Report of Statistics of Criminal and Other Offenses,* Ottawa: Information Canada, 1971. Data for provinces of Alberta and Quebec excluded.

38  Canada: Statistics Canada, *Juvenile Delinquents,* Ottawa: Information Canada, 1971.

39  Edmund W. Vaz, "The 'Straight' World of Middle-Class High School Kids" in James E. Gallagher and Ronald D. Lambert, *Social Process and Institution: The Canadian Case,* Toronto: Holt, Rinehart and Winston of Canada Ltd., 1971, 174-186.

40  Allan Mazur and Leon S. Robertson, *Biology and Social Behavior,* New York: The Free Press, 1972, 56-60.

to assume the social roles of wife and mother, and their general socialization has prepared many for these positions. The relatively limited range of role choices prescribed for women has meant that certain general behavior and attitudinal expectations have developed concerning the general female role. For example, often they have been expected to be nurturant, to forego taking the initiative, to be more chaste than their husbands and to enjoy housekeeping and childrearing duties.[41] Employment opportunities have been somewhat restricted, and greatly differentiated from those of men, and in the professional and corporate business worlds there are few women who hold positions of executive authority.

'Cross culturally the more distinct and different the roles of the sexes, the wider the reported disparity between crime rates of the sexes.'[42] One question that arises is: what happens as cultures approximate 'unisexuality?' What happens when women gain equal opportunity with men in the fields of work, as they become equal partners socially, and begin taking fewer commands and making more demands of the men they live with? How will this affect the crime and delinquency rates among them?

Certainly institutional change will help remove obstacles for occupational mobility and professional advancement, and it will open up avenues for the improved status of women. However, the opportunities for legitimate and illegitimate behavior are not parts of autonomous, distinct kinds of social organization. In order to deviate, to cut corners and to commit crime, one does not step from one separate world into another. If the occasions and means for success multiply in the legitimate, conventional worlds, so will the temptations increase to employ illegitimate means, and opportunities unfold for criminal practice. This is not to suggest that women will soon become muggers, engage in armed robbery, or that girls will go about armed in gangs.[43] However, as women increasingly assume positions of trust, so will they increasingly encounter opportunities for embezzlement. As more women move into the professions, they will acquire the expertise and the appropriate attitudes to engage in unethical practices like fee splitting,

---

41  William J. Goode, "Family Disorganization" in Robert K. Merton and Robert Nisbet, *Contemporary Social Problems,* New York: Harcourt Brace Jovanovich, Inc., (3rd edition) 1972, 535.

42  Nettler, *op. cit.,* 102.

43  However, the crime rates for adult females of crimes with an offensive weapon, robbery, breaking and entering, theft of an automobile, theft of more, and less than $50, and fraud have increased since 1962. Canada: Statistics Canada: *Crime Statistics,* Various Reports, Ottawa: Information Canada, 1962-1970. Furthermore, a *Statistics Canada* report released recently indicates a major increase in violent crimes committed by women between 1966 and 1971. *The Toronto Star,* Sept. 18, 1975.

ambulance chasing, unnecessary surgery, and methods of cheating the government, and where they are elected to public office their opportunities for crimes such as fraud, bribery and kickbacks, will flourish. Sex is no barrier against corruption.[44]

As women increase in the ranks of the professionally and occupationally successful, so will they augment the number of failures—women who have fallen by the occupational wayside. How will they react to their misery and disenchantment? What forms will their adaptation take? Will they, for example, seek full-time refuge in the more traditional roles of wife and mother? Will they retreat into a higher-class phalanx of alcoholics? Or become female Willy Lohmans? Or perhaps enter the more established deviant female occupational spheres, e.g., better class call-girl prostitution?

The convenience and novelty of opportunities for crime, previously unexperienced, may make certain kinds of illegality temporarily appealing to many women. Moreover, at least for some time, the prevailing image of the general female role, with its affiliated feminine graces, may divert attention and suspicion from women who engage in occupational kinds of crime.[45]

The same is no less true for juveniles. Customarily there are some crimes disproportionately committed by girls. In Canada in 1973 63.2 percent of the incorrigibility cases and 70 percent of immorality cases were girls.[46] But large-scale transformation has characterized the social and cultural worlds of boys and girls, especially those of the middle and upper classes. Youths are encouraged, and opportunities are structured, to actively engage in a wide variety of heterosexual activities and relationships. Traditional sex roles have undergone considerable transformation, and girls are strongly urged to participate in the worlds of work and scholarship, to assume positions of leadership and to engage in uniquely social events with boys. These changes are also mirrored in their delinquencies. Recent research indicates that both boys and girls engage in similar forms of delinquency, and that the quantity and quality of the delinquency likely reflects the role expectations of these youths. Something approaching a 'role con-

---

44  Philadelphia's Magisterial Mess, *Time Magazine,* Oct. 1, 1965.

45  There is reason to believe that traditionally, women offenders received a better deal than male offenders before the bar of justice. Perhaps women are now receiving certain kinds of equality a little sooner than they had anticipated. Recently the appelate division of the Alberta Supreme Court ruled that 'sentences for men and women should be, in principle, equal.' See the *Kitchener-Waterloo Record,* Feb. 2, 1974.

46  Canada: Statistics Canada: *Juvenile Delinquents,* Ottawa: Information Canada, 1973.

vergence' may be occurring among middle and upper-class youths which includes both delinquent and non-delinquent activities.[47]

One of the verities about the sociology of deviance is that we have accumulated a considerable storehouse of information about delinquency and crime among lower class people.[48] Admittedly, not all of this information is top quality, but at least these data are available for inspection and responsible speculation, and sometimes they offer clues for the direction that future research should take. However, our knowledge of juvenile and adult crime among the upper social strata remains shrouded in mystery. We know relatively little about the patterns of delinquency and crime at these levels; our knowledge of the organization of such illegal behavior is almost non-existent, and we remain in need of an empirically based, public image of the middle and upper-class delinquent, and of the white collar criminal. Of the illegal conduct among upper-class women we know less. Theoretically-based research must pinpoint the upper strata for study, and both the legitimate and illegitimate conduct that transpires must be investigated—the frequency of the acts, the styles that they take, and the social circumstances under which they occur. Increasingly we are gathering data about delinquency among middle-class youths, but we know almost nothing about the conduct of boys who attend expensive private schools. Some limited information that exists suggests that proportionately more delinquent acts are reported by these boys than by boys who attend public schools.[49] Are there perhaps subcultural dimensions to the delinquency and crime that occur at these levels? Are there forms of illegal behavior that are institutionalized among upper class youths? Or is their illegal behavior more an individual matter? Are there deviant career lines among upper-class persons? What are the variable relationships among positions of power in society and the forms that crime takes among upper-class persons? How serviceable is crime and delinquency for such people, and for which of their needs is deviance especially functional? These are only a few of the kinds of questions whose answers will enable us to better understand the relationship between deviance (especially crime and delinquency) and socioeconomic status.

---

47    Nancy Barton Wise, "Juvenile Delinquency Among Middle-Class Girls," in Edmund W. Vaz (ed.), *Middle-Class Juvenile Delinquency,* New York: Harper and Row, 1967, 179-188.

48    Much of this information is based on research conducted in American cities and towns. If we know less about deviance in Canada it is because we haven't done the research. Perhaps as a first step what we need are some carefully designed, theoretically oriented, descriptive studies of the various worlds of deviants.

49    Vaz, *Delinquency and the Youth Culture: Upper and Middle-Class Boys,* 37-38.

# Subcultural Worlds

To talk as we have, of the social worlds of people, implies cultural variation in the larger society. It suggests that there are smaller worlds—cultural and behavioral pockets—within the larger system that are important in the lives of people. It is never the whole world that matters to us, but the smaller number of relatively limited worlds to which most of us belong. These include families and occupations, religious and political groups, and innumerable informal worlds such as street-corner worlds, back-stage worlds, locker-room worlds and the diverse worlds of drifters, beach boys, ski-bums and the social elite. These are smaller collectivities of persons, often of similar backgrounds, who regularly meet together; they do the same work, encounter similar problems, suffer the same stresses and heartaches, and very often share the same pleasures. In the process of their interaction there emerges a subculture—an informal (sometimes partly formal) variably coordinated set of relatively explicit norms, attitudes and definitions of situations—a differentially influential way of life, that takes hold, and thereafter guides the thinking and conduct of participating members. We participate in these worlds as actors, in roles. However, we are not restricted to any single world; sometimes we skip in and out of these smaller worlds with a certain regularity, depending on their social and cultural payoffs for us, as, for example, do 'weekenders'—high school or university students, or office workers, who leave their relatively conventional worlds on weekends to participate actively in less conventional Bohemian worlds. On Mondays they return to high school, university or their permanent jobs.[1] In a different setting there is the tough gang boy who holds a job during the day and spends his evenings hanging on the street corner.[2]

The similarity in attitude and perspective among participants does not perforce reflect a collective basis. This must always be empirically established. The common legitimation of conduct (reflected in the subjective interpretation of norms by group members) is often a sound indication of a collective foundation for the resemblance in subcultural attitudes and norms.[3] As members increase their participation in these smaller worlds the resultant attitudes, knowledge and recurrent associations tend to reinforce the basis of their social congress.

The term subculture refers to a shared frame of reference, but it is something more than this. Very often it is an established way of life, i.e., a world of special techniques, judgments and attitudes, a way of dealing with problems, defining situations and categorizing people. It generates its own social milieux, garbed and distinguished by human overtones. It fosters its own customs and traditions, respects its own myths and legends, and furnishes its own rewards. It produces its own code of ethics and provides its own control mechanisms and sanctions for keeping members in line. Most important, it provides the support of sympathetic others—persons with whom we feel comfortable, who can appreciate our problems, and to whom we may look for counsel.

Subcultures often serve as adaptive mechanisms for coping with structurally produced stresses and maladjustments of the larger systems of which they are part. Members respond to these problems in various ways; sometimes they adjust to their situation by performing less desirable and sometimes illegal services for the larger system. Occasionally these subcultures function relatively autonomously, and are permitted to engage in conduct that would be condemned elsewhere. For example, black Africville (located

---

1 Reginald G. Smart and David Jackson, *The Yorkville Subculture: A Study of the Life Styles and Interactions of Hippies and Non-Hippies,* Toronto: Addiction Research Foundation, 1969, 15-18.

2 James F. Short, Jr., Introduction to the abridged edition of Frederic M. Thrasher, *The Gang,* Chicago: The University of Chicago Press, 1968, xxxvi.

3 William A. Westley, *Violence and the Police,* Cambridge, Massachusetts: The MIT Press, 1970, 120-121.

in white Halifax) was not a socially disorganized area, and remained a community where the majority of residents were related by kinship ties. However, it was known as a 'place to go for bootleg booze and conviviality' and an area for 'drinking and carousing'. It became a 'deviance service centre.'[4] Furthermore the norms and customs of the subculture are usually intimately related to the interests of its members, and emerge from the routine experiences, and recurrent, selective relationships arising from the nature of their association. Sometimes these group solutions serve to deaden the pain of routine, compensate for incompetence and ignorance, or improve one's status or material rewards. For example, in order to compensate for their carelessness at work and to expedite the flow of work, aircraft workers learn quickly to 'commit the most serious crime of workmanship,' i.e., to use the tap (a tool used for inserting a bolt through a wing section into a nut).[5] To cope with the hourly anxiety of being hooked on heroin yet maintain a cool image, the cat will employ any con-like technique to get money.[6] To augment their sometimes meager income cabdrivers soon learn how to steal from their bosses, and salesmen who consider themselves overworked and underpaid steal regularly from their companies.

These are not all deviant subcultures, and in the majority of cases these men are law-abiding, respectable, trustworthy members of society. But subcultural conduct is often practised in recurrent, collective ways. To a considerable extent behavior becomes withdrawn from individual discretion. However, to preserve identities, to foster the proper impressions and to help eliminate the doubt and ambivalence about one's conduct, subcultures also provide the appropriate kinds of rationalizations and justifications. Thus, despite public obloquy, prostitutes keep psychologically intact by believing that they are not doing anything that other women don't do, that their services help reduce the amount of rape and murder and the number of broken homes in the community, and that they provide certain 'psychotherapeutic services' for men who are lonely, unloved, and troubled.[7] Policemen legitimate their

---

4 Donald H. Clairmont and Dennis Magill, *Africville: The Life and Death of a Canadian Black Community*, Toronto: McClelland and Stewart Ltd., 1974, 92-134.

5 Joseph Bensman and Israel Gerver, "Crime and Punishment in the Factory: The Function of Deviancy in Maintaining the Social System", *American Sociological Review*, Vol. 28, 1963, 588-598.

6 Harold Finestone, "Cats, Kicks, and Color," *Social Problems*, Vol. 5, 1957, 3-13.

7 James H. Bryan, "Occupational Ideologies and Individual Attitudes of Call Girls," in Earl Rubington and Martin S. Weinberg (eds.), *Deviance: An*

use of force on the basis that it is vital to establish respect for the police, and that it is in the interests of the community to use force against the felon and the sex pervert.[8] Workers who are surrounded by goods and merchandise in factories and warehouses feel little compunction about stealing if the objects are slightly damaged or spoiled or have been on the shelf so long that they are not apt to be sold.[9] The cabdriver who keeps a twenty dollar bill given him in error by a passenger argues that, 'They give you orders and tell you where to go, they puke in your car, and you've got to clean it yourself.'[10] This sounds like the delinquent who justifies his aggression against homosexuals by saying that, 'They had it coming to them' or 'They deserve what they got.'[11]

Of course subcultures are only analytically distinguishable from groups, and groups usually try to present themselves to the community in the best possible light, e.g., they foster images of themselves. But not any image will do. The conceptions advanced by groups are often attempts to achieve, promote or otherwise sustain the appearance of respectability in their activities.[12] Typically, it is the professions that epitomize the quality of respectability in the work world. On the other hand, relatively low-ranked occupations which attempt to professionalize their work are also trying to increase their respectability. National Hockey League teams attempt to foster the image of respectability when players are televised discussing the significance of higher education, or when they are shown contributing to charitable causes, or espousing insurance plans for the family. The tactic of changing the name of one's work is another means of attempting to promote the image of respectability for one's occupation, e.g., janitors who call

*Interactionist Perspective*, New York: The Macmillan Company, 1968, 286-295; James H. Bryan, "Apprenticeships in Prostitution," *Social Problems*, Vol. 12, 1965, 289-297. For evidence on Montreal prostitutes who work as call girls and also as hustlers see Clive K. Copeland and Norris A. McDonald, "Prostitutes are Human: An Unorganized Counter-Institution," in H. Taylor Buckner, *Deviance, Reality, and Change*, New York: Random House, 1971, 261-269.

8   Westley, *op. cit.*, 121-123.

9   Clifton D. Bryant (ed.), *Deviant Behavior: Occupational and Organizational Bases*, Chicago: Rand McNally College Publishing Company, 1974, 170-171.

10   Edmund W. Vaz, *The Metropolitan Taxi-Driver: His Work and Self-Conception*, Unpublished M.A. Thesis, Department of Sociology, McGill University, 1955.

11   Gresham M. Sykes and David Matza, "Techniques of Neutralization: A Theory of Delinquency," *American Sociological Review*, Vol. 22, 1957, 664-670.

12   See the fine article by Donald W. Ball, "The Problematics of Respectability," in Jack D. Douglas (ed.), *Deviance and Respectability: The Social Construction of Moral Meanings*, New York: Basic Books, Inc., Publishers, 1970, 326-371.

themselves superintendents; nightwatchmen who call themselves custodians; garbage collectors who are sanitary engineers, or strippers who refer to themselves as artists, and perhaps sociologists who call themselves scientists.[13] Other groups promote different images. When fighting-oriented gangs assume names such as Dragons, Cobras, Vikings or Rattlers they are not trying to evoke images of respectability. Finally, although the game is played with a softball, minor league ball players refer to the game as fastball; it sounds more professional and it avoids a bush league image.[14]

Subcultures also provide their own myths and legends. Sometimes these are the extraordinary exploits of subcultural alumni— the boxing world is replete with legends of the feats of exceptional boxers[15]; among cabdrivers there is the story of the driver who 'picked up a $100 load.'[16] Among street cats there is the legendary hero who is such a skilled con artist 'that he can sell State street' to his victim.[17] Myths sometimes help support psychologically the publicly disesteemed; for example, there is a myth among homosexuals that they are especially sensitive and artistic.

There are also the prevailing images and pictures of the people with whom subcultural members must do business. Whether a person is a client, patient, customer, or 'sucker' makes a difference in how he is treated. These too are subcultural products. When every man is perceived as a 'John' or a 'trick' it is easy for prostitutes to pretend. Strippers are shocked and quickly disillusioned at the sexual exhibitionism of the men in the front rows who gape at their performances; soon all men are considered degenerates and this is one reason why strippers sometimes find a lesbian relationship more appealing and less hazardous than a relationship with a man.[18] Among some middle-class Canadian boys, girls are classified as 'prestige girls' (girls whose demands

---

13  For a discussion of the world of work, see Everett C. Hughes, *Men and Their Work*, New York: The Free Press, 1958.

14  Brian Messerschmidt, *"Sociological Analysis of the Rostick Juvenile Fastball Team,"* term paper submitted for Sociology 101 course; Department of Sociology, University of Waterloo, April, 1975.

15  For example, see S. Kiron Weinberg and Henry Arond, "The Occupational Culture of the Boxer," *The American Journal of Sociology*, Vol. 57, 1952, 460-469.

16  In fact the writer did 'pick-up' a $125 'load.' Approximately 550 miles later he 'cashed-in' $35 to his boss. Although an extreme case it suggests the extent to which stealing is possible among cabdrivers. An analysis of stealing as normative behavior among cabbies is found in Vaz, *op. cit.*, 117-156.

17  Finestone, *op. cit.*, 5.

18  Charles H. McCaghy and James K. Skipper, Jr., "Lesbian Behavior as an Adaptation to the Occupation of Stripping" in Clifton D. Bryant, *Deviant Behavior: Occupational and Organizational Bases*, 154-164; Marilyn Salutin,

are high, e.g., big cars, money, and countless small attentions),
'average girls' (girls with good personalities, who are the same
with everyone), and 'sluts' (girls who 'go the limit', who 'do it with
everybody').[19] In the jazz world short shrift is given anyone who
doesn't play jazz; outsiders are called 'squares', and commercial
music is sometimes considered 'mickey mouse'; and among some
groups to be 'straight' is to be conventional, unimaginative and
uninspiring.

To call something subcultural means that the participation
of persons in social activities and relationships is influenced by
their perception of the same norms; customs and perspectives are
shared only among those who stand to profit from them, and who
find in one another a sympathetic moral climate within which
these group standards may flourish.[20] But although a subculture
is a smaller, less diversified unit it is not culturally homogeneous.

Like the larger culture it too is culturally variable and the
extent to which its norms and values cohere, and the degree of
their institutionalization must be empirically known. Although
the institutionalization of norms does not guarantee the integration of a subculture it is easier to teach and learn the prevailing
ideas and norms when they receive the moral support of others.
It is important also to establish the supply and consistency of the
norms, for an inadequate supply of norms is apt to breed disorien-
tation among members—the absence of pegs on which to hang
one's daily conduct.[21]

There is no clearcut distinction between small social worlds
and conventional society; they are not autonomous, independent
entities, and they cannot survive apart from the larger social system. If crime and delinquency infuse the underworld, its distinc-
tiveness from the larger social context is merely one of degree. It
is highly questionable whether the crime and delinquency-

"Stripper Morality," in Craig L. Boydell, Carl F. Grindstaff and Paul C.
Whitehead, *Deviant Behavior and Societal Reaction,* Toronto: Holt, Rinehart and
Winston of Canada, Ltd., 1972, 532-546.

19   See Edmund W. Vaz, *A Sociological Interpretation of Middle-Class Juvenile
Delinquency.* unpublished Ph.D. Dissertation, Dept. of Sociology, Indiana
University, 1965.

20   Throughout this section we have relied heavily on the work of Albert K.
Cohen, *Delinquent Boys,* Glencoe, Illinois: The Free Press, 1955; Albert K.
Cohen, "Research in Delinquent Subcultures", *The Journal of Social Issues,* Vol.
14, No. 3, 1958. More recently see Albert K. Cohen, "Social Control and
Subcultural Change", *Youth and Society,* Vol. 3, 1972, 259-276. See also David
O. Arnold, *Subcultures,* Berkeley: The Glendessary Press, 1970.

21   Harold Fallding, *The Sociological Task,* Englewood Cliffs, New Jersey: Prentice-
Hall, Inc., 1968, 94-95.

oriented lower-class world can be totally shut off and remain un-affected by the larger society.[22] It is more likely true that small criminal worlds are an inseparable part of the larger society, and at various points interpenetrate with it, e.g., at race tracks, night clubs, brothels, poolrooms and restaurants, motels and 'hotels of assignation'.[23] Similarly, in suburban Montreal, high schools set the stage for a more open style of drug use. They provided an excellent market place for the distribution of drugs which were stored in lockers, and contacts among young people were strengthened through their use.[24] In part, smaller worlds reflect in varying ways the larger conventional society, and in turn help shape and nourish its style and cultural content.

All smaller worlds, e.g., criminal worlds, are to some extent dependent on and receive support from the parent society. This is the major source for most of the money, skills, values, material objects, and professional services essential for successful criminal operations. For example, among safecrackers, the values and norms that circumscribe their work, the special techniques em-ployed in cracking safes, the instruments and tools such as dyna-mite sticks, detonators and fuses, besides medical and legal connections, are all drawn from the larger system.[25] Similarly, the work of the prostitute clearly reflects the attitudes and values of the legitimate professions (e.g., service for a price, dispassionate role performance, and minimal discrimination in choice of clien-tele). The tiny world of the secret abortionist, who may work with a medical colleague, oftentimes depends on the professional ser-vices of the neighborhood pharmacist, a partially trained nurse, a rooming-house owner and perhaps a taxi company. Again, for active participation in the middle-class youth culture adolescents are directly dependent on their parents for goods, services, and above all, for predictable use of the family automobile.

In general the majority of persons who violate the law are recruited from conventional society. However, some of those who

---

22  Walter Miller's discussion of the lower-class culture as a generating milieu of delinquency among gangs suggests this. See Walter Miller, "Lower Class Culture as a Generating Milieu of Gang Delinquency", *Journal of Social Issues,* Vol. 14, 1958, 5-19; David Matza, *Delinquency and Drift,* New York: John Wiley & Sons, Inc., 1964, 33-67.

23  Walter Lippman, "The Underworld as Servant" in Gus Tyler, *Organized Crime in America,* Ann Arbor: The University of Michigan Press, 1962, 62.

24  John McMullan, "Suburbia in Transition: Patterns of Cannabis Use and Social Control in a Suburban Community," in H. Taylor Buckner (ed.), *Observations on the Normalization of Cannabis,* unpublished collection of papers, Dept. of Sociology, Concordia University, 1972.

25  Peter Letkemann, *Crime as Work,* Englewood Cliffs, New Jersey: Prentice-Hall, Inc., 1973.

have progressed through society's criminal farm system—the smaller subculture of delinquency—have become 'heavies' and moved into the world of adult crime. At their work these men are professionals; like golf or pool hustlers and card sharks, they begin their training early, pursue their careers with purpose and skill, take pride in their work, and are often successful in their endeavors.[26] There is minimal similarity in background between these men and white-collar criminals, embezzlers, or persons in the legitimate professions who violate the law.[27]

In a more obvious manner the world of organized crime is associated with the larger society in the provision of illicit goods and services, e.g., prostitution, gambling facilities, drugs, loansharking, and black market goods.[28] Moreover, the world of syndicated crime is perennially successful in its business enterprises, not only by circumventing law enforcement agencies, but by working in conjunction with them, i.e., by corrupting officials at various levels of government.[29] It is also true that syndicated crime has established itself in the world of legitimate business; businesses run by La Cosa Nostra are not necessarily illegitimate.[30] Some are

26  Subcultures of delinquency also provide opportunities for young delinquents to move into organized crime. For example, see Irving Spergel, *Racketville, Slumtown, Haulburg: An Exploratory Study of Delinquent Subcultures,* Chicago: The University of Chicago Press, 1964, 30-62. For recruitment to violence and organized crime see Gilbert Geis, "Violence and Organized Crime", *The Annals of the American Academy of Political and Social Science,* Vol. 364, 1966, 87-95.

27  Don C. Gibbons, *Society, Crime and Criminal Careers,* Englewood Cliffs, New Jersey: Prentice-Hall, Inc., 1973, 260-354.

28  For example, read the *Task Force Report: Organized Crime,* The President's Commission on Law Enforcement and Administration of Justice, Washington, D.C.: U.S. Government Printing Office, 1967; Estes Kefauver, *Crime in America,* Garden City, N.Y.: Doubleday and Company, 1951; Gus Tyler, *Organized Crime in America,* Ann Arbor: The University of Michigan Press, 1962; Donald R. Cressey, *Theft of the Nation,* Harper & Row, Publishers, 1969; William F. Whyte, *Street Corner Society,* Chicago: The University of Chicago Press (Enlarged Edition) 1955. For data on organized crime in Canada, see the *Report of the Honourable Mr. Justice Wilfrid D. Roach as a Commissioner Appointed Under The Public Inquiries Act By Letters Patent* dated Dec. 11, 1961, also the *Report of the Ontario Police Commission on Organized Crime, January 31st, 1964;* W.E. Mann and Lloyd G. Hanley, "Mafia in Canada" in W.E. Mann (ed.), *Deviant Behaviour in Canada,* Toronto: Social Science Publishers, 1968, 132-158.

29  For example, read Donald R. Cressey, *Theft of the Nation,* 248-289; John A. Gardiner and David J. Olson, "Wincanton: The Politics of Corruption" in *Task Force Report: Organized Crime,* 61-79. A good review of the symbiotic relations among politics, corruption and law enforcement is found in Stuart L. Hills, *Crime, Power and Morality,* Scranton: Chandler Publishing Company, 1971, 119-129.

30  Of the 58 known hoodlums who attended the gangland meeting at Apalachin, New York on November 14, 1957, 50 had arrest records, 35 had conviction

acquired and conducted quite legally. Others, of course, are acquired and run by means devious and coersive. It seems that La Cosa Nostra members have a virtual monopoly on some legitimate businesses in North America, such as distribution of cigarette vending machines and juke-boxes, and they also own a variety of legitimate retail firms, bars, banks, restaurants, apartment houses, food corporations, office buildings and factories.[31] As a result, La Cosa Nostra is one of America's largest business enterprises.[32]

In a smaller context, it is also true that there is overlap between the police and the criminal world, and that there is a steady flow of information from the criminal culture to police agencies.[33] Also, the boundaries between some legitimate worlds like that of professional boxing, and the criminal world are typically blurred. Because many of the persons affiliated with professional boxing likely originate from the criminally established sectors of society, they are often easily susceptible to criminal overtures. In this way the world of organized crime is often involved in manipulating (sometimes successfully) the outcome of contests on which large sums of money are wagered. There are also some legitimate service occupations, e.g., cabdrivers, hotel doormen and bellhops, that are especially well suited in helping to meet the public's need for illicit goods and services. Some 'hustling' cabdrivers augment their earnings by working in conjunction with call girls, and gambling establishments; others have their own 'private numbers'.[34]

The continuity in crime and deviance is mirrored also in the sharing of attitudes, norms and values between the world of organ-

---

records and 23 had spent time in jail or penitentiary as a result of these convictions, and there were many other illegal activities in which they were engaged. Yet 9 of these hoodlums were or had been in the coin-operated machine business; 16 were engaged in trucking or garment manufacturing; 10 owned grocery stores or markets; 17 owned restaurants or taverns; 11 were engaged in importing and exporting businesses and 9 were involved in the construction business. Others were engaged in a variety of other legitimate businesses. Read "An Underworld Convention", from the Final Report, Select Committee on Improper Activities in the Labor or Management Field, U.S. Senate, 1960, reported in Gus Tyler, *Organized Crime in America,* 19-37; Kefauver, *Crime in America,* 205-217; Charles Grutzner, "Organized Crime and the Businessman" (editor's title), in John E. Conklin (ed.), *The Crime Establishment,* Englewood Cliffs, New Jersey: Prentice-Hall, Inc., 1973, 105-119; Donald R. Cressey, *Theft of the Nation,* 100-108.

31 Donald R. Cressey, *Criminal Organization: Its Elementary Forms,* London: Heinemann Educational Books, Ltd., 1972, 18-40.

32 *Ibid.,* 22.

33 William A. Westley, *op. cit.,* 40-42; Jerome H. Skolnick, *Justice Without Trial: Law Enforcement in Democratic Society,* New York: John Wiley & Sons, Inc., 1967, 112-138; Letkemann, *op. cit.,* 43.

34 Vaz, *The Metropolitan Taxi-Driver: His Work and Self Conception,* 185-200.

ized crime and conventional society—the almighty dollar looms large in the motivation of both criminal and non-criminal behavior. Not only is there considerable overlap in the values shared by both worlds, but the values of "mobility, status and respectability operate in the underworld in a way analagous to their workings in the 'upperworld'."[35] Bloch and Geis write that, 'Organized criminals are among the most socially mobile persons in the United States, advancing with startling single-generation swiftness from the lower rungs of society into positions of power and wealth.'[36] Often their criminal and violent means of ascent become lost or otherwise disappear on the way. For example, Al Capone received 1,000 fan letters per day, as many as some movie stars.[37] Further interconnections between both worlds are apparent in the frequent indifference or ambivalence of large sectors of society toward many forms of criminal endeavor like gambling, prostitution, and corporate crime. However, there is so little public knowledge of corporate crime and of the operations and thinking of 'corporate criminals', that no distinct image is available of the role of white collar criminal.[38]

A final example is the overlap that exists between the worlds of black adults and adolescents in lower-classed, depressed neighborhoods of large cities. These are areas where petty theft, crime, robbery, small-time burglary, policy and drug operations are widespread. Yet there is a sharing of attitudes, perspectives and values between adolescents and adults. Typically in such areas both adolescent and adult blacks encounter serious economic disabilities which greatly jeopardize their social mobility, and limit their planning for the future. Competition exists 'among all age levels for excitement wherever it may be found—from a bottle, a battle or a broad.'[39] There is also a distinct permissive climate among adult blacks in their relations with adolescents, so much so that institutional arrangements which separate adults and young people do not appear to operate. For example, "a father

---

35   Eric L. McKitrick, "The Study of Corruption", in Seymour M. Lipset and Neil J. Smelser (eds.) *Sociology: The Progress of a Decade,* Englewood Cliffs: Prentice-Hall, Inc., 1961, 455; Daniel Bell, "Crime as a Way of Life", in Marvin E. Wolfgang, Leonard Savitz and Norman Johnston (eds.), *The Sociology of Crime and Delinquency,* New York: John Wiley and Sons, Inc., 1962, 213-225.

36   Herbert A. Bloch and Gilbert Geis, *Man, Crime, and Society* (Second Edition), New York: Random House, 1970, 197.

37   *Ibid.,* 197.

38   See Gibbons, *op. cit.,* 327-353.

39   James F. Short, Jr., and Fred L. Strodbeck, *Group Process and Gang Delinquency,* Chicago: The University of Chicago Press, 1965, 214.

might approach a boy and ask him to 'be careful' and not 'get the girl in trouble' rather than to stop sexual relations.'[40] Moreover, it is sometimes difficult 'to tell where life in the street leaves off and formal institutional life begins.'[41] For instance, during the summer months it is not unusual for adolescent boys to spend their evenings hanging about in the park drinking, smoking pot and fooling around with girls. When the older people begin leaving, the boys will engage in sexual relations with the girls. A worker's report states, ' . . . Jake will lay a broad right on the bench but most of them will take the girl off somewhere to one of these junked cars and lay her there . . . . '[42]

In these areas the idea of a stable legitimate marriage is not shared by adults or adolescents. What have been termed 'serial monogomy mating patterns' are common, and families sometimes have a "procession of 'uncles' moving in and out" of the home.[43] Here also, older, experienced women who have lived a life on the streets hook a younger man, so that he will 'pay for the groceries' while they live together. From these experienced women younger adolescent girls learn how to attract boys, and sucker them into paying for the upkeep of the living arrangements and the baby should there be one.[44] Such relationships and shared perspectives show forcibly that adolescents in these neighborhoods are relatively free of adult supervision, and that overlap seemingly blends two worlds into one.

Active participation in a deviant subcultural world is always variable. Even in tightly-knit, structurally consolidated, 'delinquent subcultures', where members congregate regularly, and there is alleged agreement in the norms, attitudes and values, members are not equally committed to the delinquent enterprise. Nor are 'certain forms of delinquent activity' apt to be 'essential requirements' of dominant role performance.[45] Notwithstanding

---

40  *Ibid.,* 36.

41  *Ibid.,* 214.

42  *Ibid.,* 36. This is part of a report by a detached worker affiliated with the gangs.

43  Walter Miller refers to the 'female-based household' in which a male parent is either absent from the household, present only sporadically, or, when present, only minimally or inconsistently involved in the support and rearing of children. See Walter Miller, *Lower Class Culture as a Generating Milieu of Gang Delinquency,* 5-19; Harrison E. Salisbury, *The Shook-Up Generation,* Greenwich, Conn: Fawcett Publications, 1958, 16. Very similar data were obtained about gang boys from French families in Paris: see Edmund W. Vaz, "Juvenile Gang Delinquency in Paris", *Social Problems,* Vol. 10, 1962, 23-24.

44  Short and Strodbeck, *op. cit.,* 37.

45  See Richard A. Cloward and Lloyd E. Ohlin, *Delinquency and Opportunity,* Glencoe, Illinois: The Free Press, 1960, 7.

the heavy delinquent activity of some youths, subcultural norms do not 'commit adherents to their misdeeds.' Although delinquency is doubtlessly encouraged under a variety of conditions, there is apt to be a series of extenuating circumstances which enables members to opt for something less than illegality if they so desire. The delinquent subculture does not constrain members to illegal operations.[46] Similarly, cabdrivers are not constrained to steal from their employers, professional hockey players are not committed to unrestrained aggressive conduct on the ice, and not every police officer is committed to the norm of secrecy. The commitment and active participation of members will depend largely on the payoffs that they receive for their behavioral and emotional investment. The larger and more rewarding the dividends for subcultural involvement, the fewer side bets members are apt to make in their role as subcultural participants.

# The Emergence of Subcultural Worlds

In a previous section we noted that human problems are not randomly distributed throughout the social system, and that socioeconomic location makes a difference in the number, variety and significance of the problems that characterize our everyday lives. But problems related to, and perhaps generated by, our socioeconomic position are not the only important issues that confront us. The formal and informal social roles that we occupy, our sex, the particular kinds of work that we do, and our ethnicity are also crucial in influencing the issues that we face and the troubles that befall us. At the same time they equip us differentially in our ability to tackle and handle many of our problems. For example, the roles of teenager, 'being middle aged' or 'senior citizen' make a difference in the problems and anxieties that we experience; they modify the meaning of success for us, and influence our goals and our chances of reaching them. How does the role of 'being mature' affect our attitudes towards adventure, excitement and risk in our daily living? As we assume more responsible roles are we more concerned with payoffs and less with ideals in our day-to-day affairs? Similarly, a person's sex makes a difference in the variety of work roles that are available; truck drivers, pimps and safecrackers tend to be male[47], while secretaries, prostitutes and strippers are usually female, and this invariably affects the kinds of stresses and strains that they encounter. Briefly, the criteria by

---

46  Matza, *Delinquency and Drift,* 33-67.

47  Bill Chambliss (ed.), *Box Man,* New York: Harper and Row, Publishers, 1972, 1-24; Letkemann, *op. cit.,* 1973.

which we judge ourselves (and by which others judge us) vary according to such variables, and are influenced also by the particular worlds in which we live.

When we refer to problems we mean more than the daily dilemmas, anxieties, and stresses that aggravate our ground-level activities. We have in mind the more permanent troubles, the relatively inflexible, challenging problems that persistently disrupt our daily lives. There are problems associated with the kinds of work we do in society and problems typical of the professions or endemic to the service occupations. For example, the cabdriver serves a variety of publics—the young and the old, the poor and the extravagant, the comic, the drunk and the prostitute; similarly, the waitress has her customers, the janitor his tenants, the movie star her fan clubs and the heroin addict his contacts, and each of these roles has its problems. There are problems of status deprivation and of alienation, problems of maintaining self-respect as a perennial member of a low-status occupation, problems encountered by minority groups, the handicapped, the poor, and the deviant.[48] These are nagging, daily problems that grind inexorably at our self-respect unless effective solutions are found.

An important question is whether there are available culturally prescribed solutions to these problems. How effective are they? It is disquieting to consider the societally institutionalized remedies for status deprived, lower-class youths trying to make it in a world of middle-class institutions. The encouragement of academic perseverence, personal determination, parental obedience, and moral fortitude, the establishment of settlement houses, expanded recreational facilities and social work assistance are regrettable solutions for this stratum of youths. Neither the availability nor the quality of these kinds of solutions is apt to alleviate the status pinch of lower-class youngsters.

Whatever solutions we devise or generate for our problems are most likely to be effective if they are acceptable according to the moral standards and criteria by which we conduct our daily affairs. Similarly, we will not wish to act in a manner that signifies roles with which we seek to avoid identification. To some extent the symbolism of our behavior must jibe with the kinds of roles that we are prone to claim and the terms in which we wish to view ourselves. On both of these counts, i.e., the acceptability of our

---

48  For a discussion of the plight of the poor in Canada read Ian Adams, William Cameron, Brian Hill and Peter Penz, *The Real Poverty Report*, Edmonton: M.G. Hurtig Limited, 1971; the Special Planning Secretariat, "This Too is Canada," in Craig L. Boydell, Carl F. Grindstaff and Paul C. Whitehead, *Critical Issues in Canadian Society*, Toronto: Holt, Rinehart and Winston of Canada Limited, 1971, 161-166.

behavior to our conscience and to the selves that we claim, we are dependent on others. At the best of times it is difficult to 'go it alone'. Even Thoreau and Robinson Crusoe brought with them their respective cultural luggage. It is therefore crucially important that our solutions appeal to those others to whom we look for recognition and approval, and to those groups with whom we wish to associate and be identified. We have already remarked that the strength of our ties to these reference groups will greatly influence the likelihood of our violating their expectations without experiencing pangs of guilt and moral uncertainty. Whether it is peddling dope, stealing cars or making love to the boss's daughter we are not apt to be very successful unless we believe that someone approves of our conduct. The stronger the conviction that those groups (or others) that matter to us support our beliefs and approve of our proposed conduct, the easier it will be to act.

But our group membership is never altogether stable; there is always an ongoing alignment of groups in which we seek membership, and a social climate where we will be behaviorally welcome and attitudinally at home. The duration of our stay and the strength of our membership will depend largely on the kinds of payoffs and meanings that these groups hold for us. It is also true that we are differentially involved in such groups. Our emotional investments will vary, and we devote varying amounts of time and energy to their upkeep. Some groups and institutions usually exert a relatively permanent impact on our lives, e.g., our family, occupation, religion, and social class. Other groups and relationships, even if they are shortlived, may nevertheless leave their mark and influence our destinies—our stay at university, a brief but intimate friendship, marriage, a love affair, or religious experience. It is essential, indeed it is a condition of our sanity, that we find refuge in affiliations with others. As we change worlds and realign our group memberships we acquire changed perspectives of the world, and our interpretation and reinterpretation of ourselves and of the larger world undergo modification. Thus we are continually alert for others with whom we fit,[49] who share and reinforce our convictions, persons and groups who, by their actions and words, confirm our attitudes, help sustain and give credit to our beliefs, and are receptive to our solutions to the problems.

But what happens when culturally available solutions to our problems remain hopelessly ineffective, when established guide-

---

49  This was one of the main problems experienced by Holden Caulfield: he was troubled morally and spiritually about the manner in which people lived, and he also felt that he would never find others with whom he could fit. J.D. Salinger, *The Catcher in the Rye*, Boston, Massachusetts: Little, Brown and Company, Inc., 1968.

lines for action are dead ends, and the problems persist, dragging us down irresistably? Although there is nothing sacrosanct about institutionalized courses of action, conformity to established ways remains the plight of most lower-status persons burdened with problems of poverty, status deprivation, alienation, and frustration. It may be their inability to sever reference group ties, or their early socialization to middle-class, established values and norms that deter them from widespread deviance. Thus they conform, perhaps with mixed feelings of self-contempt, and frustration at the futility of their actions. Of course, there will be others who will, at least ostensibly, do their own thing, irrespective of the approval and recognition of others.[50] But will not the remainder—laden with similar problems—require assistance? Perhaps there are solutions 'not yet embodied in action' and therefore not yet culturally available that might better suit their problems.[51] Faced with a paucity of meaningful guidelines, and the blatant failure of existing solutions to their troubles they look elsewhere for direction. Perhaps by circumstance and disposition, since each person is receptive to any sign of assistance, persons faced with similar problems provide a social climate especially conducive to the florescence of new cultural forms—subcultural answers to their problems. Perhaps each becomes something akin to a reference group for the other. Under these conditions increased involvement in joint activities is apt to breed progressive commitment to whatever behavioral solutions appear meaningful and rewarding.

What is the dynamic process whereby subcultures become solutions to the problems of persons similarly circumstanced? The first sustained effort to develop a general theory of subcultures is found in *Delinquent Boys* by Albert K. Cohen. In this book Cohen tackles the status problems of lower-class youths in society, and argues that the delinquent subculture is a suitable solution to their status deprivation. The dynamic process involved in the emergence of this collective solution, i.e., of subcultures in general, is masterfully elaborated by Cohen.

> **The crucial condition for the emergence of new cultural forms is the existence, *in effective interaction with one another, of a number of actors with similar problems of adjustment.* These**

---

50 Theoretically this is not likely possible; some persons (perhaps many) actually believe that their conduct is not influenced by others. In recent years many university students insisted on 'doing their own thing' during the summer vacation. Not unexpectedly many ended up doing very much the same things in the kibbutzim in Israel, or in London, Amsterdam or other European cities.

51 Albert K. Cohen, *Delinquent Boys,* Glencoe, Illinois: The Free Press, 1955, 59.

may be the entire membership of a group or only certain members, similarly circumstanced, within the group. Among the conceivable solutions to their problems may be one which is not yet embodied in action and which does not therefore exist as a cultural model. This solution, except for the fact that it does not already carry the social criteria of validity and promise the social rewards of consensus, might well answer more neatly to the problems of this group and appeal to its members more effectively than any of the solutions already institutionalized. For each participant, this solution would be adjustive and adequately motivated provided that he could anticipate a simultaneous and corresponding transformation in the frames of reference of his fellows. Each would welcome a sign from the others that a new departure in this direction would receive approval and support. But *how does one know* whether a gesture toward innovation will strike a responsive and sympathetic chord in others or whether it will elicit hostility, ridicule and punishment? *Potential* concurrence is always problematical and innovation or the impulse to innovate a stimulus for anxiety.

The paradox is resolved when the innovation is broached in such a manner as to elicit from others reactions suggesting their receptivity; and when, at the same time, the innovation occurs by increments so small, tentative and ambiguous as to permit the actor to retreat, if the signs be unfavorable, without having become identified with an unpopular position. Perhaps all social actions have, in addition to their instrumental, communicative and expressive functions, this quality of being exploratory *gestures.* For the actor with problems of adjustment which cannot be resolved within the frame of reference of the established culture, each response of the other to what the actor says and does is a clue to the directions in which change may proceed further in a way congenial to the other and to the direction in which change will lack social support. And if the probing gesture is motivated by tensions common to other participants it is likely to initiate a process of *mutual* exploration and *joint* elaboration of a new solution. My exploratory gesture functions as a cue to you; your exploratory gesture as a cue to me. By a casual, semi-serious, non-committal or tangential remark I may stick my neck out just a little way, but I will quickly withdraw it unless you, by some sign of affirmation, stick *yours* out. I will permit myself to become progressively committed but only as others, by some visible sign, become likewise committed. The final product, to which we are jointly committed, is likely to be a compromise formation of all the participants to what we may call a cultural process, a formation perhaps unanticipated by any of them. Each actor may contribute something directly to the growing product, but he may also contribute indirectly by encouraging others to advance, inducing them to retreat, and suggesting new avenues to be explored. The product cannot be ascribed to any one of the participants; it is a real "emergent" on a group level.

We may think of this process as one of mutual conversion. The important thing to remember is that we do not first convert ourselves and then others. The acceptability of an idea to oneself depends upon its acceptability to others. Converting the other is part of the process of converting oneself...

The emergence of these "group standards" of this shared frame of reference, is the emergence of a new subculture. It is cultural because each actor's participation in this system of norms is influenced by his perception of the same norms in other actors. It is *sub*cultural because the norms are shared only among those actors who stand somehow to profit from them and who find in one another a sympathetic moral climate within which these norms may come to fruition and persist. In this fashion culture is continually being created, re-created and modified wherever individuals sense in one another like needs, generated by like circumstances, not shared generally in the larger social system. Once established, such a subcultural system may persist, but not by sheer inertia. It may achieve a life which outlasts that of the individuals who participated in its creation, but only so long as it continues to serve the needs of those who succeed its creators.[52]

Cohen proceeds to show that the delinquent subculture is a collective response to the status deprivation of lower-class boys living in a world infested with middle-class institutions.

Participation in the delinquent subculture provides these boys with status; therefore, it is a viable solution to their status problems. For Cohen, the delinquent subculture functions mainly as a world apart; there is no tempering with middle-class norms, values and attitudes, there is no ambiguity in the delinquent response. Lower-class delinquency attacks the middle classes where it hurts most—in their love of property. These boys steal property and destroy it, and they get their kicks in the process. The delinquent solution is the categorical reversal of middle-class stand-

---

52  Cohen, *Delinquent Boys,* 59-61, 65. Reprinted with permission of Macmillan Publishing Co., Inc. Copyright by The Free Press, a Corporation, 1958.

ards. In this way it provides lower-class boys with status against youths from all corners of society. It provides them with others, similarly circumstanced, who support their depredations; it provides beliefs, attitudes, perspectives, and a rhetoric which help guide their conduct and motivate their action. Equally important, it provides lower-class boys with criteria for status that are essentially standards that they can meet, unlike middle-class criteria against which they come off second best. Moreover, participation in the delinquent subculture helps neutralize doubt, and provides moral reinforcement for a sometimes ambivalent conscience. Hence, these substantial payoffs, plus the fact that the lower-class boy is fully aware that outside his gang his status is low, help keep him actively engaged in delinquent pursuits.[53]

---

53  Our emphasis is on Cohen's account of the dynamic process involved in the emergence of subcultures in general, not on the validity of the specific theory of the delinquent subculture.

# The Social Organization of Deviant Behavior

# 10

If persons expect to work together to reach agreed-upon goals, their activities must be something more than an ad lib flow of events. Whether it is constructing a school building, managing a baseball team or teaching sociology, the successful accomplishment of the activity requires some degree of planning. Similarly, an illegal lottery, a brothel, car theft and dope trafficking must be planned; some element of rationality must be included if the groups are to work effectively and remain in business.

The term organization means 'putting into working order' the various roles of a group of persons. It is the rational coordination of roles and the prescribed and proscribed activities associated with them, that generates efficiency and 'continuous purposive activity of a specified kind,[1] and facilitates the achievement of goals. Without organization the activity is intermittent.

Like many other activities, especially those which involve risks, deviant behavior is undertaken for a reward. This may be a sexual payoff, it may be power as a result of military coup, it may be a bank heist or turning a trick where the reward is money, or it may be two students planning to crib for a passing grade on

---

1   Max Weber, *The Theory of Social and Economic Organization,* London: William Hodge and Company Limited, 1947, 204.

an examination. In each instance the planning is instrumental, designed to achieve a goal—to maximize a payoff.

It is customary to refer to the 'formal' and 'informal' social organization of activities, as if there were two intrinsically different kinds of organization. Sometimes we equate the term formal with official groups, and informal with unofficial groups. Nothing could be farther from the truth. There are not some groups that are formal organizations and other groups that are informal organizations.[2] It seems likely that any organization of activities will exhibit some formal elements—roles that are at least relatively explicit, and according to which members orient their conduct—and informal elements—rules and roles that are not explicitly prescribed.

An important source of predictability in the behavior of members of a group is the extent to which their behavior is oriented to common rules. This increases the rationality of behavior since 'any one person's rationality in action is severely limited unless he can count on what others will do in particular circumstances.'[3] Any activity that is undertaken to increase rationality in an enterprise is an effort to maximize its organization.

It is important to remember that the organization of both deviant and non-deviant activities is always variable. For example, when two youngsters run through an apartment building stealing pennies from milk bottles, their conduct is not completely spontaneous.[4] Involved in this prankish conduct is some rudimentary role differentiation; there is an, albeit temporary, specialization of tasks: one boy acts as the lookout while the other does the stealing. To the extent that the boys agree about their respective roles and about sharing the money, this helps coordinate their delinquent acts. However, this behavior is best seen more as play than work, and therefore the element of spontaneity is perhaps more illuminating than the planning. Should their depredations persist, the element of play is still apt to predominate. Certainly, no long-term delinquent goals are envisaged, and role differentiation is elementary; indeed, the youths are likely to switch roles in the

---

2 Theodore Caplow, *Principles of Organization,* New York: Harcourt, Brace and World, Inc., 1964, 22.

3 Harry M. Johnson, *Sociology: A Systematic Introduction,* New York: Harcourt, Brace and World, Inc., 1960, 291.

4 The fun element in delinquency is found in Frederic M. Thrasher, *The Gang,* (abridged edition), Chicago: The University of Chicago Press, 1968, 74-77; Clifford R. Shaw, *The Jack-Roller,* Chicago: The University of Chicago Press, 1966, 47-56; Clifford R. Shaw and Henry D. McKay, *Social Factors in Juvenile Delinquency, A Study of the Family, and the Gang in Relation to Delinquent Behavior for the National Commission on Law Observance and Enforcement,* (no date nor publisher) 117-120.

course of the activity. Moreover, there are no established rules by which their acts are governed. In brief, the element of rationality included in the delinquent activity is minimal and short lived.

On the other hand, a prison break sometimes requires relatively long-term planning and intelligence, and price-fixing among large business organizations is not without careful consideration and planning.[5] When we read that 'the raiders . . . must have spent much of Saturday and Sunday [using] homemade thermal lances to cut through a two foot thick steel door and grille' to escape with three million dollars, there is little doubt that technical expertise, intelligence, and considerable planning were required.[6] Similarly, the following excerpt illustrates the careful coordination of roles, the effort to improve performance through rehearsal and to maximize precautions against detection.

> **Lemay, he said, went to New York to buy walkie-talkie equipment used in the operation. Lemay's private island north of Montreal was used for dynamite practice and for equipment tests. An office across the street from the bank was rented as a lookout office and on the weekend of June 23, 1961, there was a dress rehearsal during which drilling and blasting were begun and power lines for lights and equipment were put in place.**
>
> **Encountering difficulties in trying to get through the wall with the tools they had brought, Lemay and Roland Primeau made a trip north to obtain dynamite, he said. The second attempt also brought little success and they finally ran short of dynamite.**
>
> **Lajoie said other plans were made and at Lemay's suggestion he had gone to St. Jerome to get the drills lengthened.**
>
> **The casing of the bank was also on the weekend of June 23, Lajoie said. He said, he, Lemay, Primeau and Andre Lemieux scouted around the area on the Friday. Lemieux, he said, opened the side door to the building housing the bank with a key supplied by Lemay.[7]**

However, the above example does not necessarily reflect an established group with a stable membership and common identity, whose rationally coordinated roles are singularly oriented to achieving criminal goals. The distinction should be noted between

---

5 For example, see Gilbert Geis, 'The Heavy Electrical Equipment Antitrust Cases of 1961,' in Gilbert Geis (ed.), *White-Collar Criminal: The Offender in Business and the Professions,* New York: Atherton Press, 1968, 103-118.

6 See the *Kitchener-Waterloo Record,* Nov. 13, 1967, 1.

7 See *The Globe and Mail,* Toronto, Nov. 22, 1966.

an established kind of criminal group, e.g., an organized pick-pocket group that may work together for years,[8] and a number of highly skilled men who temporarily pool their resources, coordinate their skills and maximize their efforts to 'pull a job'. While the element of rationality characterizes their efforts to successfully accomplish the job, once the caper is completed they are likely to disband and may never again work together.

The planning or organization of social activities usually requires some repetition of events, which usually demands an 'unequivocal roster of members.'[9] This applies to deviant as well as to conventional groups. A constant turnover in membership precludes an established patterning of events and the development of a permanent collective identity. For example, the constantly shifting membership in boys' gangs usually prevents any form of stable organization to their activities from developing. Although legitimate groups often go to considerable lengths to magnify their identities, understandably some criminal groups attempt to hide or camouflage theirs. However, members of the group must be identifiable to each other. But something more is required. For example, boys may congregate at a street corner, but their contacts may be irregular, new members may appear each night, no real sense of belonging will develop, role differentiation will be elementary, and this will certainly preclude a common identity from emerging.

For the regularity of interaction to persist some minimal scheduling of activities is required.[10] The willy-nilly gathering of members and undertaking of events prevent predictable patterning of activities from developing. Yet the scheduling of events is no guarantee of their organization. Moreover, daily routine activities—a kind of elementary programming of events—is not the same thing as rational planning.[11]

The every day and night hanging activities of street corner boys (both young and old) is an example of informal daily interaction. These tiny cultures-in-the-making, from which embryonic configurations of roles sometimes emerge, are usually something less than structurally established. Yet more or less the same roster of youths come together on a regular basis, and their habitual association may last for many years. Even when members leave

---

8  David W. Maurer, *Whiz Mob,* New Haven, Conn: College and University Press, 1964, 88.

9  Caplow, *op. cit.,* 13.

10  Caplow, *op. cit.,* 13.

11  Caplow, *op. cit.,* 13-16.

the neighborhood, they return often to be with their friends.[12] Gradually there emerges a patterning of activities and a configuration of relationships. Over time these relationships become daily patterns and expectations which lend a modicum of stability to the groups.

Although the patterns of interaction among these boys are largely routine, the nature and flow of their behavior can be intense.[13] Furthermore, a variety of delinquent or criminal practices may be included in their repertoire of activities. Yet the roles that do emerge are less than clearcut, their obligations usually lack specificity, there is no mechanism for recruiting others when members move elsewhere, and there are no clearly established goals to their corner activities. Sometimes nominal identification exists, and shared attitudes, perspectives and sentiments develop, but whatever structure exists 'is not necessarily perceived as serving collective purposes.'[14] In brief, only a trace of rationality characterizes their practices; there is little planning or organization to such events. Certainly these groups are not organized towards achieving criminal or deviant goals.

In contrast, the professional in crime requires more than technical expertise in order to ply his trade successfully. According to one career burglar, '[He] must have patience. [He] must study. [He] must be disciplined.'[15] Moreover, the professional works systematically; he plans his work and target/victim in advance, sometimes for months. The professional also takes prior precautions for avoiding punishment in case of apprehension.[16] The fence and the 'fix' are crucial roles in this process. The fence is the receiver of stolen goods, but he also receives orders for special objects of value which he conveys to the thief. Cressey writes that 'The professional criminal expects that every case will be fixed.'[17] This means that someone must be corrupted, and someone must do the corrupting. In large criminal organizations like

---

12   William Foote Whyte, *Street Corner Society,* Chicago: The University of Chicago Press, 1969, 255.

13   Walter B. Miller, 'Lower Class Culture as a Generating Milieu of Gang Delinquency,' *Journal of Social Issues,* Vol. 14, 1958, 5-19; Walter B. Miller, Hildred S. Geertz and Henry S. G. Cutter, 'Aggression in a Boys' Street-Corner Group,' *Psychiatry,* Vol. 24, 1961, 283-298.

14   Donald R. Cressey, *Criminal Organization,* London: Heinemann Educational Books, 1972, 10.

15   Nicholas Pileggi, 'The Year of the Burglar,' in Clifton D. Bryant (ed.), *Deviant Behavior: Occupational and Organizational Bases,* Chicago: Rand McNally College Publishing Company, 1974, 396.

16   Donald R. Cressey, 'Delinquent and Criminal Structures,' in Robert K. Merton and Robert Nisbet (eds.), *Contemporary Social Problems,* New York: Harcourt Brace Jovanovich, Inc., 1971, 160.

La Cosa Nostra, there is at least one organizational position for corrupter. 'The corruptee position is occupied by a public official who, for a fee, insures that the group can operate with relative immunity from the penal process.'[18] As a Box Man states, 'Every town has a criminal lawyer who is a fix ... A fix has got it all fixed before you go to court ... You know what you're gonna get before you go down to court.'[19] The fix can take a number of forms. Victims may be persuaded to accept restitution, the police may be paid off, a witness may be 'convinced' to testify falsely, the prosecutor may be persuaded to drop charges against the accused or, when everything else fails, the judge may be bribed to be lenient in his decision.

Moreover, if the criminal group is to persist for any length of time a division of criminal skills is needed. We have noted already that some of these skills require a long apprenticeship; nevertheless, the careful coordination of such expertise is indispensable for the success of the enterprise. The best example of a criminal group that relies on the precision-like execution of multiple skills is the pick-pocket mob.[20] Finally, unlike the majority of persons who violate the law, the professional criminal goes about his work in a businesslike manner. His performance is controlled and rationally motivated towards a successful and profitable conclusion. Bravado, spontaneity and the careless display of toughness are the marks of the amateur, not the professional.

# The Social Organization of Gang Delinquency

Some years ago Clifford Shaw and Henry McKay established empirically that the large bulk of juvenile delinquency was conducted in groups.[21] But this is only part of the story. Groups vary widely

---

17  Cressey, *Delinquent and Criminal Structures,* 160; Edwin H. Sutherland, *The Professional Thief,* Chicago: The University of Chicago Press, 1937, 218-222; Bruce Jackson, *Outside the Law: A Thief's Primer,* New Brunswick, New Jersey: Transaction Books, Rutgers University, 1972, 130-139.

18  Cressey, *Delinquent and Criminal Subcultures,* 162; Donald R. Cressey, *Theft of the Nation,* New York: Harper and Row, Publishers, 1969, 248-289; Peter D. Chimbos, 'Some Aspects of Organized Crime in Canada: A Preliminary Review,' in W. E. Mann (ed.), *Social Deviance in Canada,* Toronto: The Copp Clark Publishing Company, 1971, 179-182.

19  Bill Chambliss (ed.), *Box Man,* New York: Harper and Row, Publishers, 1972, 98-99.

20  David W. Maurer, *Whiz Mob,* New Haven, Conn: College and University Press, 1964; Sutherland, *The Professional Thief,* 44-48.

21  Clifford R. Shaw and Henry McKay, *Social Factors in Juvenile Delinquency, A Study of the Community, The Family, and the Gang in Relation to Delinquent Behavior,* for the National Commission on Law Observance and Enforcement, (no

in their social organization and leadership, the degree of their cohesion, and the kind and amount of their delinquency.

From an early age most boys, whatever their socioeconomic location, belong to some kind of group or what they usually prefer to call 'gang.' The term 'gang' often evokes an image of a tightly knit group with an established identity, enthusiastic participation, and coordinated roles designed to achieve agreed-upon criminal goals. But this image bears little resemblance to the groups to which the majority of boys belong. Most of these gangs are neither clearly organized, nor oriented to delinquent ends. In his study of street gangs in Toronto, Rogers suggests that there is nothing intrinsically bad with gangs; any good or bad element resides first, in the nature of the companionship involved, and in the purposes and activities of the gang as a whole. Indeed, gang life may have many desirable elements worth cultivating like group loyalty.[22]

There are apt to be proportionately more juvenile gangs located in the lower socioeconomic strata of society, but this does not mean that most gangs engage regularly in delinquency. Some do, most do not. The majority of gangs are little more than groups of boys who hang together on a more-or-less regular basis, with little or no structure to their activities. However, there are also social gangs, athletic gangs, club gangs and gangs associated with particular neighborhoods. The members of these gangs are emotionally stable youths, and the large majority of their activities are social in nature; the boys organize dances and other recreational events, engage in discussions, arrange athletic competitions and participate on sports teams. Mutual attraction and the desire to engage in social affairs seem to motivate these boys to join gangs. The leaders are often the most popular members, and possess the required qualities of leadership. Some members engage in delinquent practices, but the gangs are not delinquency oriented, nor is their incipient organization directed to the realization of criminal ends. In fact, the regular activities of these gangs often reflect their accord with the values and sentiments of the larger society.[23]

# Thrasher's Gangs

The first extensive sociological investigation of boys' gangs was conducted by Frederic Thrasher, while a graduate student at the University of Chicago and submitted as a Ph.D. dissertation in

---

date or publisher), 191-199.

22  Kenneth H. Rogers, *Street Gangs in Toronto,* Toronto: The Ryerson Press, 1945,41.

23  Martin R. Haskell and Lewis Yablonsky, *Crime and Delinquency,* Chicago: Rand McNally College Publishing Company, 1974, 510-518.

1926. This is a study of 1313 different gangs, and remains the best analysis of the formation, location and cultural content of big-city gangs.[24]

Thrasher discovered that gangs were located primarily in the interstitial zones of the city, deteriorated 'poverty-belt' areas adjacent to the central business district, long considered the breeding ground for many forms of crime and delinquency.[25] He suggested that gangs were 'formed spontaneously and then integrated through conflict.' Face to face contacts, 'milling movement through space as a unit, conflict and planning' were also major characteristics; the result of these processes was the growth of a 'tradition, unreflective internal structure, *esprit de corps,* solidarity, morale, group awareness and attachment to a local territory.'[26]

Thrasher was fully aware of the variation among gangs and referred to 'diffuse', 'solidified', 'conventionalized' and 'criminal' types of gangs. He suggested that the gang may develop the features of a 'secret society' with initiation ceremonies, rituals, codes and so forth. But he failed to 'conceptualize such differences in a way which would account for them or relate them systematically to other (variable) characteristics of gangs or gang boys.'[27] Also absent from his account is the detailed analysis of the organization, structure and behavior of gangs that is found in some contemporary research studies.[28]

In discussing the growth and formation of adult criminal gangs, Thrasher refers to a 'certain criminal residue upon whom gang training has, for one reason or another, taken fast hold.'[29] The most salient features contributing to gang boys' undertaking a criminal career are the "experiences and associations undergone in so-called 'reform' and penal institutions."[30] These statements are likely equally valid today, yet they fail to stipulate the essential social process and relationships among variables which explain why some gang boys become adult criminals and others do not.

24  Frederic M. Thrasher, *The Gang,* Chicago: The University of Chicago Press, 1927.

25  Frederic M. Thrasher, *The Gang,* (abridged edition with a New Introduction by James F. Short, Jr.) Chicago: The University of Chicago Press, 1968, 6.

26  *Ibid.,* 46. See also Frank Tannenbaum, *Crime in the Community,* New York: Columbia University Press, 1951, 8-17.

27  Thrasher, *The Gang,* (abridged edition with a New Introduction by James F. Short, Jr.), xxii.

28  *Ibid.,* xvii-xxiv.

29  *Ibid.,* 287.

30  *Ibid.,* 288.

Knowledge of the processes involved in this matter continues to elude us.[31]

Thrasher was aware also of the importance of status among gang members, and was sensitive to the considerable role differentiation that characterized some gangs. Yet he failed to systematically spell out the subtle relationships among roles, and how their interaction influenced behavioral variation in the gang. In his discussion of conflict and fighting, he tends to lump together different forms of conflict like gang fighting, family feuds, and warfare among adult criminal gangs, as if they were the same kind of behavior. Thus he fails to 'conceptualize the difference between conflict which is carried out as one of the focal activities of the gang, and conflict which is functional to other purposes.'[32]

# Fighting Gangs

Around 1946 in the city of New York a number of apparently senseless killings were carried out by juvenile gangs. A 'detached worker program', in which trained workers are sent into depressed neighborhoods to contact and work with gangs, was begun, and the New York City Youth Board has continued this work with juvenile gangs.[33] The material on gangs gathered by the Youth Board and reported in *Reaching the Fighting Gang* distinguishes four types of groups.

One type tends to emerge and develop around a particular location such as a street corner or candy store; its members grow up together and occasionally engage in collective activities. There is very little anti-social behavior among them and they seldom fight other gangs. A second type is usually associated with a social-athletic club; members engage in sports, but these groups seldom fight other groups although individual members may fight occasionally. The third type is what the Youth Board calls the group in conflict, the fighting gang. The organization for fighting varies

---

31 Gerald D. Robin, 'Gang Member Delinquency in Philadelphia,' in Malcolm W. Klein (ed.), in collaboration with Barbara G. Myerhoff, *Juvenile Gangs in Context*, Englewood Cliffs, New Jersey: Prentice-Hall, Inc., 1967, 23.

32 Thrasher, *The Gang*, (abridged edition with a New Introduction by James F. Short, Jr.), xxii.

33 *Reaching the Fighting Gang*, New York City Youth Board, 1960; Walter Bernstein, 'The Cherubs are Rumbling,' *The New Yorker*, Sept. 21, 1957; C.K. Meyers, *Light the Dark Streets*, Greenwich, Conn.: Seabury Press, 1957; P.C. Crawford, D.I. Mulamud and J.R. Dumpson, *Working with Teen-Age Gangs*, New York Welfare Council, 1950; S.V. Jones, 'The Cougars—Life with a Brooklyn Gang,' *Harper's*, Vol. 209, Nov. 1954; an early work on gangs was written by Herbert Asbury, *The Gangs of New York*, New York: Alfred A. Knopf, 1928.

among these gangs, and members engage in a variety of anti-social acts; fighting between gangs occurs, and often the boys are armed and extremely violent. The fourth group is the thoroughly delinquent or 'pathological' type; usually it consists of a small number of boys who are especially difficult for detached workers to work with.

The street or fighting gangs were found typically in 'high hazard' neighborhoods, depressed areas full of poverty and overcrowded with slum dwellings where social disorganization is the norm, adult hostility is high and there are few recreational facilities. Living in a milieu of violence, anxiety, and fear, where adult crime is widespread, boys learned quickly to think of violence as a normal quality of daily living, and at a young age delinquency was regarded as part of everyday life.[34]

Gang members ranged in age from twelve to twenty-two years, and their ethnic composition often reflected the ethnic population of their neighborhoods. These gangs were typically organized vertically or horizontally. Vertical organization was along age lines with a large gang having attached tenuously to it, different age groups, e.g., 'Tots' (eleven to thirteen years), 'Juniors' (thirteen to fifteen years) and 'Seniors' (seventeen years and over). When gang members moved to other parts of the city they sometimes maintained their membership in the gang; this form of horizontal organization sometimes included divisions of youths from different neighborhoods.

It is important to remember that the organization of these fighting gangs was loose, variable and tenuous; whatever coordination of roles developed remained intact only for a limited period of time. Membership was continually shifting, and the size of gangs was unstable. Intra-group friction was frequent, and continuously developing factions within the gang disturbed its cohesiveness, so that at times the 'group forms and dissolves in rapid succession.'[35] Furthermore, the autocracy of leadership and the constant baiting and verbal infighting among members, produced an emotionally unstable climate where fighting often erupted.

More recently Yablonsky reported on fighting gangs.[36] He found that the organization of what he called the violent gang was very unclear. Internal aggression, conflict, and hostility characterized relationships among members. The continual fluctuation in

---

34  See for example, *Reaching the Fighting Gang,* 17; Clifford R. Shaw, *The Jack-Roller,* 47-56; Rogers, *Street Gangs in Toronto,* 43-64.

35  *Reaching the Fighting Gang,* 12-60.

36  Lewis Yablonsky, "The Violent Gang," New York: The Macmillan Company, 1962.

membership gave it a 'chameleonlike quality', and since the violent gang maintained a 'state of partial organization', Yablonsky used the term 'near group' to highlight its fluid group qualities.[37] Yablonsky also found that gang members were generally sociopathic personalities, and that the most disturbed boys were the core members and leaders. He suggested that violent activities of these gangs were an especially satisfactory means of adjustment for gang members.[38]

# Delinquent Subcultures

The work of Albert K. Cohen does not deal specifically with the social organization of juvenile gangs. However, his general theoretical perspective on the emergence of subcultures, and the delinquent subculture in particular, has resulted in a body of systematically related statements about deliquent subcultures and gangs, and has stimulated a number of empirical studies.

In his book *Delinquent Boys: The Culture of the Gang,* Cohen was concerned primarily with three problems.[39] The major theoretical problem was to account for cultural innovation, i.e. the emergence of subcultures. He posed the question: 'How is it possible for cultural innovations to emerge while each of the participants in the culture is so powerfully motivated to conform to what is already established?'[40] We have already noted his general statement that, 'The crucial condition for the emergence of new cultural forms is the existence, *in effective interaction with one another, of a number of actors with similar problems of adjustment.* '[41] The second problem was based on the methodological premise that the 'explanation of any phenomenon consists of the demonstration that it conforms to a general theory applicable to all phenomena of the same class.'[42] His task was to explain the delinquent subculture as a special case of his general statement on subcultures.

---

37  Lewis Yablonsky, 'The Delinquent Gang as a Near-Group,' *Social Problems,* Vol. 7, 1959, 108-117; Yablonsky, *The Violent Gang,* 222-233.

38  Unfortunately Yablonsky resorts to a psychological explanation of violence among gangs and, as Kobrin notes, he offers little independent evidence to substantiate his notion that gang members are 'sociopaths.' See Solomon Kobrin's review of Lewis Yablonsky, "The Violent Gang," *American Sociological Review,* Vol. 28, 1963, 316-317.

39  Albert K. Cohen, *Delinquent Boys,* Glencoe, Illinois: The Free Press, 1955; Albert K. Cohen and James F. Short, Jr., 'Research in Delinquent Subcultures,' *The Journal of Social Issues,* Vol. 14, 1958, 20-37.

40  Cohen, *Delinquent Boys,* 59.

41  *Ibid.,* 59.

42  Cohen and Short, *Research in Delinquent Subcultures,* 20.

Cohen describes the delinquent subculture (which does not include all juvenile crime) as non-utilitarian, malicious, negativistic, versatile, and hedonistically oriented. He says that much of the stealing by delinquents is not for gain, but for 'the hell of it'; that there is a kind of 'malice apparent' in their delinquencies; they delight in defying the rules themselves, and their behavior is considered right precisely because it is wrong by the standards of the larger society. Cohen's third problem was to account for the regular distribution of delinquency in the working-class areas of large cities, and to explain in particular its cultural content, i.e., its malicious, negativistic and non-utilitarian qualities.

The status of people derives from how they stand in the eyes of others, especially those others who are important to them. For young people, the school situation is where many of their social rewards are located and where most of their evaluation by others takes place. Customarily, high schools are institutions where middle-class standards tend to prevail, and they are staffed by middle-class persons with middle-class values and perspectives. These standards subsume such things as academic ability, high levels of achievement, verbal fluency, the ability to delay gratification for long-run goals, and the typical middle-class criteria of good behavior.

If most young people are judged according to middle-class standards it means that working-class youths continuously find themselves in unfair competition for status and social recognition. Working-class boys are poorly equipped to compete with middle-class youths in what are essentially middle-class games played in middle-class institutions. A damaging consequence for working-class youths is that they are deprived of status in school, and in most other walks of middle-class life. Because they cannot measure up to the 'middle-class measuring rod' they are more likely to experience daily humiliation, failure, and social disapproval. As Cohen writes, '. . . they are caught up in a game in which others are typically the winners and they are the losers and alsorans.'[43] At every turn they are deprived of status. This is their *common problem of adjustment.*

But options are available to them. They may withdraw from the middle-class game and 'break clean with middle-class morality'; they can set up their own game with their own rules in which they are better equipped to participate. The theft and destruction

---

43   Albert K. Cohen, *Deviance and Control,* Englewood Cliffs, New Jersey: Prentice-Hall, Inc., 1966, 65.

of property, and the violation of middle-class norms and values is precisely such a game. Besides, is not the middle class, with its middle-class 'measuring rod', the cause of their status deprivation? However, delinquency is not approached in one fell swoop.

Cultural innovation, in this case the delinquent subculture, covers a wide range of exploratory acts and its emergence is likely to be tentative, uncertain and ambiguous, and to proceed in small probing steps. Each person's act triggers the responses of others which are clues to the direction in which change may proceed. Through 'mutual exploration and joint elaboration' the process proceeds in acts so small that the final product is a joint compromise, a 'real emergent on a group level.'[44]

But there is a further problem with which these boys must contend. Implicit in the Cohen theory is the considerable internalization of middle-class norms and values by working-class youths. This means that engaging in delinquent practices violates the dominant values and norms that one has already internalized. However, the violation of strongly felt norms and values generates guilt and provokes feelings of anxiety. One major device for overcoming anxiety is reaction formation, an exaggerated, abnormally strong response that is inappropriate to the stimulus that evoked the anxiety. Regardless of the "unintelligibility of the response, the 'over-reaction' becomes intelligible when we see that is has the function of reassuring the actor against an *inner* threat to his defenses as well as the function of meeting an external situation on its own terms."[45] Not content with stealing objects these youths destroy them in the process; seldom do they steal merely for profit. They flout their thefts, and gleefully defy middle-class norms and values. Their primary target is the property of the middle classes. This behavior assures the boys that resurgence of those internalized norms and values that threaten their choice of delinquency will not occur, and simultaneously assuages their sense of guilt.[46] Having recourse to the reaction-formation concept, Cohen is able to explain the malicious, non-utilitarian and negativistic qualities of the behavior.

We have noted already that the delinquent subculture is a viable solution to the status deprivation of working-class boys. Cohen suggests that the delinquent response operates best when it is a group solution. It provides these youths with others like themselves who support their actions, share their attitudes and who provide them with moral reinforcement when they experi-

---

44  Cohen, *Delinquent Boys*, 61.

45  *Ibid.*, 133.

46  However, empirical evidence does not support the reaction-formation

ence doubt about their conduct. Most important, the delinquent subculture provides them with criteria for status according to which they are successful against all comers. The major cost for participating in the delinquent subculture is that their social status is limited to their fellow delinquents only.

His theory accounts for the location of the delinquent subculture in the working-class sectors of urban areas, and helps explain its particular cultural qualities. It should be noted that these qualities (maliciousness, negativism and non-utilitarianism) comprise a common core of elements that are shared by subcultural variants. This means that the delinquent subculture is of the 'garden variety' from which other subcultural types have their structural and cultural roots.[47] It is also true that the theory does not deny to these youths alternative solutions to their common problems of status deprivation. For example, not all boys become delinquent. Some become corner boys; they grow up, get jobs and live out their lives, unmotivated and defeated, in working-class areas. A few manage the college route and become a 'success', but this is a rough road, and the possibility of failure looms large along the way.

An important question remains: does the theory account for any of these alternative solutions? A telling criticism and the major shortcoming is that it fails to inform us why a particular choice is made. Why do some boys become delinquent, and others corner boys? Why don't all boys take the college route?[48]

# Subcultural Variety

Daily accounts of what was happening in the urban ghettos of big cities undermined the notion of a single delinquent subculture, and suggested instead, subcultural variety. The theoretical perspective of Richard A. Cloward and Lloyd E. Ohlin is in the Merton and Cohen tradition, and is something of an extension of

---

hypothesis. See James F. Short, Jr. and Fred L. Strodbeck, *Group Process and Gang Delinquency*, Chicago: The University of Chicago Press, 1965, 72-76; Albert J. Reiss, Jr. and Albert L. Rhodes, 'Delinquency and Social Class Structures,' *American Sociological Review*, Vol. 26, 1961, 729-730.

47  Cohen and Short, *Research in Delinquent Subcultures*, 24-33.

48  David J. Bordua, 'Some Comments on Theories of Group Delinquency,' *Sociological Inquiry*, Vol. 32, 1962, 245-260; other criticisms can be found in John I. Kitsuse and David C. Dietrick, 'Delinquent Boys: A Critique,' *American Sociological Review*, Vol. 24, 1959, 208-215; Harold L. Wilensky and Charles N. Lebeaux, *Industrial Society and Social Welfare*, New York: Russell Sage Foundation, 1958, 187-207.

this perspective.[49] It sees deviance resulting from the uneven distribution of legitimate and illegitimate opportunities for reaching culturally preferred goals in society. It emphasizes the lack of fit between the cultural and social structures in society. Specifically, it notes that lower-class youth are blocked in their access to legitimate opportunities for attaining success goals which leads to their intense feelings of frustration. Under such conditions they are likely to seek alternative routes. At this point Cloward and Ohlin add a new theoretical twist to their proposal. They suggest that illegitimate opportunities are also unevenly distributed in the system, and this strongly influences the kinds of alternative solutions or delinquent subcultures that develop.[50] In effect, it is the differential social organization of certain sectors of society that facilitates the learning and performance of delinquent activities and the growth of delinquent subcultures.[51]

In areas where organized crime and some forms of professional crime are accepted and established, and where conventional and criminal values overlap, big-time criminals often occupy differential positions in conventional groups. Criminals serve as role models for neighborhood delinquents, and personal contacts with criminals increase boys' prestige in the eyes of their peers. It is in these communities where a *criminal subculture* takes hold. Technical skills, loyalty, dependability, intelligence and hard work—characteristics of the successful businessman—are highly valued among adult criminals, and resident delinquents are aware of this. Violence is deplored, and adult criminals use their power to maintain a quiet and stable community. The systematic learning of criminal techniques and norms is achieved through the integration of different age levels of boys. Experiences with criminals, fences, the police, politicians, and other adults whose activi-

---

49  See Robert K. Merton, *Social Theory and Social Structure,* (revised and enlarged edition), New York: The Free Press, 1967, 131-194. For a sound review of work done with the concept of anomie see Marshall B. Clinard (ed.), *Anomie and Deviant Behavior,* New York: The Free Press of Glencoe, 1964.

50  Richard A. Cloward and Lloyd E. Ohlin, *Delinquency and Opportunity,* Illinois: The Free Press of Glencoe, 1960. Richard A. Cloward, 'Illegitimate Means, Anomie, and Deviant Behavior,' *American Sociological Review,* Vol. 24, 1959, 164-176.

51  For a critical examination of the concept of illegitimate opportunity, read Cohen, *Deviance and Control,* 109-111. The structure of opportunity and the actor's response to it in anomie theory is examined in processual terms by Albert K. Cohen, 'The Sociology of the Deviant Act: Anomie Theory and Beyond,' *American Sociological Review,* Vol. 30, 1965, 9-14; also Cohen, *Deviance and Control,* 111-113. See also Cloward and Ohlin, *Delinquency and Opportunity,* 145-147.

ties straddle the criminal and conventional worlds, are the crucial sources of folklore and learning for young adults. Adult criminals and structures make opportunities available for achieving success, and boys often aspire to acceptance by and in them and work towards it.

According to these writers, different social conditions produce subcultural variation. In areas characterized by population movement, changing land use, and the continual dispersal of traditional residents, organizational stability is badly stunted. There is little organized effort to achieve cooperation in the community and this general instability precludes adults from exercising effective control over youngsters. Minimal integration of criminal and conventional values hinders the stable establishment of criminal groups. Crime is sporadic, criminal careers seldom flourish, and very few criminal roles exist for youths to emulate. Neither legitimate nor illegitimate opportunities are available for success, and the relative absence of conventional controls allows violence to erupt. Such conditions give rise to the *conflict subculture*—a subculture of fighting gangs, where toughness and violence are major criteria for achieving a 'rep.' and where the values of courage, honor and the defense of the gang are prized. For these boys violence is congruent with their early home and street socialization, and provides an outlet for their status frustration and lack of opportunities.

Young adults who cannot make it successfully in the conventional world or in either the criminal or gang-oriented worlds often become detached from the remainder of society, and retreat into a small world of their own. This is the *retreatist-subculture*— a world dominated by a search for intense, sensuous experiences. It is a drug-ridden world of street cats, where the careful presentation of a cool sophisticated front is, in reality, an anxiety-ridden guise to camouflage the bleak prospects of being hooked on drugs.[52]

The conception of the delinquent subculture carries with it the notion of dedication and commitment by its members to the subcultural norms and values. According to these writers, membership in a delinquent subculture is a full-time-consuming activity that infuses the lives of gang boys.[53] The inexorable constraint on gang boys to participate in delinquent practices is mirrored in the criteria for gang membership suggested by Cloward and Ohlin.

---

52  See Alfred R. Lindesmith and John Gagnon, 'Anomie and Drug Addiction,' in Clinard, *Anomie and Deviant Behavior*, 180-181.

53  Read David Matza, *Delinquency and Drift*, New York: John Wiley & Sons, Inc., 1964, 1-64.

They write that a delinquent subculture is one in which certain forms of delinquent activity are essential requirements for the performance of the dominant roles supported by the subculture. Delinquent behavior is required as a 'demonstration of eligibility for membership or leadership status.'[54] However, empirical research has yet to discover juvenile gangs where such stringent criteria prevail. As Matza writes' . . . the subculture of delinquency itself is a synthesis between convention and crime, and . . . the behavior of many juveniles, . . . is influenced but not constrained by it.'[55] Nor is there any evidence of the highly specialized types of delinquent subculture suggested by these writers. For example, Spergel described in considerable detail three types of subculture which he metaphorically termed Racketville, Slumtown and Haulburg plus a drug-using form of adaptation, but in no instance did he uncover a dominant delinquent subculture that precluded the presence of other delinquent patterns.[56] In *Racketville* youths experienced pressure to employ the criminal means that were available to them. Varied forms of illegal enterprise, like loan-sharking rackets, gambling and policy flourished, which provided criminal learning opportunities for youths. Conventional and criminal orientations and values overlapped, and the highly integrated neighborhood facilitated the use of interpersonal networks as a way of achieving success goals via illegitimate means.[57] *Slumtown* was a deteriorated area, where youths were very restricted in either legitimate or illegitimate opportunities for economic success and social mobility. Conventional and adult criminal groups were minimally related, and there was limited integration of different age groups. The values and expectations of honor, courage and fighting skills loomed large, and the ability to achieve and maintain a reputation as a gang fighter was strongly valued. In *Haulburg* Spergel found an area where avenues to conventional and criminal success goals were partially closed. Semi-organized criminal activities offered youths some limited opportunity for success. Haulburg was mainly a subculture of theft;[58] youths engaged in shoplifting, burglary, forgery and theft of automobiles

---

54   Cloward and Ohlin, *Delinquency and Opportunity*, 7.

55   Matza, *op. cit.*, 47-48.

56   Irving Spergel, *Racketville, Slumtown, Haulburg*, Chicago: The University of Chicago Press, 1964.

57   The integration of conventional and criminal value systems is examined in Solomon Kobrin, 'The Conflict of Values in Delinquency Areas,' *American Sociological Review*, Vol. 16, 1951, 653-661.

58   In this regard compare the 'instrumental-theft' patterns that characterize gangs in Córdoba, Argentina. See Lois B. DeFleur, *Delinquency in Argentina: A Study of Córdoba's Youth*, Washington State University Press, 1970, 141-146.

and scooters; some boys were quite skilled in stealing techniques, but in general, thefts were neither well planned nor carefully executed, and seldom did an entire group engage in robbery.

Spergel also located a drug-using pattern of adaptation. This was not an exclusive subculture, but a type of response used by older adolescents and young adults to help overcome certain social class and role pressures. Sometimes these young persons were no longer acceptable to delinquent groups and they turned to drugs to ease their transition to adult status. This was not a retreatist subculture, since drug users often held conventional or criminal jobs in the neighborhood in order to obtain money to support their habit and thereby 'remained at least partially integrated with both conventional and criminal systems.'[59]

Another study has highlighted a fighting gang's conspicuous striving for status and visibility.[60] This visibility was achieved in the neighborhood by resorting to conflict and violence, and the gang's reputation in the community 'rested solely on their accomplishments as fighters.'[61] Nearly all juvenile gangs are versatile in their illegal activities. This gang was no different. Besides violence, their depredations included theft, strong-arm robbery and burglary. The group, which contained a large number of low-status Mexicans, was characterized by 'swagger, assaultiveness and recklessness.' However, fluctuation and inconsistency characterized their activities as a group, and gang members seldom participated in an activity as an entire group.

Behavioral versatility in crime and delinquency is typical of big-city juvenile gangs.[62] But this should not surprise us; these are gangs of adolescents and young adults, and technical specialization in criminal skills takes time, practice and discipline—qualities that are not likely encouraged in these areas. These slum-infested sectors are rough places in which to grow up. The realization of highly preferred cultural goals is severely restricted for these youths. Moreover, these boys often come from broken homes, and their early socialization, both in the family and on the streets, is of little help in meeting the standards for achievement in society. These are sectors where smalltime hoodlums and petty criminals

---

59  Spergel, *op. cit.,* 62.

60  Solomon Kobrin, Joseph Puntil, and Emil Peluso, 'Criteria of Status Among Street Gangs' in James Short, Jr., (ed.), *Gang Delinquency and Delinquent Subcultures,* New York: Harper and Row, Publishers, 1968, 178-208.

61  Short, *Gang Delinquency and Delinquent Subcultures,* 185.

62  Thrasher, *The Gang* (abridged edition), 1968. See also James Short, Jr., Ray A. Tennyson and Kenneth I. Howard, "Behavior Dimensions of Gang Delinquency," *American Sociological Review,* Vol. 28, 1963, 411-428.

are permanent residents, 'policy' is a household word[63] and the presence of differentially oriented criminal subcultures further complicates the likelihood of these boys becoming a success in the conventional world. Theft is common, widespread, and utilitarian in these sectors; burglary, robbery, shoplifting, and purse snatching are also common practices. Yet it is true that not all boys engage in theft activities.[64]

The evidence suggests that on all fronts lower-class gang boys are losers, and they are faced with strong feelings of status frustration.[65] Not only are they blocked from occupational advancement and social mobility in the larger society, but they perceive few opportunities for improving their lot.[66] Even when they try to become serious about conventional middle-class matters like assuming responsible family relationships, they are derided by gang members.[67] Moreover, their harsh everyday experiences are not likely to encourage realistic hopes. They lack technical skills, their academic performance is typically low, and their relatively narrow range of social experiences and role-playing opportunities outside of the gang hinder the development of satisfactory social skills and role-playing abilities for most non-gang situations. Thus, the peer group assumes crucial importance as a source of status.[68] The

---

63 Policy, 'numbers' or 'bolita' are different names for a highly organized 'protected' gambling enterprise that operates in defiance of the law. The player bets that he can guess what three digit number like 2-7-9 will come up in a predetermined tabulation, e.g., the total amount of money taken in at a particular race track on a given day. Players bet as little as a quarter and sometimes as much as ten dollars. Usually they have one chance in a thousand to win; winning numbers are paid at odds of about 500 to 1. See Donald R. Cressey, *Theft of a Nation,* New York: Harper & Row, Publishers, 1969, 134-139; St. Clair Drake and Horace Cayton, " 'Policy': Poor Man's Roulette" in Robert D. Herman (ed.), *Gambling,* New York: Harper & Row, Publishers, 1967, 3-10.

64 Walter B. Miller, "Theft Behavior in City Gangs," in Klein and Myerhoff, *Juvenile Gangs in Context,* 37.

65 Short and Strodbeck, *Group Process and Gang Delinquency,* 230-234.

66 *Ibid.,* 268-269. See also Delbert S. Elliott, "Delinquency and Perceived Opportunity," *Sociological Inquiry,* Vol. 32, 1962, 216-227.

67 See James F. Short, Jr., "Social Structure and Group Processes in Explanation of Gang Delinquency," in Muzafer Sherif and Carolyn W. Sherif (eds.), *Problems of Youth: Transition to Adulthood in a Changing World,* Chicago: Aldine Publishing Company, 1965, 173-174; James F. Short, Jr., Fred L. Strodbeck and Desmond S. Cartwright, "A Strategy for Utilizing Research Dilemmas: A Case from the Study of Parenthood in a Street Corner Gang," *Sociological Inquiry,* Vol. 32, 1962, 192-193.

68 Short and Strodbeck, *Group Process and Gang Delinquency,* 217-247. Social disability does not characterize all boys' gangs. In some Chicano communities it is a code of personal honor and a network of rules regulating interpersonal propriety (the violation of which must be defended) that helps sustain the traditions of fighting gangs. See Ruth Horowitz and Gary Schwartz, "Honor,

group norms and values generate means and methods of achievement which are not prescribed in the conventional society.[69] The gang becomes the immediate audience for most of their activities, and is the most immediate source of rewards and punishments. As a result, gang boys spend considerable time with each other, and become dependent on gang relationships and contacts for psychological support and interpersonal gratification.[70]

But these gangs lack formal structure, and so are unstable and unable to provide any kind of firm support to gang members. Moreover, they are neither sufficiently dependable nor cohesive to properly satisfy the social and interpersonal needs of their members. Ghettos do not breed feelings of trust and respect for one's fellow man. Socialization in lower-class sectors very likely produces a general feeling of suspicion and distrust of everyone; this wariness seems to spill over into gang relationships. Daily life on the streets is often intense, and includes persistent verbal and physical aggression among gang members,[71] in the form of verbal baiting and insults, e.g., 'playing the dozens', 'playing house', 'sounding', 'signifying', kidding and physical roughhousing, a function of which is to gain status at the expense of others.[72] This produces a climate of intense concern for status management among members. These kinds of daily intra-group activities are extremely stressful, requiring that boys possess the capacity for intimate, intense, persistent interaction, and only boys who can meet the criteria for this intense interaction remain gang members. Thus, daily gang activities are a selective mechanism for gang

Normative Ambiguity and Gang Violence," *American Sociological Review*, Vol. 39, 1974, 238-251.

69   Short, "Social Structure and Group Processes in Explanation of Gang Delinquency," in Sherif and Sherif, *Problems of Youth: Transition to Adulthood in a Changing World*, 161.

70   Of course Thrasher was aware of this years ago. See Thrasher, *The Gang*, (abridged edition with a New Introduction by James F. Short, Jr.,) 1968. Also see Tannenbaum, *Crime and the Community*, 8-11.

71   Miller, *Lower Class Culture as a Generating Milieu of Gang Delinquency*, 14-15; also Miller, Geertz and Cutter, "Aggression in a Boys' Street-Corner Group" in Short, *Gang Delinquency and Delinquent Subcultures*, 56-78; Spergel, *Racketville, Slumtown, Haulburg*, 80.

72   The street-corner hanging activities of gang members are characterized by the continuous systematic exchange of insults. Variations include obscene remarks about the family members of opponents. The idea is to counter the insult with a more insulting remark. This activity is a form of social control; it enables boys to display their verbal virtuosity, and requires hair-trigger responsiveness to be successful. Ralph F. Berdie, "Playing the Dozens," *The Journal of Abnormal and Social Psychology*, Vol. 42, 1947, 120-121. For an examination of the functions of these games, see Matza, *Delinquency and Drift*, 52-55.

membership.[73] There also prevails an undercurrent of aggression and hostility in gang relationships. Admittedly, close ties between boys do develop, but the precarious nature and crucial significance of status within the gang means that 'one is subject to challenge from many quarters,' and the threat exists that 'one may have to prove one's self against his closest friend' at any time.[74] It may be that involvement in delinquency is a compensatory means of overcoming these accumulated stresses and anxieties of daily living on the streets. Moreover, gang fights and violence directed against other gangs, serve temporarily to knit gang members against a common enemy.[75]

In some neighborhoods fighting seems to be a 'full-time preoccupation' in the effort to achieve and maintain a 'rep.'[76] The demonstration of 'heart' which signifies toughness and daring is all important to these boys. "To be called a 'guy' who has 'heart' symbolized the achievement of the sought-after ultimate goal."[77] Although fighting is important for the gang and gang members, it occupies only a small fraction of a boy's time; yet fighting does not occur without rhyme or reason, as a spontaneous outburst of aggression. At the same time, boys are ambivalent towards violence since they are fully aware that they may be seriously injured. Nevertheless, it is likely that gang rules encourage 'the suppression of squeamishness;' boys put up a tough front and usually are ready to defend turf and reputation.[78]

The size of gangs is variable,[79] and although the history of some gangs is part of the neighborhood folklore, there is little or no evidence that these gangs are coordinated rationally to attain exclusively criminal goals, or that there is agreement among gang

---

73  Miller, *Lower-Class Culture as a Generating Milieu of Gang Delinquency,* 14.

74  Short and Strodbeck, *Group Process and Gang Delinquency,* 233. Miller suggests insightfully that expressions of affection between 'tough' males in these areas are disguised as their opposite, and take the form of "ostensibly aggressive verbal and physical interaction (kidding, 'ranking,' roughhousing, etc.)." Read Miller, *Lower Class Culture as a Generating Milieu of Gang Delinquency,* 9.

75  Short, "Social Structure and Group Processes in Explanation of Gang Delinquency," in Sherif and Sherif, *Problems of Youth: Transition to Adulthood in a Changing World,* 162-185.

76  Spergel, *op. cit..* 43; Kobrin, Puntil and Peluso, "Criteria of Status Among Street Groups," in Short, *Gang Delinquency and Delinquent Subcultures;* Miller, *Lower Class Culture as a Generating Milieu of Gang Delinquency.* 16-17. For a fictional account read Warren Miller, *The Cool World.* Greenwich, Connecticut: Fawcett Publications, 1964.

77  Spergel, *op. cit.,* 43.

78  Cohen and Short, *Research in Delinquent Subcultures,* 25.

79  It was Yablonsky who exploded the myth of the multi-divisioned, tightly organized, fighting gang among young adults. Read Yablonsky, *The Violent Gang,* 4-110.

members about common goals. Nor is there any evidence that these gangs resemble the kinds of criminally-oriented subcultures hypothesized by Cloward and Ohlin. For example, in one technically sophisticated project the workers failed 'to locate a full blown criminal group, or more than one drug-using group, despite [their] highly motivated effort to do so . . . .'[80] The only full-fledged group exclusively organized towards a criminal activity— theft—was a clique of eight boys who were also members of a larger group. In their street activities they engaged in the regular round of drinking and hanging patterns, but they did not participate as a distinguishable unit. 'Only in their pattern of theft activities were they a clique.'[81] This clique operated successfully for two years; their planned criminal affairs resembled 'semi-professional' theft, but in no way did they approximate a fully developed criminal subculture.[82]

In fighting-oriented gangs it is the relatively tenuous, hierarchical organization of roles that reflects their conflict and fighting orientation. These gangs often have positions such as president, vice-president, war counsellor and so on. Some groups have quite clearly established functionaries, but in most gangs these positions are informal, and are more expressive than instrumental; role obligations are seldom specific, and tasks remain unclear. Yet these roles are another basis for acquiring status; there is a kind of 'ceremonial deference' that surrounds these roles; boys covet these positions and sometimes compete for them.[83]

These gangs are not homogeneous nor is there necessarily strong norm commitment except, for example, in individual and group status-threatening kinds of situations.[84] Conflict-oriented gangs are usually fluid, relatively loose entities. Membership is constantly changing, boys come and go, and there is no established method of keeping track of members; unless they are leaders they are seldom missed. Fighting and violence are differentially distributed among gangs. Some gangs seem to thrive on inter-gang fighting and violent activities. Other gangs seem less dependent on violence and gang fighting for their reputations. Much of the everyday activities of gang boys involve the effort to achieve, in-

---

80  Short and Strodbeck, *Group Process and Gang Delinquency*, 13.

81  Short, Tennyson and Howard, *Behavior Dimensions of Gang Delinquency*, 426-427.

82  *Ibid.*, 427; Cohen and Short, *Research in Delinquent Subcultures*, 27-28.

83  Short and Strodbeck, *Group Process and Gang Delinquency*, 200.

84  Short, Strodbeck and Cartwright, *A Strategy for Utilizing Research Dilemmas: A Case from the Study of Parenthood in a Street Corner Gang*, 185-202; Short and Strodbeck, *Group Process and Gang Delinquency*, 206-207; Matza, *Delinquency and Drift*, 33-67.

crease, or guard their hardwon status within the gang. This is notably true of gang leaders whose positions are precarious at best, and are often being challenged. Usually it is the core members, especially the leaders, who engage in fighting and violence. Thus, violence among these boys is best seen developing in a situation where there is a threat to one's personal status or the status of the gang.

It has been suggested that participation in violent encounters is not necessarily a result of a hedonistically-oriented definition of the situation. Rather a boy may engage in a rational evaluation of the circumstances, i.e., he will 'size up the situation' in which he finds himself.[85] While recognizing the importance of not losing status within the gang, they simultaneously recognize that varying kinds of violence are societally prohibited, and contain the possibility of apprehension and incarceration. Thus, a boy likely considers the risk of 'joining the action', and getting caught and sent to prison, and calculates this against the near certainty of the immediate loss of status in the eyes of important others for failure to participate. It seems likely that a boy rationally assesses, on the basis of previous experiences and neighborhood knowledge, the odds of the most serious outcome occurring. A decision to join the action is understandable given the remote probability of the most serious outcome occurring, i.e., getting caught and jailed. It is not necessarily true that delinquents always desire violent action, but a boy will run the risk of these undesired outcomes because the rewards and probabilities associated with the gamble seem, from his point of view, to outweigh the disadvantages. Boys gamble, and sometimes they lose.[86]

However, encounters between members of different gangs in fact seldom erupt into serious violence. There is more likely an exchange of taunts, threats of attack, and name-calling. Members play it tough, talk a good fight, and sometimes lay plans for violence; neither side backs down nor gives ground. Thus, there are no losers in these confrontations. Such episodes are often sufficient to elate gang members; they confer status on both gangs and temporarily stimulate cohesion within them. When fights do erupt, they are usually short lived; often they are more 'humbug' than anything else—skirmishes that are relatively unimportant and

---

85  What follows is based on the insightful analysis by Short and Strodbeck, *Group Process and Gang Delinquency,* 248-264; Short, Strodbeck and Cartwright, *A Strategy for Utilizing Research Dilemmas: A Case from the Study of Parenthood in a Street Corner Gang,* 198-201.

86  Short and Strodbeck, *Group Process and Gang Delinquency,* 251.

quickly brought under control.[87] Once the status of the gang is maintained, and the reputations and images of individual members are untarnished, nothing is felt to be lost.[88] Neither side perceives itself as a loser.

---

87   James F. Short, Jr., and Fred L. Strodbeck, "Why Gangs Fight," in Short, *Gang Delinquency and Delinquent Subcultures,* 249-250. See also Short and Strodbeck, *Group Process and Gang Delinquency,* 203-207.

88   Short and Strodbeck, *Group Process and Gang Delinquency,* 202.

# Conclusion

In conclusion we ought to say something about the social control of deviance, the various processes and structures, both formal and informal, that operate to prevent, reduce or otherwise temper the amount of deviance occurring. These processes may be manifestly organized and socially understood by the man on the street as the prevailing mechanisms for the control of deviance, e.g., the police, probation officers, judges and the law courts. These are the structures whose main job it is to do something about deviance, especially about crime and delinquency. However, this is only part of the apparatus of social control.

Most social control goes largely unnoticed in society.[1] As persons organize their lives so do they regulate their activities. Social control is implicit in the ways of men and women, and it is a built-in aspect of their social organization.[2] This is because the interdependence, exchange and complementary needs that exist among people are satisfied according to established ways. When one member of the group departs from the accepted way of doing things it usually affects other members adversely, and deviance is met with resistance in one form or another.[3] This implies that the kinds of controls operating will partly reflect the

---

1  Harry M. Johnson, *Sociology: A Systematic Introduction*, New York: Harcourt, Brace & World, Inc., 1960, 581.

2  George C. Homans, *The Human Group*, New York: Harcourt, Brace and Company, 1950, 281-312.

3  Homans, *op. cit.*, 282; Harry C. Bredemieir and Richard M. Stephenson, *The Analysis of Social Systems*, New York: Holt, Rinehart and Winston, Inc., 1962, 167.

kinds of social organization by which persons govern themselves. Informal controls operate primarily where social interaction is face to face, but in a complex, formal milieu more complicated controlling mechanisms are required.

The high rate of failure in our efforts to systematically reduce or otherwise control crime and delinquency does not reflect so much our lack of knowledge as it does the quality of the knowledge that we possess, and the problems seemingly inherent in implementing control programs. Admittedly, we have accumulated considerable knowledge about the determinants of crime and delinquency in society, yet our theories are of limited help since they are scarcely more than relatively systematic perspectives on different kinds of deviant behavior. The variables, and their interrelationships are enormously complex, their operationalization often arbitrary and always less than exact. Also, the values of the variables remain unknown to us, which precludes their precise manipulation. Thus, at this stage we cannot rely too heavily on our theories as valid explanations of criminal conduct. Moreover, since there is no obvious step from a theory of deviant behavior to the deliberate means for its control, the implications of our theories for the reduction of deviance are not necessarily a reliable basis for action.

But there are other problems to be overcome. There is the tendency to equate deviance with evil, and conformity with good. Even if it were possible, it is highly doubtful whether it would be wise to eliminate all forms of deviance from society.[4] Both deviance and conformity are functional for society, and contribute to its stability. Moreover, it may be that some forms of deviance, like juvenile delinquency, serve as a valuable safety value for the large majority of youngsters, and that the elimination of delinquency, like the elimination of prostitution, would generate more serious problems.[5] This means that we cannot disavow all forms of deviance and support every instance of conformity. Both deviance and conformity must be examined and judged according to the social costs that they exact and the contributions that they make to the society. It is important always to specify what kind of deviance is being tackled, e.g., white-collar crime, organized crime, delinquent gangs, fraud, prostitution. We have noted already that not all kinds of deviance are equally costly to society. In comparison with organized crime, prostitution, smoking pot and most forms

---

4   Richard A. Cloward, "The Prevention of Delinquent Subcultures: Issues and Problems," in John R. Stratton and Robert M. Terry (eds.), *Prevention of Delinquency*, New York: The Macmillan Company, 1968, 287.

5   Stratton and Terry, *Prevention of Delinquency*, 1968.

of juvenile delinquency pall into insignificance. The questions are: under what circumstances, at what cost, and at the neglect of what other problems does society wish to deal with a particular form of deviance?[6]

Our knowledge of deviance always comes in packages of complex variables and factors. It is the varying combinations of these variables that determine the amount and kinds of deviance that occur. This suggests that different programs for preventing deviance may be undertaken at different points in the social structure. For example, we may focus our attention on the social branding and segregation (sometimes termed rehabilitation) of deviants, in order to prevent them from contaminating others with their behavior and attitudes, e.g., by incarcerating them in lock-ups, jails, reformatories and penitentiaries. A second alternative is to try and improve the 'treatment' of criminals, which suggests that criminals are sick persons who are best handled by psychiatrists, psychologists and social workers. Another possibility is to initiate a large-scale program designed to eliminate certain kinds of deviants, e.g., an intensive police crackdown on prostitutes, or dealers in hard drugs. We may wish to legislate more repressive laws like mandatory long-term sentences without parole for narcotics offenders. Or, in line with a prominent sociological theory of delinquent gangs, we may wish to distribute more equitably the legitimate means of success, so that those who are economically and socially deprived can get a better deal from life.[7] Of course, there are other possibilities as well.

Each point of intervention requires, very likely, its own form of social organization, technical skills, and resources. One problem is to establish what form of organization, and what kinds of skills are best suited for the prevention program being implemented. A further problem is to establish whether our concepts are amenable to practical manipulation. There is also the task of generating agreement among the various groups in the community that are differentially responsible and involved in deviance control. Their organizational and ideological differences are reflected often in their conflicting attitudes towards continuing programs of deviance prevention. If such programs are to be successful these con-

---

6  Edmund Vaz, "Deviance and Conformity: The Issue of Marihuana Use," in Dennis Forcese and Stephen Richer (eds.), *Issues in Canadian Society: An Introduction to Sociology,* Scarborough, Ontario: Prentice-Hall of Canada, Ltd., 1975, 337.

7  Read Richard A. Cloward and Lloyd E. Ohlin, *Delinquency and Opportunity,* Illinois: The Free Press Co., Glencoe, 1960. Also read Albert K. Cohen, *Deviance and Control,* Englewood Cliffs, New Jersey: Prentice-Hall, Inc., 1966, 37-40.

flicting perspectives must be overcome, and harmonious relationships sustained among them.[8] Ironically, any new group that becomes involved in such programs usually has a still newer set of attitudes and perspectives, and becomes a further source of potential conflict.

An important question is who is going to foot the bill for controlling deviance in society? It is seldom the tally in dollars that pinches most. Were programs for the reduction of deviance to involve a major upheaval in the social structure, i.e., the transformation of people's lives, it is the cost in attitudes, sentiments, and values, and the disruption of established life-styles that people would be unwilling to pay. But this should not surprise us. Deviants, especially those who are publicly labeled, seldom rank high among those who warrant our special consideration, and we are not prone to sacrifice ourselves on their account. However well-meaning our intentions it is difficult to see how this will change much.

Instead of structural surgery, we resort usually to a band-aid approach to the problem. We increase the number of psychiatrists, psychologists and social workers, introduce guidance and counseling officers in high schools and universities, or develop special youth branches of police departments; we may open 'free schools' where youths can do more or less as they please, or we may construct differentially open reformatory systems. Sometimes, in cases where the deviance is widespread, e.g., smoking pot, drinking, car theft or sexual behavior, and involves large numbers of middle and upper middle-class youths, we might change or modify the laws. What was criminally prohibited yesterday becomes legally acceptable today; for example, we lower the drinking age to 18 years, or we reduce the penalty for first or second offenders of the marijuana laws, or when the rate of car thefts increases rapidly, we recognize a new category of car theft termed 'joy-riding' which calls for a lesser penalty. Similarly, in such instances we usually attempt to educate the public. These educational programs may include courses given in high schools, television programs, special films, or government pamphlets and brochures. In the long run nothing much changes; the rates of crime and delinquency remain relatively constant, with minor fluctuations attributable to gradual transformations in the social structure. If

8   Walter B. Miller, "Inter-institutional Conflict as a Major Impediment to Delinquency Prevention," in Stratton and Terry (eds.), *Prevention of Delinquency,* 120-127. also LaMar T. Empey, "Crime Prevention: The Fugitive Utopia," in Daniel Glaser (ed.), *Handbook of Criminology,* Chicago: Rand McNally College Publishing Co., 1974, 1103-1104.

there is a considerable change it is due usually to changes in the criminal code.

With our present level of knowledge, we can never be altogether certain whether our programs of deviance control do more good than harm. We can seldom anticipate the undesirable side effects of our intervention.[9] In our efforts to control the vices of men and women, and thereby create a better society, we sometimes enact more repressive laws. Rather than tempering our vices, this usually creates a larger population of criminals. For example, in the United States, the Prohibition Era which was begun by the adoption of the Eighteenth Amendment in 1920, spawned a large-scale, criminally organized liquor industry, and a vast network of speakeasies that provided outlawed liquor on demand. Moreover, efforts to enforce the Eighteenth Amendment were a colossal failure.[10] In a more recent context the strategy of sending street workers into high delinquency areas to work with tough gangs of adolescent youths backfires occasionally, and breeds unexpected violence. Gangs that do not acquire an attached worker become envious, and attack those gangs that do have social workers. By displaying such violence these gangs attempt to indicate their need for an attached worker.[11]

At all times in evaluating the success of programs of deviance control the costs as well as the results must be considered. The question arises as to whether our efforts at reducing deviance really make a difference in the quantity and quality of deviance occurring. With respect to the reduction of crime and juvenile delinquency our efforts have been less than encouraging. There is one thing only of which we can be certain—whatever changes occur are due to a multiplicity of variables acting concurrently.[12] Should there result from our program an appreciable reduction in deviance, we can never be sure what aspects of the program caused the change, and secondly, whether such change in the rates and amount of deviance might not have occurred without our intervention.

---

9   Cohen, *Deviance and Control*, 37-40. We have relied somewhat on Cohen's work in this section.

10   James A. Inciardi, "Vocational Crime," in Daniel Glaser (ed.), *Handbook of Criminology*, Chicago: Rand McNally College Publishing Company, 1974, 363-364.

11   Reported in Johnson, *Sociology: A Systematic Introduction*, 584, based on the work of Walter B. Miller, "The Impact of a Community Group Work Program on Delinquent Corner Groups," *Social Service Review*, Vol. 31, no. 4, 1957, 390-406. Recently a full-fledged anti-VD campaign was undertaken in Saskatchewan. The result was that an image emerged of Saskatchewan as a hotbed of the disease. The *Kitchener-Waterloo Record*, Tue., June 17, 1975.

12   Cohen, *Deviance and Control*, 37-40.

Like all social behavior our responses to deviance are never willy-nilly, but are normatively regulated. This implies that those groups and agencies responsible for the control and prevention of deviance are themselves likely to break rules in the course of their duties. Neither formal nor informal control agents are special kinds of people, nor are they immune to the forces and processes operating to produce deviance in society. Therefore, we should not be surprised when we hear of the cruelty of parents towards their children, of the viciousness of prison guards and the staffs of correctional institutions towards their inmates, or of the immorality of priests. Nor should we be shocked to learn of corruption among our law enforcement agencies, that inspectors and politicians as well as judges can be bribed, that cheating, malingering, favoritism and wickedness are found among the institutions designed to watch over us. As Albert K. Cohen suggests ' . . . we have travelled full circle and are confronted with the problem of the social control of the agencies of control.' The question is: 'Who will guard the guardians?'[13]

---

13  *Ibid* ., 40.

# Selected Bibliography

AHLSTROM, WINTON A. and ROBERT J. HAVIGHURST. *400 Losers.* San Francisco: Jossey-bass, Inc., Publishers, 1971.

AKERS, R. "Socio-economic Status and Delinquent Behavior: A Retest," *Journal of Research in Crime and Delinquency,* Vol. 1, 1964.

AMIR, MENNACHEM. "Patterns of Forcible Rape," in Marshall B. Clinard and Richard Quinney (eds.), *Criminal Behavior Systems.* New York: Holt, Rinehart and Winston, Inc., 1967.

ARNOLD, WILLIAM R. "Continuities in Research: Scaling Delinquent Behavior," *Social Problems,* Vol. 13, No. 1, 1965.

ASBURY, HERBERT. *The Gangs of New York: An Informal History of the Underworld.* New York: Alfred A. Knopf, 1928.

BALL, DONALD W. "The Problematics of Respectability," in Jack D. Douglas (ed.), *Deviance and Respectability: The Social Construction of Moral Meanings.* New York: Basic Books, 1970.

BALTZELL, E. DIGBY. *An American Business Aristocracy.* New York: Collier Books, 1962.

BARBER, BERNARD. *Social Stratification: A Comparative Analysis of Structure and Process.* New York: Harcourt, Brace and Company, 1957.

BARBER, BERNARD B. and ALEX INKELES (eds.). *Stability and Social Change.* Boston: Little, Brown and Company, 1971.

BARTH, ALAN. *The Price of Liberty.* New York: The Viking Press, 1961.

BASS, RICHARD. "Montreal's Homosexual Community: Why It Is Different," in H. Taylor Buckner (ed.), *Urban Life Styles: St. Catherine Street—Friday Night.* Unpublished collection of papers, Department of Sociology, Concordia University, 1972.

BECKER, HOWARD S. "Notes on the Concept of Commitment," *The American Journal of Sociology,* Vol. 66, 1960.

————. *Outsiders: Studies in the Sociology of Deviance.* New York: The Free Press of Glencoe, 1963.

————. "Review of Mary Owen Cameron, 'The Booster and the Snitch'," *The American Journal of Sociology,* Vol. 70, March, 1965.

BECKER, HOWARD S. (ed.). *The Other Side.* New York: The Free Press of Glencoe, 1964.

BECKER, HOWARD S. et. al. (eds.). *Institutions and the Person.* Chicago: Aldine Publishing Company, 1968.

BELL, DANIEL. "Crime as an American Way of Life," *The Antioch Review,* Summer, 1953.

BELL, ROBERT R. *Social Deviance.* Homewood, Illinois: The Dorsey Press, 1971.

BENSMAN, JOSEPH and ISRAEL GERVER. "Crime and Punishment in the Factory: The Function of Deviancy in Maintaining the Social System," *American Sociological Review,* Vol. 28, 1963.

BERDIE, RALPH F. "Playing the Dozens," *The Journal of Abnormal and Social Psychology,* Vol. 42, 1947.

BERNSTEIN, WALTER. "The Cherubs are Rumbling," *The New Yorker,* Sept. 21, 1957.

BERGER, PETER L. *Invitation to Sociology.* Garden City, New York: Doubleday and Company, 1963.

BIDERMAN, A.D. et al. "Report on a Pilot Study in the District of Columbia on Victimization and Attitudes Toward Law Enforcement, Field Surveys 1," *President's Commission on Law Enforcement and Administration of Jus-*

*tice.* Washington, D.C.: U.S. Government Printing Office, 1967.

BLACK, DONALD J. "Police Control of Juveniles," *American Sociological Review,* Vol. 35, 1970.

BLACK, DONALD J. and ALBERT J. REISS, JR. "Patterns of Behavior in Police Citizen Transactions," Section 1 of *Studies of Crime and Law Enforcement in Major Metropolitan Areas,* Vol. 11. Washington, D.C.: U.S. Government Printing Office, 1967.

BLACKSTOCK, HARVEY. *Bitter Humour.* Toronto: Burns and MacEachern Ltd., 1967.

BLOCH, HERBERT H. and GILBERT GEIS. *Man, Crime and Society* (2nd edition). New York: Random House, 1970.

BLOCH, HERBERT and ARTHUR NIEDERHOFFER. *The Gang: A Study in Adolescent Behavior.* New York: Philosophical Library, 1958.

BLUMER, HERBERT. *The World of Youthful Drug Use.* Berkeley, California: School of Criminology, University of California, 1967.

BOHLKE, R. "Social Mobility, Stratification Inconsistency and Middle-Class Delinquency," *Social Problems,* Vol. 8, 1961.

BOLES, JACQUELINE and A.P. GARBIN. "Stripping for a Living: An Occupational Study of the Night Club Stripper," in Clifton D. Bryant, *Deviant Behavior: Occupational and Organizational Bases.* Chicago: Rand McNally Publishing Company, 1974.

BORDUA, DAVID J. "Recent Trends: Deviant Behavior and Social Control," *The Annals of the American Academy of Political and Social Science,* Vol. 369, 1967.

————. "Some Comments on Theories of Group Delinquency," *Sociological Inquiry,* Vol. 32, 1962.

BOYDELL, CRAIG L. "Public Opinion and the Criminal Law: An Empirical Test of Public Attitudes Toward Legal Sanctions," in Craig L. Boydell, Carl F. Grindstaff and Paul C. Whitehead (eds.), *Deviant Behavior and Societal Reaction.* Toronto: Holt, Rinehart and Winston of Canada, 1972.

BOYDELL, CRAIG L. and CARL F. GRINDSTAFF. "Public Attitudes Toward Legal Sanctions for Drug and Abortion Offences," *The Canadian Journal of Corrections,* Vol. 13, 1971.

BOYDELL, CRAIG L., CARL F. GRINDSTAFF and PAUL C. WHITEHEAD (eds.). *Deviant Behavior and Societal Reaction.* Toronto: Holt, Rinehart and Winston of Canada, 1972.

BRECHER, EDWARD M. and Editors of the Consumers Reports. *Licit and Illicit Drugs.* Mount Vernon, New York: Consumers Union, 1972.

BRIM, ORVILLE G. JR. and STANTON WHEELER. *Socialization After Childhood: Two Essays.* New York: John Wiley & Sons, 1966.

BRYAN, JAMES H. "Apprenticeships in Prostitution," *Social Problems,* Vol. 12, 1965.

————. "Occupational Ideologies and Individual Attitudes of Call Girls," in Earl Rubington and Martin S. Weinberg (eds.), *Deviance: An Interactionist Perspective.* New York: The Macmillan Company, 1968.

BRYANT, CLIFTON D. *Deviant Behavior: Occupational and Organizational Bases.* Chicago: Rand McNally Publishing Company, 1974.

BUCKNER, H. TAYLOR. *Deviance, Reality and Change.* New York: Random House, 1971.

BUCKNER, H. TAYLOR. (ed.). *Observations on the Normalization of Cannabis.* Unpublished collection of papers, Department of Sociology, Concordia University, 1972.

————. *Urban Life Styles: Observations in Montreal—'72.* Unpublished collection of papers, Department of Sociology, Concordia University, 1972.

———. *Urban Life Styles: St. Catherine Street—Friday Night.* Unpublished collection of papers, Department of Sociology, Concordia University, 1972.

BURKE, KENNETH. *Permanence and Change.* Indianapolis: The Bobbs-Merrill Company, Inc., 1965.

CAMERON, MARY OWEN. *The Booster and the Snitch: Department Store Shoplifting.* New York: The Free Press of Glencoe, 1964.

CAPLOW, THEODORE. *Principles of Organization.* New York: Harcourt, Brace and World, Inc., 1964.

CASPARIS, JOHN and EDMUND W. VAZ. "Social Class and Self-Reported Delinquent Acts among Swiss Boys," *International Journal of Comparative Sociology,* Vol. 14, No. 1-2, 1974.

CHAMBLISS, WILLIAM J. and ROBERT B. SEIDMAN. *Law, Order and Power.* Reading, Massachusetts: Addison-Wesley Publishing Co., 1971.

CHAMBLISS, BILL (ed.). *Box Man.* New York: Harper and Row Publishers, 1972.

CHIMBOS, PETER D. "Some Aspects of Organized Crime in Canada: A Preliminary Review," in W.E. Mann (ed.), *Social Deviance in Canada.* Toronto: The Copp Clark Publishing Company, 1971.

CLAIRMONT, DONALD H. and DENNIS WILLIAM MAGILL. *Africville: The Life and Death of a Canadian Black Community.* Toronto: McClelland and Stewart Limited, 1974.

CLARK, JOHN P. and EUGENE P. WENNINGER. "Socio-Economic Class and Area as Correlates of Illegal Behavior Among Juveniles," *American Sociological Review,* Vol. 27, 1962.

CLINARD, MARSHALL. *The Black Market.* New York: Rinehart and Company, 1952.

CLINARD, MARSHALL B. (ed.). *Anomie and Deviant Behavior.* New York: The Free Press of Glencoe, 1964.

CLINARD, MARSHALL B. and RICHARD QUINNEY (eds.). *Criminal Behavior Systems.* New York: Holt, Rinehart and Winston, Inc., 1967.

CLOWARD, RICHARD A. "Illegitimate Means, Anomie and Deviant Behavior," *American Sociological Review,* Vol. 24, 1959.

CLOWARD RICHARD A. and LLOYD E. OHLIN. *Delinquency and Opportunity.* Glencoe, Illinois: The Free Press, 1960.

COHEN, ALBERT K. *Delinquent Boys.* Glencoe, Illinois: The Free Press, 1955.

———. "Deviant Behavior and Its Control," in Talcott Parsons (ed.), *American Sociology.* New York: Basic Books, 1968.

———. *Deviance and Control.* Englewood Cliffs, New Jersey: Prentice-Hall, Inc., 1966.

———. "Social Control and Subcultural Change, *"Youth and Society,* Vol. 3, 1972.

———. "The Sociology of the Deviant Act: Anomie Theory and Beyond," *American Sociological Review,* Vol. 30, 1965.

———. "The Study of Social Disorganization and Deviant Behavior," in Robert K. Merton, Leonard Broom and Leonard S. Cottrell (eds.), *Sociology Today: Problems and Prospects.* New York: Basic Books, 1959.

COHEN, ALBERT K. and JAMES F. SHORT, JR. "Juvenile Delinquency," in Robert K. Merton and Robert A. Nisbet (eds), *Contemporary Social Problems.* New York: Harcourt, Brace and World, Inc., 1961.

———. "Research in Delinquent Subcultures," *The Journal of Social Issues,* Vol. 14, No. 3, 1958.

COHEN, STANLEY (ed.). *Images of Deviance.* Middlesex, England: Penguin Books Ltd., 1971.

COLEMAN, JAMES. *The Adolescent Society.* New York: The Free Press, 1961.

CONKLIN, JOHN E. *The Impact of Crime.* New York: Macmillan Publishing Co., Inc., 1975.

CONKLIN, JOHN E. (ed.). *The Crime Establishment.* Englewood Cliffs, New Jersey: Prentice-Hall, Inc., 1973.

CONNOR, WALTER, D. "The Manufacture of Deviance: The Case of the Soviet Purge 1936–1938," *American Sociological Review,* Vol. 37, 1972.

COOK, SHIRLEY J. "Canadian Narcotics Legislation, 1908–1923: A Conflict Model Interpretation," *The Canadian Review of Sociology and Anthropology,* Vol. 6, No. 1, 1969.

COOLEY, CHARLES H. *Human Nature and the Social Order.* New York: Charles Scribner's Sons, 1902.

COPELAND, CLIVE L. and NORRIS A. McDONALD. "Prostitutes are Human Beings: An Unorganized Counter-Institution," in H. Taylor Buckner, *Deviance, Reality and Change.* New York: Random House, 1971.

COUSINEAU, D.F. and J.E. VEEVERS. "Incarceration as a Response to Crime: The Utilization of Canadian Prisons," *The Canadian Journal of Corrections,* Vol. 14, No. 1, 1972.

CRAWFORD, P.C., D.I. MULMUD and J.R. DUMPSON. *Working with Teen-Age Gangs.* New York Welfare Council, 1950.

CRESSEY, DONALD R. *Criminal Organization: Its Elementary Forms.* London: Heinemann Educational Books, Ltd., 1972.

———. "Delinquent and Criminal Structures," in Robert K. Merton and Robert Nisbet (eds.), *Contemporary Social Problems.* New York: Harcourt, Brace Jovanovich, Inc., 1971.

———. *Other People's Money.* Glencoe, Illinois: The Free Press, 1953.

———. *Theft of the Nation.* New York: Harper and Row, Publishers, 1969.

CRESSEY, DONALD R. (ed.). *Crime and Criminal Justice.* Chicago: Quadrangle Books, 1971.

DAVIS, ALAN J. "Sexual Assaults in the Philadelphia Prison System," in John Gagnon and William Simon (eds.), *The Sexual Scene.* Aldine Publishing Company, 1970.

DAVIS, KINGSLEY. *Human Society.* New York: Macmillan Company, 1949.

———. "Prostitution," in Robert K. Merton and Robert Nisbet (eds.), *Contemporary Social Problems.* New York: Harcourt, Brace and World, Inc., 1961.

DeFLEUR, LOIS B. *Delinquency in Argentina.* Washington State University Press, 1970.

DENTLER, R.A. and K.T. ERIKSON. "The Functions of Deviance in Groups," *Social Problems,* Vol. 7, 1959.

DENTLER, ROBERT A. and LAWRENCE J. MONROE. "Social Correlates of Early Adolescent Theft," *American Sociological Review,* Vol. 26, No. 5, 1961.

DESROCHES, FRED. "Regional Psychiatric Centres. A Myopic View," *Canadian Journal of Criminology and Corrections,* Vol. 15, 1973.

———. "Patterns in Prison Riots," *Canadian Journal of Criminology and Corrections,* Vol. 16, 1974.

DOBRINER, WILLIAM M. *Social Structures and Systems.* Pacific Palisades: Goodyear Publishing Company, 1969.

DOUGLAS, JACK D. *The Social Meanings of Suicide.* Princeton, New Jersey: Princeton University Press, 1973.

DOUGLAS, JACK D. (ed.), *Deviance and Respectability: The Construction of Moral Meanings.* New York: Basic Books, 1970.

DOWNES, DAVID. *The Delinquent Solution: A Study in Subcultural Theory.* New York: The Free Press of Glencoe, 1966.

DRAKE, ST. CLAIR and HORACE CAYTON. " 'Policy': Poor Man's Roulette," in Robert D. Herman (ed.), *Gambling.* New York: Harper and Row, Publishers, 1967.

DURKHEIM, EMILE. *The Division of Labor,* (trans. by George Simpson). Glencoe, Illinois: The Free Press, 1949.

———. *The Rules of Sociological Method,* (trans. by Sarah A. Solvay and John H. Mueller, and edited by George E.G. Catlin). Glencoe, Illinois: The Free Press, 1950.

———. *Suicide,* (trans. by John A. Spaulding and George Simpson). Glencoe, Illinois: The Free Press, 1951.

ENNIS, P.H. "Criminalization in the United States: A Report of a National Survey," *A Report of a Research Study Submitted to The President's Commission on Law Enforcement and Administration of Justice.* Washington, D.C.: U.S. Government Printing Office, 1967.

ERICKSON, MAYNARD L. and LAMAR T. EMPEY. "Court Records, Undetected Delinquency, and Decision-Making," in Donald R. Cressey and David A. Ward (eds.), *Delinquency, Crime and Social Process.* New York: Harper and Row, Publishers, 1969.

ERIKSON, K.T. "Notes on the Sociology of Deviance," *Social Problems,* Vol. 9, 1962.

ERIKSON, KAI T. *Wayward Puritans: A Study in the Sociology of Deviance.* New York: John Wiley and Sons, Inc., 1966.

FALLDING, HAROLD. *The Sociological Task.* Englewood Cliffs, New Jersey: Prentice-Hall, Inc., 1968.

FAULKNER, ROBERT R. *Violence, Camaraderie, and Occupational Character in Hockey.* Unpublished paper, Department of Sociology, University of Massachusetts, 1971.

FINESTONE, HAROLD. "Cats, Kicks and Color," *Social Problems,* Vol. 5, 1957.

FOOTE, NELSON N. "Identification as the Basis for a Theory of Motivation," *American Sociological Review,* Vol. 16, 1951.

FRIEDSON, ELIOT. "Visibility as Social Deviance," in Marvin Sussman (ed.), *Sociology and Rehabilitation.* American Sociological Association with the Rehabilitation Administration, U.S. Department of Health, Education and Welfare, 1965.

GAGNON, JOHN H. and WILLIAM SIMON (eds.). *The Sexual Scene.* Chicago: Aldine Publishing Company, 1970.

GANDY, JOHN M. "The Exercise of Discretion By The Police as a Decision-Making Process in the Disposition of Juvenile Offenders," *Osgoode Hall Law Journal,* Vol. 8, 1970.

GARFINKEL, HAROLD. "Conditions of Successful Degradation Ceremonies," *The American Journal of Sociology,* Vol. 61, 1956.

GARDNER, JOHN A. and DAVID J. OLSON. "Wincanton: The Politics of Corruption," in *Task Force Report: Organized Crime.* The President's Commission on Law Enforcement and Administration of Justice. Washington, D.C.: U.S. Government Printing Office, 1967.

GEIS, GILBERT. "The Heavy Electrical Equipment Antitrust Cases of 1961," in Gilbert Geis (ed.), *White-Collar Criminal: The Offender in Business and the Professions.* New York: Atherton Press, 1968.

———. "Violence and Organized Crime," *The Annals of the American Academy of Political and Social Science,* Vol. 364, 1966.

GEIS, GILBERT (ed.). *White-Collar Offender: The Offender in Business and the Professions.* New York: Atherton Press, 1968.

GIBBONS, DON C. *Society, Crime and Criminal Careers.* Englewood Cliffs, New Jersey: Prentice-Hall, Inc., 1973.

GIBBS, J. "Conceptions of Deviant Behavior: The Old and the New," *The Pacific Sociological Review,* Vol. 9, 1966.

GLASER, DANIEL (ed.). *Handbook of Criminology.* Chicago: Rand McNally College Publishing Company, 1974.

GLASER, DANIEL. "Victim Survey Research: Theoretical Implications," in Anthony L. Guenther (ed.), *Criminal Behavior and Social Systems.* Chicago: Rand McNally and Company, 1970.

GLUECK, SHELDON and ELEANOR. *Unraveling Juvenile Delinquency.* Cambridge: Harvard University Press, 1950.

GOFFMAN, ERVING. *Behavior in Public Places.* New York: The Free Press, 1963.

———. *Encounters: Two Studies in the Sociology of Interaction.* The Bobbs-Merrill Company, Inc., 1961.

———. "The Nature of Deference and Demeanor," *American Anthropologist,* Vol. 58, 1956.

———. *The Presentation of Self in Everyday Life.* Edinburgh: University of Edinburgh Social Sciences Research Centre, 1958.

———. *Stigma: Notes on the Management of Spoiled Identity.* Englewood Cliffs, New Jersey: Prentice-Hall, Inc., 1964.

GOLDMAN, NATHAN. *The Differential Selection of Juvenile Offenders for Court Appearance.* National Research and Information Center: National Council on Crime and Delinquency, 1963.

GOODE, WILLIAM J. "Family Disorganization," in Robert K. Merton and Robert Nisbet (eds.), *Contemporary Social Problems.* New York: Harcourt, Brace, Jovanovich, Inc., (3rd edition), 1972.

GOULDNER, ALVIN W. "The Norm of Reciprocity: A Preliminary Statement," *American Sociological Review,* Vol. 25, No. 2, 1960.

GRUTZNER, CHARLES. "Organized Crime and the Businessman," (editor's title), in John E. Conklin (ed.), *The Crime Establishment.* Englewood Cliffs, New Jersey: Prentice-Hall, Inc., 1973.

HAGEN, JOHN J. "The Labelling Perspective, the Delinquent, and the Police: A Review of the Literature," *The Canadian Journal of Corrections,* Vol. 14, 1972.

HALL, JEROME. *Theft, Law and Society.* Indianapolis: The Bobbs-Merrill Co., Inc., 1939.

HARTUNG, FRANK E. *Crime, Law and Society.* Detroit: Wayne State University Press, 1966.

HASKELL, MARTIN R. and LEWIS YABLONSKY. *Crime and Delinquency.* Chicago: Rand McNally College Publishing Company, 1974.

HASSLER, RICHARD M. "Junkies in White: Drug Addiction among Physicians," in Clifton D. Bryant, *Deviant Behavior: Occupational and Organizational Bases.* Chicago: Rand McNally Publishing Company, 1974.

HAWKINS, GORDON. "God and the Mafia," in John E. Conklin (ed.), *The Crime Establishment.* Englewood Cliffs, New Jersey: Prentice-Hall, Inc., 1973.

HILLS, STUART L. *Crime, Power and Morality.* Scranton: Chandler Publishing Company, 1971.

HIRSCHI, TRAVIS. *Causes of Delinquency.* Los Angeles: University of California Press, 1969.

HOFFMAN, MARTIN. *The Gay World.* New York: Basic Books, 1968.

HOMANS, GEORGE C. *The Human Group.* New York: Harcourt, Brace and Company, 1950.

HOOD, ROGER and RICHARD SPARKS. *Key Issues in Criminology.* New York: World University Library, McGraw-Hill Book Company, 1970.

HOROWITZ, RUTH and GARY HOROWITZ. "Honor, Normative Ambiguity and Gang Violence," *American Sociological Review,* Vol. 39, 1974.

HUGHES, EVERETT C. "The Sociological Study of Work: An Editorial Forward," *The American Journal of Sociology,* Vol. 57, March, 1952.

HUMPHREYS, LAUD. *Tearoom Trade.* Chicago: Aldine Publishing Company, 1970.

INCIARDI, JAMES A. "Vocational Crime," in Daniel Glaser (ed.), *Handbook of Criminology.* Chicago: Rand McNally College Publishing Company, 1974.

JACKSON, BRUCE. *Outside the Law: A Thief's Primer.* New Brunswick, New Jersey: Transaction Books, Rutgers University, 1972.

JARVIS, GEORGE K. "Ecological Analysis of Juvenile Delinquency in a Canadian City," in Craig L. Boydell, Carl F. Grindstaff and Paul C. Whitehead (eds.), *Deviant Behavior and Societal Reaction.* Toronto: Holt, Rinehart and Winston of Canada Ltd., 1972.

JOHNSON, HARRY. *Sociology: A Systematic Introduction.* New York: Harcourt, Brace and World, Inc., 1960.

JONES, S.V. "The Cougars—Life with a Brooklyn Gang," *Harper's,* Vol. 209, Nov. 1954.

KADISH, SANFORD H. "Overcriminalization," in Leon Radzinowicz and Marvin E. Wolfgang (eds.), *The Criminal in Society,* (Vol. 1 of *Crime and Society* ). New York: Basic Books, 1971.

KEFAUVER, ESTES. *Crime in America.* Garden City, N.Y.: Doubleday and Company, 1951.

KITSUSE, JOHN I. "Societal Reactions to Deviant Behavior," *Social Problems,* Vol. 9, 1962.

KITSUSE, JOHN I. and AARON V. CICOUREL. "A Note on the Uses of Official Statistics," *Social Problems,* Vol. 11, No. 2, 1963.

KITSUSE, JOHN I. and DAVID C. DIETRICK. "Delinquent Boys: A Critique," *American Sociological Review,* Vol. 24, 1959.

KLEIN, MALCOLM W. (ed.), in collaboration with Barbara G. Myerhoff, *Juvenile Gangs in Context.* Englewood Cliffs, New Jersey: Prentice-Hall, Inc., 1967.

KOBRIN, SOLOMON. "The Conflict of Values in Delinquency Areas," *American Sociological Review,* Vol. 16, 1951.

———. "Review of Lewis Yablonsky, 'The Violent Gang'," *American Sociological Review,* Vol. 28, 1963.

KOBRIN, SOLOMON, JOSEPH PUNTIL and EMIL PELUSO. "Criteria of Status Among Street Gangs," In James F. Short, Jr. (ed.), *Gang Delinquency and Delinquent Subcultures.* New York: Harper and Row Publishers, 1968.

KOCHMAN, THOMAS. "Rapping in the Black Ghetto," *Transaction,* Vol. 6, No. 4, 1969.

KUNDRATS, ULDIS. *Adolescence, Role Commitment and Middle-Class Delinquency.* Unpublished M.A. Thesis, Department of Sociology, University of Waterloo, 1975.

KUPFER, GEORGE. *Middle-Class Delinquency in a Canadian City.* Unpublished Ph.D. Dissertation, University of Washington, 1966.

KVARACEUS, WILLIAM and WALTER B. MILLER. *Delinquent Behavior: Culture and the Individual.* Washington: National Education Association, 1959.

LEMERT, EDWIN M. *Human Deviance, Social Problems, and Social Control.* Englewood Cliffs, New Jersey: Prentice-Hall, Inc., 1967.

———. "Paranoia and the Dynamics of Exclusion," *Sociometry,* Vol. 25, 1962.

———. *Social Pathology.* New York: McGraw-Hill, 1951.

LETKEMANN, PETER. *Crime as Work.* Englewood Cliffs, New Jersey: Prentice-Hall, Inc., 1973.

LEVER, JANET. "Soccer As a Brazilian Way of Life," in Gregory P. Stone ed.), *Games, Sport and Power.* New Brunswick, New Jersey: Transaction Books, E.P. Dutton and Company, 1972.

LEWIS, ARTHUR H. *Carnival.* New York: The Trident Press, 1970.

LIEBOW, ELLIOTT. *Tally's Corner.* Boston: Little, Brown and Company, 1967.

LINDESMITH, ALFRED R. *The Addict and the Law.* Bloomington: Indiana University Press, 1965.

——. *Opiate Addiction.* Evanston, Ill.: The Principia Press of Illinois, (no date).

LINDESMITH, ALFRED R. and JOHN GAGNON. "Anomie and Drug Addiction," in Marshall Clinard (ed.), *Anomie and Deviant Behavior.* New York: The Free Press of Glencoe, 1964.

LINDESMITH, ALFRED R. and ANSELM L. STRAUSS. *Social Psychology* (revised edition). New York: Holt, Rinehart and Winston, 1968.

LIPPMAN, WALTER. "The Underworld as Servant," in Gus Tyler (ed.), *Organized Crime in America.* Ann Arbor: The University of Michigan Press, 1962.

LOFLAND, JOHN. *Deviance and Identity.* Englewood Cliffs, New Jersey: Prentice-Hall, Inc., 1969.

LOWSKY, IRIS. "C'est Un Depart," in H. Taylor Buckner (ed.), *Urban Life Styles: Observations in Montreal—'72.* Unpublished collection of papers, Department of Sociology, Concordia University, 1972.

LUCAS, REX A. *Minetown, Milltown, Railtown.* Toronto: University of Toronto Press, 1971.

LYND, ROBERT S. *Knowledge For What?.* New York: Grove Press, Inc., 1964.

MANN, W.E. (ed.), "Deviant Behaviour in Reformatory," in *Deviant Behaviour in Canada.* Toronto: Social Science Publishers, 1968.

MANN, W.E. and L.G. HANLEY. "The Mafia in Canada," in W.E. Mann (ed.), *Deviant Behaviour in Canada.* Toronto: Social Science Publishers, 1968.

MATZA, DAVID. *Becoming Deviant.* Englewood Cliffs, New Jersey: Prentice-Hall, Inc., 1969.

——. *Delinquency and Drift.* New York: John Wiley and Sons, Inc., 1964.

MATZA, DAVID and GRESHAM M. SYKES. "Juvenile Delinquency and Subterranean Values," *American Sociological Review,* Vol. 26, No. 5, 1961.

MAURER, DAVID W. *Whiz Mob.* New Haven, Conn.: College and University Press, 1964.

MAZUR, ALAN and S. ROBERTSON. *Biology and Social Behavior.* New York: The Free Press, 1972.

MCCAGHY, CHARLES H. and JAMES K. SKIPPER, JR. "Lesbian Behavior as an Adaptation to the Occupation of Stripping," in Clifton D. Bryant, *Deviant Behavior: Occupational and Organizational Bases.* Chicago: Rand McNally Publishing Company, 1974.

MCDONALD, LYNN. "Crime and Punishment in Canada: A Statistical Test of the 'Conventional Wisdom'," *Canadian Review of Sociology and Anthropology,* Vol. 6, 1969.

MCINTOSH, MARY. "Changes in the Organization of Thieving," in Stanley Cohen (ed.), *Images of Deviance.* Middlesex, England: Penguin Books Ltd., 1971.

MCKITRICK, ERIC L. "The Study of Corruption," in Seymour M. Lipset and Neil J. Smelser (eds.), *Sociology: The Progress of a Decade.* Englewood Cliffs, New Jersey: Prentice-Hall, Inc., 1961.

MCMULLAN, JOHN. "Suburbia in Transition: Patterns of Cannabis Use and Social Control in a Suburban Community," in H. Taylor Buckner (ed.), *Observations on the Normalization of Cannabis.* Unpublished collection of papers, Department of Sociology, Concordia University, 1972.

MEAD, GEORGE HERBERT. *Mind, Self and Society.* Chicago: University of Chicago Press, 1934.

MERTON, ROBERT K. *Social Theory and Social Structure.* New York: The Free Press (revised edition), 1967.

MERTON, ROBERT K. and ROBERT NISBET (eds.). *Contemporary Social Problems.* New York: Harcourt, Brace and World, Inc., 1961.

———. *Contemporary Social Problems* (3rd edition). New York: Harcourt, Brace Jovanovich, Inc., 1971.

MESSERSCHMIDT, BRIAN. *Sociological Analysis of the Rostick Juvenile Fastball Team.* Term paper submitted for Sociology 101 course, Department of Sociology, University of Waterloo, April, 1975.

MILLER, WALTER B. "The Impact of a Community Group Work Program on Delinquent Corner Groups," *Social Service Review,* Vol. 31, No. 4, 1957.

———. "Inter-institutional Conflict as a Major Impediment to Delinquency Prevention," in John R. Stratton and Robert M. Terry (eds.), *Prevention of Delinquency.* New York: The Macmillan Company, 1968.

———. "Lower Class Culture as a Generating Milieu of Gang Delinquency," *Journal of Social Issues,* Vol. 14, No. 3, 1958.

———. "Theft Behavior in City Gangs," in Malcolm W. Klein (ed.), *Juvenile Gangs in Context.* Englewood Cliffs, New Jersey: Prentice-Hall, Inc., 1967.

———. "Violent Crimes in City Gangs," *The Annals of the American Academy of Political and Social Science,* Vol. 364, March, 1966.

MILLER, WALTER B, HILDRED GEERTZ and HENRY S.G. CUTTER. "Aggression in a Boys' Street-Corner Group," in James F. Short, Jr. (ed.), *Gang Delinquency and Delinquent Subcultures.* New York: Harper and Row Publishers, 1968.

MILLER, WARREN. *The Cool World.* New York: Fawcett Publications, 1964.

MILLS, C. WRIGHT. *The Power Elite.* New York: Oxford University Press, 1957.

———. "Situated Actions and Vocabularies of Motive," *American Sociological Review,* Vol. 5. No. 6, 1940.

MURPHY, FRED J., MARY M. SHIRLEY and HELEN L. WITMER. "The Incidence of Hidden Delinquency," *American Journal of Orthopsychiatry,* Vol. 16, 1964.

MYERS, G.K. *Light The Dark Streets.* Greenwich, Conn.: Seabury Press, 1957.

MYERS, GUSTAVUS. *History of the Great American Fortunes,* Vol. 1, Chicago: Charles H. Kerr and Co., 1910.

NEASE, BARBARA. "Measuring Juvenile Delinquency in Hamilton," in Craig L. Boydell, Carl F. Grindstaff and Paul C. Whitehead (eds.), *Deviant Behaviour and Societal Reaction.* Toronto: Holt, Rinehart and Winston of Canada Ltd., 1972.

NETTLER, GWYNN. *Explaining Crime.* New York: McGraw-Hill Book Company, 1974.

PACKER, H.L. *The Limits of the Criminal Sanction.* Stanford: Stanford University Press, 1968.

PAGE, GARY S. "Social Nudism: The Social Organization of Southern Ontario Nudist Camps," in W.E. Mann (ed.), *Social Deviance in Canada.* The Copp Clark Publishing Company, 1971.

PARSONS, TALCOTT. *Essays in Sociological Theory Pure and Applied.* Glencoe, Illinois: The Free Press, 1949.

———. *The Social System.* Glencoe, Illinois: The Free Press, 1951.

PARSONS, TALCOTT (ed.), *American Sociology.* New York: Basic Books, 1968.

PILEGGI, NICOLAS. "The Year of the Burglar," in Clifton D. Bryant (ed.), *Deviant Behavior: Occupational and Organizational Bases.* Chicago: Rand McNally College Publishing Company, 1974.

PILIAVIN, IRVING and SCOTT BRIAR. "Police Encounters with Juveniles," *The American Journal of Sociology,* Vol. 70, No. 2, 1964.

PLIMPTON, GEORGE. *Mad Ducks and Bears.* New York: Bantam Books, 1974.

POLSKY, NED. *Hustlers, Beats and Others.* Chicago: Aldine Publishing Company, 1967.

PORTER, JOHN. *The Vertical Mosaic.* Toronto: University of Toronto Press, 1966.

PORTERFIELD, AUSTIN L. *Youth in Trouble.* Fort Worth: The Leo Potishman Foundation, 1946.

QUINNEY, RICHARD. "Occupational Structure and Criminal Behavior: Prescription Violation by Retail Pharmacists," *Social Problems,* Vol. 11, 1963.

RADZINOWICZ, LEON and MARVIN E. WOLFGANG. (eds.), *Crime and Justice* (3 vols.). New York: Basic Books, 1971.

*Reaching the Fighting Gang.* New York City Youth Board, 1960.

REISS, ALBERT J. JR., "The Social Integration of Queers and Peers." *Social Problems,* Vol. 9, 1961.

REISS, ALBERT J. JR., and ALBERT L. RHODES. "The Distribution of Juvenile Delinquency in the Social Class Structure," *American Sociological Review,* Vol. 26, No. 5, 1961.

*Report of the Honourable Mr. Justice Wilfred D. Roach as a Commissioner Appointed Under The Public Inquiries Act by Letters Patent,* Dec. 11, 1961.

ROBIN, GERALD D. "Gang Member Delinquency in Philadelphia," in Malcolm W. Klein (ed.), in collaboration with Barbara G. Myerhoff, *Juvenile Gangs in Context.* Englewood Cliffs, New Jersey: Prentice-Hall, Inc., 1967.

ROGERS, KENNETH H. *Street Gangs in Toronto.* Toronto: The Ryerson Press, 1945.

ROSENBERG, BERNARD and HARRY SILVERSTEIN. *The Varieties of Delinquent Experience.* Waltham, Massachusetts: Blaisdell Publishing Co., 1969.

ROSS, HERMAN R. *Juvenile Delinquency in Montreal.* Unpublished Master's Thesis, Department of Sociology, McGill University, 1932.

ROTH, LORNA. "The Olympic Player: A Study of Pool Hall Regulars," in H. Taylor Buckner (ed.), *Urban Life Styles: St. Catherine Street—Friday Night.* Unpublished collection of papers, Department of Sociology, Concordia University, 1972.

RUBINGTON, EARL and MARTIN S. WEINBERG (eds.). *Deviance: An Interactionist Perspective.* New York: The Macmillan Company, 1968.

SALISBURY, HARRISON E. *The Shook-Up Generation.* Greenwich, Conn.: Fawcett Publications, 1958.

SALUTIN, MARILYN. "Stripper Morality," in Craig Boydell, Carl F. Grindstaff and Paul C. Whitehead (eds.), *Deviant Behaviour and Societal Reaction.* Toronto: Holt, Rinehart and Winston of Canada, 1972.

SCHEFF, THOMAS J. *Being Mentally Ill: A Sociological Theory.* Chicago: Aldine Publishing Company, 1966.

SCHUR, EDWIN. *Crimes Without Victims.* Englewood Cliffs, New Jersey: Prentice-Hall, Inc., 1965.

———. *Labeling Deviant Behavior.* New York: Harper and Row, Publishers, 1971.

SCHWARTZ, LOUIS B. "Morals and the Model Penal Code," in Leon Radzinowicz and Marvin E. Wolfgang (eds.), *The Criminal in Society* (Vol. 1 of *Crime and Justice*). New York: Basic Books, 1971.

SCHWENDINGER, HERMAN and JULIA. "Delinquent Stereotypes of Probable Victims," in Malcolm W. Klein (ed.), in collaboration with Barbara G. Myerhoff, *Juvenile Gangs in Context.* Englewood Cliffs, New Jersey: Prentice-Hall, Inc., 1967.

SCOTT, MARVIN B. *The Racing Game.* Chicago: Aldine Publishing Company, 1968.

SCOTT, ROBERT A. *The Making of Blind Men.* New York: Russell Sage, 1969.

SEELEY, JOHN R., ALEXANDER SIM and ELIZABETH W. LOOSLEY. *Crestwood Heights.* New York: Basic Books, 1956.

SELLIN, THORSTEIN. *Culture Conflict and Crime.* New York: Social Science Research Council, Bulletin No. 41, 1938.

SHANLEY, FRED J. "Middle-Class Delinquency as a Social Problem," *Sociology and Social Research,* Vol. 51, 1965.

SHAW, CLIFFORD R. *The Jack-Roller: A Delinquent Boy's Own Story.* Chicago, Ill.: The University of Chicago Press, 1966.

SHAW, CLIFFORD R. and HENRY D. MCKAY. *Juvenile Delinquency and Urban Areas.* Chicago: The University of Chicago Press, 1942.

———. *Social Factors in Juvenile Delinquency, A Study of the Family, and the Gang in Relation to Delinquent Behavior for the National Commission on Law Observance and Enforcement,* (no date or publisher).

SHORT, JAMES F. JR. "Social Structure and Group Processes in Explanations of Gang Delinquency," in Muzafer Sherif and Carolyn W. Sherif (eds.), *Problems of Youth: Transition to Adulthood in a Changing World.* Chicago: Aldine Publishing Company, 1965.

SHORT, JAMES F. JR. and F. IVAN NYE. "Extent of Unrecorded Juvenile Delinquency: Tentative Conclusions," *The Journal of Criminal Law, Criminology and Police Science,* Vol. 49, No. 4, 1958.

SHORT, JAMES F. JR. and FRED L. STRODBECK. *Group Process and Gang Delinquency.* Chicago: The University of Chicago Press, 1965.

———. "Why Gangs Fight," in James F. Short, Jr. (ed.), *Gang Delinquency and Delinquent Subcultures.* New York: Harper and Row Publishers, 1968.

SHORT, JAMES F. JR., FRED L. STRODBECK and DESMOND S. CARTWRIGHT. "A Strategy for Utilizing Research Dilemmas: A Case from the Study of Parenthood in a Street Corner Gang," *Sociological Inquiry,* Vol. 32, 1962.

SHORT, JAMES F. JR., RAY A. TENNYSON and KENNETH I. HOWARD. "Behavior Dimensions of Gang Delinquency," *American Sociological Review,* Vol. 28, 1963.

SILVERMAN, ROBERT A. and JAMES J. TEEVAN, JR. *Crime in Canadian Society.* Toronto: Butterworth and Co. (Canada) Ltd., 1975.

SIMMONS, J.L. "On Maintaining Deviant Belief Systems," *Social Problems,* Vol. 11, No. 3, 1964.

SKOLNICK, JEROME H. *Justice Without Trial: Law Enforcement in Democratic Society.* New York: John Wiley and Sons, Inc., 1967.

SMART, REGINALD G. and DAVID JACKSON. *A Preliminary Report on the Attitudes and Behavior of Toronto Students in Relation to Drugs.* Toronto: Addiction Research Foundation, 1969.

———. *The Yorkville Subculture: A Study of the Life Styles and Interactions of Hippies and Non-Hippies.* Toronto: Addiction Research Foundation, 1969.

SMART, R., DIANNE FEJER and JIM WHITE. *The Extent of Drug Use in Metropolitan Toronto Schools: A Study of Changes from 1968–1970.* Toronto: Addiction Research Foundation, 1971.

SMELSER, NEIL J. (ed.). *Sociology: An Introduction.* New York: John Wiley and Sons, Inc., 1967.

SMIGEL, ERWIN O. and H. LAURENCE ROSS (eds.). *Crimes Against Bureaucracy.* New York: Van Nostrand Reinhold Co., 1970.

SMITH, RICHARD AUSTIN. "The Incredible Electrical Conspiracy," in Donald R. Cressey and David A. Ward (eds.), *Delinquency, Crime and Social Process.* Harper and Row Publishers, 1969.

SPERGEL, IRVING. *Racketville, Slumtown, Haulburg.* Chicago: The University of Chicago Press, 1966.

STEBBINS, ROBERT A. *Commitment to Deviance.* Westport, Conn.: Greenwood Publishing Corporation, 1971.

STINCHCOMBE, ARTHUR L. "Institutions of Privacy in the Determination of Police Administrative Practice," *The American Journal of Sociology,* Vol. 69, No. 2, 1963.

STONE, GREGORY P. *The Social Significance of Clothing in Occupational Life.* East Lansing: Michigan State College Agricultural Experiment Station, Technical Bulletin 217, June, 1955.

STRATTON, JOHN R. and ROBERT M. TERRY (eds.). *Prevention of Delinquency.* New York: The Macmillan Company, 1968.

SUCHMAN, E.A. "The 'Hang-Loose' Ethic and the Spirit of Drug Use," *Journal of Health and Social Behavior,* Vol. 9, 1968.

SUDNOW, DAVID. "Normal Crimes," *Social Problems,* Vol. 12, 1965.

SUMNER, WILLIAM GRAHAM. *Folkways.* New York: New American Library, 1960 (first published in 1907).

SUTHERLAND, EDWIN H. *The Professional Thief.* Chicago: The University of Chicago Press, 1937.

————. *White-Collar Crime.* New York: Holt, Rinehart and Winston, 1961.

SUTTLES, GERALD D. *The Social Order of the Slum.* Chicago: The University of Chicago Press, 1968.

SYKES, GRESHAM M. *Crime and Society.* New York: Random House, 1956.

SYKES, GRESHAM M. and DAVID MATZA. "Techniques of Neutralization: A Theory of Delinquency," *American Sociological Review,* Vol. 22, 1957.

SZASZ, THOMAS. *The Myth of Mental Illness.* New York: Hoeber-Harper, 1961.

TANNENBAUM, FRANK. *Crime and the Community.* New York: Columbia University Press, 1951.

TERRY, ROBERT M. *The Screening of Juvenile Offenders: A Study in the Societal Reaction to Deviant Behavior.* Unpublished Ph.D. dissertation, University of Southern California, 1963.

THRASER, FREDERICK M. *The Gang.* Chicago: The University of Chicago Press, 1936.

TOBIAS, J.J. *Crime and Industrial Society in the Nineteenth Century.* Middlesex, England: Penguin Books Ltd., 1972.

TURKUS, BURTON B. and SID FEDER. *Murder, Inc.* New York: Farrar, Straus and Young, 1951.

TYLER, GUS (ed.). *Organized Crime in America.* Ann Arbor: The University of Michigan Press, 1962.

VAZ, EDMUND W. "Delinquency and the Youth Culture: Upper and Middle-Class Boys," *The Journal of Criminal Law, Criminology, and Police Science,* Vol. 60, No. 1, 1969.

————. "Deviance and Conformity: The Marihuana Issue," in Dennis Forcese and Stephen Richer (eds.), *Issues in Canadian Society: An Introduction to Canadian Sociology.* Scarborough: Prentice-Hall of Canada Ltd., 1975.

————. "Juvenile Delinquency in the Middle-Class Youth Culture," in Edmund W. Vaz (ed.), *Middle-Class Juvenile Delinquency.* New York: Harper and Row, Publishers, 1967.

————. *The Metropolitan Taxi Driver: His Work and Self Conception.* Unpublished Master's Thesis, Department of Sociology, McGill University, 1955.

————. "Middle-Class Adolescents: Self-Reported Delinquency and Youth Culture Activities," *The Canadian Review of Sociology and Anthropology,* Vol. 2, No. 1, 1965.

————. "The 'Straight' World of Middle-Class High School Kids," in James E. Gallagher and Ronald D. Lambert, *Social Process and Institution: The Canadian Case.* Toronto: Holt, Rinehart and Winston of Canada, Ltd., 1971.

WALLER, IRVIN. *Men Released From Prison.* Toronto: University of Toronto Press, 1974.

WALLERSTEIN, JAMES S. and C.J. WYLIE. "Our Law-Abiding Law Breakers," *Federal Probation,* Vol. 25, 1947.

WEBER, MAX. *The Theory of Social and Economic Organization* (trans. by A.M. Henderson and Talcott Parsons). New York: Oxford University Press, 1947.

WEINBERG, MARTIN S. "Sexual Modesty, Social Meanings, and the Nudist Camp," *Social Problems,* Vol. 12, 1957.

WEST, WILLIAM GORDON. *Serious Thieves: Lower-Class Adolescent Males in a Short-Term Deviant Occupation.* Unpublished Ph.D. Dissertation, Northwestern University, 1974.

WESTLEY, WILLIAM A. *Violence and the Police.* Cambridge, Massachusetts: The MIT Press, 1970.

WESTLEY, WILLIAM A. and FREDERICK ELKIN. "The Protective Environment and Adolescent Socialization," *Social Forces,* Vol. 35, 1957.

WHEELER, STANTON. "Deviant Behavior," in Neil J. Smelser (ed.), *Sociology: An Introduction.* New York: John Wiley and Sons, Inc., 1967.

WHITE, T.H. *The Age of Scandal.* Middlesex, England: Penguin Books, 1963.

WHYTE, WILLIAM FOOTE. *Street Corner Society.* Chicago: The University of Chicago Press, 1964.

WILENSKY, HAROLD L. and CHARLES N. LEBEAUX. *Industrial Society and Social Welfare.* New York: Russell Sage Foundation, 1958.

WILLIAMSON, HENRY. *Hustler.* New York: Doubleday and Company, 1965.

WINICK, CHARLES. "Physician Narcotic Addicts," in Howard S. Becker (ed.), *The Other Side.* New York: The Free Press, 1964.

WISE, NANCY BARTON. *Disregarded Delinquency: A Study of Self-Reported Middle-Class Female Delinquency in a Suburb.* Unpublished Ph.D. Dissertation, Indiana University, 1965.

WOLFGANG, MARVIN E. and FRANCO FERRACUTI. *The Subculture of Violence.* London: Tavistock Publications, 1967.

YABLONSKY, LEWIS. "The Delinquent Gang as a Near-Group," *Social Problems,* Vol. 7, 1959.

————. *The Violent Gang.* New York: The Macmillan Co., 1962.

ZAY, NICOLAS. "Gaps in Available Statistics on Crime and Delinquency in Canada," *Canadian Journal of Economics and Political Science,* Vol. 29, 1963.

# Index

Adams, Ian, 134n
Adulteress
image of, 38
Ahlstrom, Winton A., 56n
Akers, R.L., 103n, 111
Amir, Mennachem, 36n
Arnold, David O., 127n
Arnold, William R., 111
Arond, Henry, 126n
Arrests
factors influencing, 95-98
Asbury, Herbert, 148n
Ball, Donald W., 77n, 125n
Baltzell, E. Digby, 55n
Barber, Bernard, 27n, 35n, 86n
Barth, Alan, 16n
Bass, Richard, 39n
Batten, Jack, 104n
Beatty, Richmond C., 38n
Becker, Howard S., 24n, 79n, 88n, 104n, 114n
Bell, Daniel, 131n
Bell, Robert R., 9n, 23n, 28n, 58n, 76, 104n
Bensman, Joseph, 124n
Berdie, Ralph F., 159n
Berger, Peter L., 38, 39n
Bernstein, Walter, 148n
Biderman, A.D., 98
Black, Donald J., 84n, 85n, 93, 94
Blackstock, Harvey, 97n
Bloch, Herbert, 131
Blumer, Herbert, 72n
Boles, Jacqueline, 12n
Bordua, David, 84n, 85, 93, 153n
Boydell, Craig L., 12n, 33n, 85n, 107n, 127n, 134n
Bradley, Sculley, 38n
Brecher, Edward M., 47n, 49n, 89n
Bredemeir, Harry C., 164n
Briar, Scott, 84n, 94
Brim, Orville G., 57n
Broom, Leonard, 29n
Bryan, James H., 24n, 58n, 124n, 125n
Bryant, Clifton D., 12n, 23n, 114n, 125n, 144n
Buckner, H. Taylor, 15n, 39n, 41n, 58n, 76n, 125n, 128n
Burke, Kenneth, 64n, 65n
Cameron, Mary Owen, 15n, 17n
Cameron, William, 134n
Caplow, Theodore, 57n, 141n, 143n
Capone, Al, 131
Cartwright, Desmond S., 158n, 161n, 162n

Casparis, John, 103n
Cayton, Horace, 158n
Chambliss, William, 33n, 34n, 41n, 53n, 58n, 97n, 133n, 145n
Chilton, Roland, 106
Chimbos, Peter D., 145n
Cicourel, Aaron V., 92n
Clairmont, Donald H., 78, 124n
Clark, John P., 111
Clinard, Marshall B., 17n, 36n, 113n, 154n
Cloward, Richard A., 132n, 153, 154, 155, 156n, 160, 165n, 166n
Cohen, Albert K., 14n, 16n, 20n, 27n, 29, 32n, 49n, 51n, 62, 63, 75n, 76n, 86n, 89n, 98, 127n, 136, 138, 139n, 150, 151, 152, 153, 154n, 160n, 161n, 166n, 168n, 169
Cohen, Stanley, 37n
Collective conscience, 50
and the marijuana issue, 51-52
Conformity
and social system, 13
to rules, 14-15
Conklin, John E., 98n, 130n
Connor, Walter D., 51n
Cook, Shirley, 47
Cooley, Charles H., 75n
Copeland, Clive L., 58n, 125n
Correctional institutions
deviance inside, 4-5, 169
Cosa Nostra, 2, 8, 9, 16, 129, 130, 145
Cottrell, Leonard S. Jr., 29n
Courtis, M.C., 99n
Cousineau, D.F., 51n
Crawford, C.K., 148n
Cressey, Donald C., 2n, 4n, 7n, 33n, 51n, 54n, 56n, 59n, 64n, 69, 80n, 97n, 103n, 111n, 113n, 129n, 130n, 144, 145n, 158n
Culture, 53
and vocabularies of motives, 69
Cutter, Henry S.G., 144n, 159n
Dank, Barry M., 31n
Davis, Kingsley, 6n, 51n, 67n
DeFleur, Lois B., 20n, 91n, 156n
Dentler, R.A., 103n, 111
Deviant behavior
structure of, 2-5
and social system, 10
as normative system, 17-21
inevitability of deviance, 18
criteria of, 27-29
and roles, 29-32

Deviant Behavior (cont.)
 social definitions of, 43-52
 and collective conscience, 50-51
 and socialization, 53
 and personality pathology, 28-29
 and identity, 76
Dietrick, David C., 153n
Discretion
 among police officers making arrests,
  94-96
 personal, in defining deviance, 23
Disvalued behavior
 and deviant roles, 78
Do Nascimento, Edson Arantes, 38n
Douglas, Jack D., 77n, 125n
Drake, St. Clair, 158n
Dumpson, J.R., 148n
Durkheim, Emile, 50, 52
Elkin, Frederick, 44n
Elliott, Delbert S., 158n
Empey, Lamar T., 103, 167n
Ennis, P.H., 97n, 99n, 101n
Erickson, Maynard L., 103
Erikson, Kai T., 51n
Fallding, Harold, 2n, 127n
Faulkner, Robert R., 17n, 40
Feder, Sid, 2n
Fejer, Dianne, 114n
Finestone, Harold, 77n, 124n
Forcese, Dennis, 71n, 166n
Form, William H., 35n
Friedson, Eliot, 82n, 83n
Gagnon, John H., 54n, 58n, 155n
Gallagher, James E., 118n
Gandy, John M., 85n
Gangs
 variation of, 147-149
 behavioral versatility of, 157-158
 and fighting, 160-163
 daily activities of, 159-160
 informal structure of, 159-161
Garbin, A.P., 12n
Gardiner, John A., 129n
Garfinkel, Harold, 82n, 87n
Garvin, Andrew, 71n
Geer, Blanche, 104n
Geertz, Hildred S., 144n, 159n
Geis, Gilbert, 129n, 131, 142n
Gerver, Israel, 124n
Gibbons, Don C., 129n, 131n
Gibney, Frank, 66n, 113n
Glaser, Daniel, 100, 167n, 168n
Goffman, Erving, 12, 13n, 79n, 81n, 88n,
 89

Goldman, Natham, 85n, 93
Goode, William J., 119n
Goodman, Paul, 66n
Gouldner, Alvin W., 24n
Grindstaff, Carl F., 12n, 33n, 85n, 107n,
 127n, 134n
Groups
 images of respectability, 125
 importance for social conduct, 135
Grutzner, Charles, 130n
Haas, Jack, 31n
Hagen, John J., 82n

Hanging activities, 143, 159
Hanley, Lloyd G., 129n
Hartung, Frank E., 54n, 67n
Haskell, Martin R., 146n
Hemingway, Ernest, 35n
Hessler, Richard M., 114n
Hill, Brian, 134n
Hills, Stuart L., 129n
Hirschi, Travis, 115n
Hoffman, Martin, 31n, 33n, 34n
Homans, George C., 164n
Homosexuality
 norms, 12
Hood, Roger, 100, 103n
Horowitz, Irving Louis, 64n
Horowitz, Ruth, 158n
Howard, Kenneth I., 157n
Hughes, Everett C., 17n, 126n
Humphreys, Laud, 12n, 39n, 54n, 91n
Identity
 and role appropriation, 74
 deviant, development, 86-89
 change of, 90-91
Illegitimate opportunity, 154
Inciardi, James A., 168n
Inkeles, Alex, 27n, 86n
Institutionalization,
 in general, 21
 in a pluralistic society, 22
Jackson, Bruce, 145n
Jackson, David, 114n, 123n
Jarvis, George K., 107n
Johnson, Harry, 24n, 53n, 62n, 141n,
 164n, 168n
Johnston, Norman, 131n
Kadish, Sanford H., 44n, 48n, 50n
Kefauver, Estes, 129n, 130n
Kennedy, Senator Edward, 20n
Kitsuse, John I., 92n, 153n
Klein, Malcolm W., 70n, 148n
Knudten, Richard D., 56n

Kobrin, Solomon, 156n, 157n, 160n
Kochman, Thomas, 36n
Kundrats, Uldis, 116n
Kupfer, George, 114n
Labeling (*see also* Identity)
  within a subsystem of institutions, 60,
    83-86
  and cultural imagery, 79
  and law enforcement agencies, 82, 84
  and the dramatization of evil, 82-83
Lambert, Ronald D., 118n
Law
  enacted, 7
  and basic sentiments, 7
  and immorality, 44-46
  and special interest groups, 45-46
Lebeaux, Charles N., 153n
Lemert, Edwin M., 78n, 88n, 89, 97n
Letkemann, Peter, 18n, 23n, 33n, 41n,
    51n, 58n, 59n, 60n, 82n, 89n, 128n,
    130n, 133n
Lever, Janet, 90n
Lewis, Arthur H., 20n
Liebow, Elliott, 62n, 75n
Lindesmith, Alfred R., 44n, 53n, 75n, 86,
    155n
Lippman, Walter, 8n, 79, 80, 128n
Lipset, Seymour, M., 131n
Lofland, John, 17n, 22n, 28n, 67n, 87n
Long, E. Hudson, 38n
Loosley, Elizabeth W., 44n, 55n
Lowsky, Iris, 41n
Lucas, Rex, 77n
Lynd, Robert S., 22
Magill, William, 78, 124n
Mann, W.E., 5, 10n, 104n, 129n, 145n
Matza, David, 20n, 28n, 32, 66n, 68n,
    125n, 128n, 133n, 155n, 156, 159n,
    161n
Maurer, David W., 53n, 143n, 145n
Mays, John Barron, 51n
Mazur, Alan, 118n
McCaghy, Charles H., 126n
McDonald, Norris A., 58n, 125n
McGrath, W.T., 98n
McIntosh, James K., 31n
McIntosh, Mary, 37n
McKay, H.D., 106, 141n, 145
McKitrick, Eric L., 131n
McMullan, John, 128n
Mead, George H., 69, 74, 75n
Merton, Robert K., 7n, 29n, 51n, 59n,
    62n, 75n, 119n, 144n, 153, 154n
Messerschmidt, Brian, 63n, 126n

Meyers, C.K., 148n
Middle-class delinquency, 113-114,
    116-117
Miller, Walter B., 16n, 108n, 128n, 132n,
    144n, 158n, 159n, 160n, 167n, 168n
Miller, Warren, 35n, 108, 109n, 160n
Mills, C. Wright, 55, 64, 113n
Minicultures, 82
Monroe, L.J., 103n, 111
Moral entrepreneurs, 48
Morality
  enforcement through criminal law,
    44-45
Motivation
  in general, 60-62
  and role-expectations, 38-41, 66
Mulamud, D.I., 148
Murphy, Fred J., 102n
Myerhoff, Barbara G., 70n, 148n
Myers, Gustavus, 113n
Narcotics (*see also* Moral entrepreneurs)
  Canadian legislation, 47-48
  and legal controls, 49-50
Nawaz, M., 56n
Nease, Barbara, 107n
Nettler, Gwynn, 93n, 95n, 100n, 113n
New York City Youth Board, 108n, 148
Nisbet, Robert A., 51n, 59n, 62n, 75n,
    119n, 144n
Norms (*see also* Rules)
  significance of, 6, 13
  as social control, 7-8, 12, 14, 48
  variability, 10, 12-13
  as enacted law, 7
  situational, 11
  and sanctions, 9-10
Nye, F. Ivan, 103n, 111
Ohlin, Lloyd, E., 132n, 153, 154, 155,
    156n, 161, 166n
Olson, David J., 129n
Packer, Herbert L., 44n, 49n
Page, Gary S., 10n
Parsons, Talcott, 49n, 66n
Peluso, Emil, 157n, 160n
Penz, Peter, 134n
Personality
  pathology, 28-29
Pileggi, Nikolas, 23n, 144n
Piliavin, Irving, 84n, 94
Plimpton, George, 8n, 40, 41n
Police
  bias in making arrests, 95
  and crime reporting, 96
  and visibility of illegal acts, 96

Polsky, Ned, 8n, 13n, 30n
Porter, John, 113n
Porterfield, Austin, 102
Prostitution
  role requirements, 58
Puntil, Joseph, 157n, 160n

Quinney, Richard, 17n, 36n

Radzinc icz, Leon, 44n, 48n
Reference groups
  normative, 62-63
  status, 63-64
Reiss, Albert J. Jr., 7n, 84n, 85n, 93, 94, 110n, 153n
Rhodes, Albert Lewis, 110n, 153n
Richer, Stephen, 71n, 166n
Roach, Justice Wilfrid D., 129n
Robertson, Leon S., 118n
Robin, Gerald, D., 148n
Robison, Sophia M., 56n
Rogers, Kenneth H., 108n, 146
Role
  and groups, 30-32
  and rules, 30
  and social control, 31
  and social change, 31-32
  definition, 32
  ambiguity, 31-32
  expectations, 33-34
  terms, 32-33
  criteria, 43
  signs, 33-37
  images, 37-38
  emotion, 38-39
  moral attributes, 39-40
  identity, 73-77
  age, 116-117
  convergence, 120-121
  and gangs, 158-162
Rosenberg, Bernard, 108n, 110, 114n
Ross, H. Laurence, 19n, 22n
Ross, Herman R., 106
Roth, Lorna, 15n, 76n
Rubington, Earl, 124n
Rules (see also Deviant behavior)
  clairity of, 11-12
  in public places, 12-13
  and social systems, 14,21
  and individuality, 14
  and conformity, 14-16
  validity of, 21
Salinger, J.D., 135n
Salisbury, Harrison, 132n
Salutin, Marilyn, 12n, 33

Sanctions
  variation, 9-10
  control of, 16
Savitz, Leonard, 131n
Sawchuk, Peter, 31n
Schafer, Stephen, 56n
Scheff, Thomas J., 87n
Schur, Edwin M., 79n, 80n, 87n
Schwartz, Gary, 158n
Schwartz, Louis B., 48n
Schwendinger, Herman, 70n
Schwendinger, Julia, 70n
Scott, Marvin B., 40
Scott, Robert A., 80n, 83n
Seeley, John R., 44n, 55n
Self-image (see also Identity)
  in general, 75-77
Self-report studies
  in general, 102-104, 110-111
  criticisms of, 111-113
Shaffir, Bill, 31n
Shanley, Fred J., 114n
Shaw, Clifford R., 60n, 106, 107n, 141n, 145, 149n
Sherif, Carolyn W., 158n, 159n, 160n
Sherif, Muzafer, 158n, 159n, 160n
Shirley, Mary M., 102n
Short, James F. Jr., 14n, 54n, 75n, 89n, 103n, 108n, 109, 110n, 111, 123n, 131n, 132n, 147n, 148n, 150n, 153n, 157n, 158n, 159n, 160n, 161n, 162n, 163n
Silverman, Robert A., 99n, 112n
Silverstein, Harry, 108n, 110, 114n
Sim, R. Alexander, 44n, 55n
Simon, William, 54n, 58n
Simmons, J.L., 90n
Skipper, James K., 126n
Skolnick, Jerome H., 130n
Slum
  living conditions, 106
  quality of delinquency, 107, 114
  legitimate marriage, 132
Smart, Reginald G., 114n, 123n
Smelser, Neil J., 45n, 87n, 131n
Smigel, Erwin O., 19n, 22n
Smith, Richard Austin, 113n
Social action
  in general, 1-2
Social control
  as reactions of others, 16
  cost of, 168-169
  problems of, 164-168
  and institutions, 82-86

Social organization
  and rationality, 141
  variability and deviant activities,
    141-144
  and role differentiation, 141
  and social control, 164
Social status
  of social roles, 41-42
  and marginal differentiation, 73n
  deprivation, among lower-class
    youths, 138-139
  and fighting gangs, 157-159
Social worlds (*see also* Subcultures)
  roles, 31
  social control, 85
  age-related roles, 116-117
  variety, 122-123
  interdependence with conventional
    world, 127-130
  recruitment, 129
Socialization
  and family structure, 54-55
  and socioeconomic location, 54-57
  of adults, 58
  and deviant roles, 57-58
  formal, 58-59
  informal, 59-60
  and motivation, 62-64
  and reference groups, 64
  and pain, 41n
Socioeconomic location
  and differential life chances, 106
  variability of delinquency, 108-109,
    113-114
Sparks, Richard, 100, 103n
Spergel, Irving, 110n, 129n, 156, 157,
    159n, 160n
Stebbins, Robert A., 87n
Stephenson, Richard M., 164n
Stinchombe, Arthur L., 95, 96n
Stone, Gregory P., 35n, 90n
Stratton, John R., 165n, 167n
Strauss, Anselm L., 53n, 75n
Stripping
  as deviant behavior, 12, 33
Strodbeck, Fred L., 14n, 54n, 108n, 109,
    110n, 131n, 132n, 153n, 158n, 160n,
    161n, 162n, 163n
Subcultures
  some characteristics of, 122-128
  problems that generate, 133-134
  dynamic process in the development
    of, 136-138
  delinquent, 136-139, 150-153

criminal, 154-155
  conflict, 155
  retreatist, 155
Suchman, E.A., 72n
Sumner, William Graham, 7n, 27n
Sussman, Marvin, 82n
Sutherland, Edwin H., 37n, 53n, 113n,
    145n
Sutter, Alan G., 33n
Suttles, Gerald D., 60n
Sykes, Gresham M., 15n, 20n, 125n
Tannenbaum, Frank, 78n, 82n, 147n
Taylor, Laurie, 9n
Teevan, James J. Jr., 99n, 112n
Tennyson, Ray A., 157n, 161n
Terry, Robert M., 84n, 165n, 166n
Thrasher, Frederic, III, 108n, 123n,
    141n, 146, 147, 148n, 157n, 159n
Tobias, J.J., 37n, 110n
Tribble, Stephen, 112n
Trust
  as social control, 19
Turkus, Burton B., 2n
Tyler, Gus, 8n, 128n, 129n, 130n
Vaz, Edmund W., 10n, 31n, 33n, 45n,
    56n, 71n, 103n, 111n, 114n, 117n,
    118n, 121n, 125n, 126n, 127n, 130n,
    132n, 166n
Veevers, J.E., 51n
Victimization studies
  in general, 98-101
Vocabulary of motives
  differential distribution of, 65
  sources, 66-69
  personalized version of, 69
  and marijuana use, 70-72
Waller, Irvin, 59n
Wallerstein, James S., 102
Ward, David A., 33n, 54n, 56n, 103n,
    111n, 113n
Weber, Max, 1n, 17n, 140n
Weinberg, Martin S., 10n, 124n
Weinberg, S. Kiron, 126n
Wenninger, Eugene P., 111
West, William Gordon, 66, 103n, 107
Westley, A. William, 4, 8n, 44n, 104n,
    123n, 130n
Wheeler, Stanton, 45n, 51n, 52, 57n, 87n
White, Jim, 114n
White, T.H., 77n
Whitehead, Paul C., 12n, 33n, 85n, 107n,
    127n, 134n
Whyte, William F., 129n, 144n
Wilensky, Harold, 153n

Williams, Robin M., 17n

Williams, Tennessee, 20n

Williamson, Henry, 90n

Winick, Charles, 114n

Wise, Nancy Barton, 121n

Witmer, Helen L., 102n

Wolfgang, Marvin E., 44n, 48n, 131n

Wylie, Clement J., 102

Yablonsky, Lewis, 108n, 146n, 149, 150, 160n

Zay, Nicolas, 97n